STRAY THOUGHTS ON INDIAN CRICKET

STRAY THOUGHTS ON INDIAN CRICKET

J. M. FRAMJEE PATEL

GYAN

Published by

GYAN

Gyan Publishing House
5, Ansari Road
Daryaganj, New Delhi-110002
Phone: 011-47034999, 9811692060
E-mail: books@gyanbooks.com

Distribution Network
gyanbooks.com
India, USA, Canada, UK, Australia

ISBN: 978-93-7225-022-0 (PB)

First Published, 1905

2nd Impression 2025

Printed at: Gyan Press, Delhi.

STRAY THOUGHTS ON INDIAN CRICKET
Author: J. M. FRAMJEE PATEL

RESPECTFULLY DEDICATED

to

Pandit Madan Mohan Malaviya,

Vice-chancellor, Benares Hindu University,

as a humble token of appreciation of his ceaseless efforts for the moral, material, and spiritual development of Indi:

BY THE AUTHOR—*AN ALUMNUS*

OF THE UNIVERSITY.

THE INDIAN SUGAR INDUSTRY

ITS PAST, PRESENT AND FUTURE.

BY

M. P. GANDHI, M.A.

Secretary, Indian Sugar Mills Association; Secretary, Indian Chamber of Commerce, Calcutta; Secretary, Federation of Indian Chambers of Commerce and Industry, (1929-30); Secretary, International Chamber of Commerce, Indian National Committee (1929-30).

FOREWORD

BY

SHETH WALCHAND HIRACHAND.

The story of the Sugar Industry in India should read like a romance in the history of Industries of any country in the World. Although India is to-day mainly an agricultural country and was first in the world to produce sugarcane and sugar, she has been for more than two generations importing the whole of her sugar requirements from foreign countries. Sugar after all is a slightly refined process near gur or jaggery which India has been making for ages. The import of sugar, even for a poor country like India, came to enormous figures, like a million tons per year, causing a drain of about Rs. 15/- crores per year. When, however, public disaffection became acute and the Government saw that various other public organisations were catching not only the imagination of the masses but were also successful in doing concrete good to the masses and there was the pressure of local agitation, the Government agreed to give real protection to this industry. It is said that even to this the Government agreed, because the introduction of this protection did not adversely affect any British Industry. Immediately after the protection was granted and within a short period like three years India will produce almost all the sugar that she requires. In spite of the acutest depression in the whole world and in spite of the shyness of Indian Capital and illiteracy nearly Rs. 20/- crores are estimated to have been invested in this industry in most modern machinery. It is a gratifying feature of this scheme of protection that almost 95 per cent of the new Sugar factories are Indian owned and managed. This to my mind is a convincing illustration of what protection can do. Not only is the country expected to produce all the sugar she requires but after 1934-35 season, it is expected that the country will have to look out for outside markets for export of her sugar.

I think at the end of the 15 years, probably earlier, we should be able to do away with protection. My reasons for thinking thus are that while the Indian Sugar Committee in 1920 would have been satisfied with a recovery of 8 per cent some of the Indian Factories are now getting an average recovery of a little above 11 per cent. Similarly it seems quite possible to get an average like that of Java of 60 tons per acre of Adsali (16 month) sugar cane crop. As a matter of fact a production of 50 tons per acre has already been attained. Similarly for plant sugar cane 45 tons per acre of Java varieties seems practicable. It might be interesting here to note that in the Deccan a Prize of Rs. 1000/- is being offered by the Maharashtra Chamber to the cane grower who gets 100 tons of sugar cane per acre. With these facts before us one is justified in thinking that at the end of 15 years of protection the country should be able to do away with protection. After all, being an agricultural country, we ought to excel in a commodity like cane. Although we are not yet an industrialised country we are producing the cheapest and the best pig iron in the world as also the best cement and comparatively cheap cement too. Similarly production of cheap sugar also is, to my mind, only a question of a few years.

The Industry has given employment to about 1500 Graduates in chemistry and mechanical Engineering plus about one hundred thousand factory workers, in these days of unemployment. This industry has found a new cash market for about sixty lakhs of tons sugar cane worth about Rs. 6 crores which gives employment to half a million agriculturists. To this splendid service and response of the Indian Industrialists the Government however have returned a kick in the shape of the excessive excise duty of Rs. 1/5 per Cwt. recently announced. The basic principle underlying the imposition of this duty is wrong inasmuchas it is founded on the idea of adding a surcharge equivalent to the excise duty. This is not fair to the industrialist as price of sugar to the consumer in the country is already much cheaper than this surcharge would justify. It is estimated that the consumer is already getting a benefit of at least about Rs. 2-10-0 per Cwt., owing to internal competition as against the surcharge of Rs. 1-5-0 which is thus not operative. The benefit to the consumer on this account alone comes therefore to about 3 crores of rupees per year.

The main argument, however, would be that a legislature and a Government having solemnly assured the industrialist of an uninterrupted protection for 15 years should not go back upon their word by adding to the basic cost of the industrialist by imposing an excise duty. If the Industrialist's profit became reduced owing to molasses not fetching any price or price of sugar falling owing to internal competition, he took these risks with open eyes and is prepared to face these; but there is no justification on any grounds of equity or business morality for the Government to add to his cost by means of an excise duty.

A careful analysis of the balance sheets of sugar companies for the 1933-34 crushing season will easily explode the theory of profiteering. I hope that this monograph will be published annually and balance sheets of a few factories will be given therein, for the information of the public, as it will be very useful.

The monograph is planned in a scientific way and should be useful to scholars desirous of studying this industry.

BOMBAY :
3rd March, 1934.

WALCHAND HIRACHAND

AUTHOR'S PREFACE

Encouraged by the appreciation and the response that my last two monographs on the Indian Cotton Textile Industry—Its Past, Present and Future, and How to Compete with Foreign Cloth, met with from the public, I have ventured to publish the present monograph on the Indian Sugar Industry—Its Past, Present and Future. The idea of this publication first originated in my mind during June, 1933, in view of the very great interest that was evinced by the public in the development of this industry after the grant of protection to it by the Government of India in April 1932. The absence of any information about the extent, the peculiar features, and the prospects of development of this industry in India, with the exception of the valuable Reports of the Indian Sugar Committee (1920) and of the Indian Tariff Board (1930) which have become obsolete with respect to several matters, impelled me to undertake a scientific research on the subject and to prepare a comprehensive monograph giving authoritative, up-to-date and reliable information pertaining to the industry, in order that it may furnish some help and guidance to the industrialists, scholars, and public men, taking a keen interest in the industrial development of this country in general, and of this industry in particular.

I have attempted to treat the subject-matter of the monograph in a scientific manner and have discussed briefly most of the important problems in a similar spirit. I have also given considerable statistical and other relevant information relating to the Sugar Industry in India, as also in other parts of the world, in order to enable a fair comparison being made of the stage of development of the industry in India with that of other countries, and to point directions in which further improvements are possible and feasible. Due to the hurry in the preparation of this monograph, several defects and deficiencies have been left therein, and I will feel very grateful if any of my readers will be good enough to make suggestions calculated to enhance the utility of this treatise in any way. I shall consider myself amply rewarded if the publication of this monograph at this juncture is helpful in crystallizing the opinion of the industrialists, the public and the Government in regard to various problems confronting the industry, e.g. fixation of prices of cane, licensing of factories, allocation of zones, utilization of by-products, directions of research, and improvement in agriculture, manufacture, etc., relations between cane-growers and sugar-manufacturers, single sugar selling organization, imposition of an excise duty on Indian factory sugar etc. and thus enabling the industry as well as the Government to concert effective measures for increasing in any manner the efficiency and prosperity of this industry, representing a total investment of over Rs. 25 crores, giving employment to over 80,000 workers, stopping the drain of about Rs. 15 crores every year, and supporting no less than 15 million agriculturists whose interests are indissolubly bound up with this industry.

I have endeavoured to show that India is situated exceptionally well in regard to manufacture of sugar from cane, and I feel that if suitable encouragement is given to this industry, India should be able not only to supply fully the quantity of sugar required by her, which she has already practically done, but also to supply sugar to other countries in the world. What is needed is a bold and continuous policy of encouragement to this industry, by the Government of this country, in appreciation of the importance and advantages of development of industries in India.

If circumstances are favourable and the need is felt, I hope to make this publication an Annual one, and to deal with the latest features in the industry in all parts of the world, in order that those interested in the development of the Indian Sugar Industry may keep abreast of the times and may be able to measure the progress made by the industry from year to year and to effect continual improvements therein, in order to enable India to rank, before long, amongst the most efficient sugar-producing countries of the world, and to supply the requirements of sugar to other parts of the British Empire, if not, indeed, to other countries of the world.

I must express my great indebtedness to my friend Mr. R. C. Srivastava, Sugar Technologist to the Imperial Council of Agricultural Research, Cawnpore, for the very valuable help he has readily given to me at all times. I am also obliged to my friends, Mr. S. P. Shah, and Mr. S. Lall, Directors of Industries, United Provinces, and Bihar and Orissa, respectively, and to Mr. Charan Das, Secretary of the Imperial Council of Agricultural Research, for the assistance they have so kindly given to me from time to time.

I must also thank Mr. B. M. Birla, Mr. J. M. Lownie, Mr. Walchand Hirachand, Mr. D. P. Khaitan, Lala Shri Ram, Mr. Noel Deerr, and other friends who have so kindly discussed with me various problems pertaining to the industry, and encouraged me in other ways in bringing out this publication. To Mr. Walchand, I am, indeed, very grateful for having kindly agreed to write a foreword to this monograph.

I have given a few striking facts about the industry in India in "The Sugar Industry at a Glance", appearing in front of the 1st page.

It would hardly be necessary for me to observe that the views expressed in this monograph are my own and have no necessary connection with the views of any of the Associations with which I have the honour to be associated.

Dated 22nd March, 1934.

C/o Indian Sugar Mills Association,
135, Canning Street, Calcutta.

M. P. Gandhi

CONTENTS OF THE MONOGRAPH.

CHAPTER III.

CHAPTER IV.

CHAPTER V.

Attention is invited

to the

Following List of Advertisers.

LIST OF ADVERTISERS

(Arranged Serially.)

THE SUGAR INDUSTRY AT A GLANCE.

1. *Sugar-Cane Factories* & Khandsari.†*

Year.	No. of Factories.	U.P.	Behar.	Factory Production Tons.	Khandsari† Production Tons.
1931-32	31	14	12	158,581	2,50,000
1932-33	57	33	19	290,177	2,75,000
1933-34	135	70	34	650,000 (Est.) (Govt.'s Estimate is 5,86,000.)	2,60,000

2. *Total Production of Sugar and Gur and Yield of Raw Sugar in Tons.*

Year.	Total Sugar (Tons).	U.P.	Behar.	Gur for direct consumption.	Yield of Raw Sugar (Gur).
		Factory Production only			
1931-32	4,78,000	66,312	75,091	27,72,000	38,80,000
1932-33	6,56,000	140,344	126,610	32,45,000	46,84,000
1933-34	10,00,000‡ (Est.)	...	.	30,00,000 (Est.)	50,67,000¶

3. *Total and Per Capita Consumption of Sugar in India.§*

Year.	Consumption of Sugar in Tons.	Per Capita Consumption in lbs.		
		Sugar.	Gur.	Total.
1932-33	9,82,000	6	17·7	23·7
1931-32	9,40,000 (Est.)	5 8	20·4	26·2
1933-34	9,40,000 (Do.)	..	...	...

---

* For a complete list of Factories, Names of Managing Agents, capacity etc., see Appendix III.

† Estimates of Khandsari Production are Conjectural. An Enquiry has been undertaken for ascertaining Khandsari Production in U. P. in 1933.

‡ Please correct the mistake in the total on page 57 where 1100000 is printed instead of 10,50,000. A deduction of 50,000 tons is made on account of damage to factories due to the recent earthquake, and late starting of several factories.

¶ India continues to lead as the largest sugar producing country in the world. Till 1931, Cuba was leading.

§ For consumption in other countries, see page 67.

4. *World's Production and Consumption (in Metric Tons).*

Year.	Total Production of Sugar.	Production from cane.	Production from Beet.	Consumption.	Excess of Production over Consumption.
1931-32	27,000,000	18,000,000	8,910,000	26,000,000	750,000
1932-33	26,000,000	17,000,000	8,000,000	25,000,000	70,000
1933-34	26,000,000	17,000,000	8,000,000	25,000,000	30,000

(These figures are approximate only)

5. *Average and Maximum Percentage Recovery in India and Java.*

Year.	India (average).	U.P. (average).	Behar (average).	Bombay (Maximum).	Java (average).
1931-32	8·89%	8·59%	9·06%	..	11·92%
1932-33	8.66%	8·55%	8·60%	11·1%	.
1933-34	9·00% (Expected).	.	..	...	...

6. *Uses of Cane.*

Year.	Percentage of Cane Crushed in Factories.	Quantity Crushed in Factories (Tons).	For *Gur* Manufacture in Tons.	By Khandsari. Tons.	For Chewing Tons.	Total Cane Crop in Tons.
1931-32	4·1%	17,83,000	29,871,000	5,000,000	5,400,000	43,316,000
1932-33	6·6%	33,50,000	34,595,000	5,500,000	5,500,000	50,000,000
1933-34	10·0% (Est.)	55,00,000	.	..	...	55,000,000 (Est.)

7. *Crushing Season and Capacity of Factories in India.*

(*a*) Average Cane-crushing capacity of Factory per day of 22 hours .. .. 600 Tons

(*b*) Average duration of Cane-crushing Season All-India in 1932-33 ... ... 134 Days

(*c*) *Maximum* Duration do. do. in 1932-33 ... 184 Days

(*d*) Average Duration do. do. in U. P. ... 144 Days

(*e*) Average Duration do. do. in Behar ... 154 Days

8. *Acreage under Sugar-Cane ; Total & Average Production of Cane per Acre.*

Year.	Total Acreage.	Acreage under Improved varieties.	Average Cane production per Acre (in Tons).	Total Cane Crop (in Tons).
1931-32	3,076,000	1,170,000	14	43,316,000
1932-33	3,321,000*	1,814,000	15	50,000,000
1933-34	3,305,000	..	16	55,000,000 (Rsti.)

* Please correct the figure on page 17, line 21, accordingly.

9. *Cost of Production of Cane per Maund.*

(*a*) Definite figures are not available. Cost of Production varies from Province to Province from annas 0-2-0 to annas 0-10-0 per Maund.

(*b*) Average Cost of Production in Bihar, according to Bihar Government's figures, is roughly between 2½ to 3 annas per Maund.

(*c*) Enquiry into Cost of Production undertaken by Imperial Council of Agricultural Research. Report awaited 1936.

10. *Average Price of Cane paid by Factories to Cultivators.*

1932-33	...	...	Rs. 0-6-0 Per Maund.
1933-34	...	...	,, 0-6-0 ,, ,,

11. *Import of Sugar into India (Value and Quantity) & Revenue therefrom.*

Year.	Quantity in Tons.	Value.	Yield of Revenue to Government of India from Import Duty.
1931-32	5,16,000	Rs. 6,01,00,000	Rs. 8,00,00,000
1932-33	3,69,500	Rs. 4,12,00,000	Rs. 6,84,00,000
1933-34	2,50,000	Rs. 2,70,00,000	Rs. 4,80,00,000
1934-35	1,10,000*	Rs.	Rs. 2,05,00,000*

12. *Import Duty on Sugar† and Sugar Candy‡ and Proposed Excise Duty on Factory Sugar.*

On Sugar ... ... Rs. 9-1-0 per Cwt.

Rs. 7-4-0 Protective Duty and Rs. 1-13-0 Surcharge.

(From April 1932 to 31st March 1934).

(*Proposed Change with effect from 1st April, 1934.*)

On Sugar ... ... Rs. 9-1-0 per Cwt.

Rs. 7-12-0 Protective Duty and Rs. 1-5-0 Equivalent Excise Duty.

13. *Excise Duty on Internal Production of Factory Sugar.*

Proposed at Rs. 1-5-0 per Cwt. (Roughly equivalent to Rs. 0-15-4·5 per maund).

With effect from 1st April, 1934.

* Government's estimate.

† Please amend Table No. 3 on pages 10,11 accordingly. For import duties on sugar in other countries, see Table No. 3.

‡ On Sugar-Candy Rs. 10-8-0 per Cwt. (from 20th February 1934) in place of Rs. 9-1-0 per Cwt.

Sugar Excise Duty Bill introduced in Assembly on 13th March 1934.
Expected Yield of Revenue 1934-35 Rs. 1,47,00,000.

14. *Price of Sugar.*

Indian (1st & 2nd Quality Average) ... Rs. 7-12-0 per Maund Ex-Factory (February 1934)

Imported Sugar, at Calcutta ... ... Rs. 10-2-0 per Maund (February 1934)

15. *Transportation Cost on Sugar.*

Railway Freight ... About 1000 miles—about Rs. 1-4-0 per Md.
Steamer ,, ... From Java to Calcutta—about Rs. 0-3-6 per Md.

16. *Expenditure on Research (through the Imperial Council).*

Total Amount spent from 1930-31 to 1933-34 ... Rs. 11 Lakhs.
,, ,, proposed to be spent upto 1937-38 ... Rs. 20 Lakhs.

21st March, 1934.

M. P. Gandhi.

THE INDIAN SUGAR INDUSTRY.

ITS PAST, PRESENT, AND FUTURE.

CHAPTER I.

Historical Survey of the Industry.

1. A GLIMPSE INTO THE PAST.

THOUGH there is a large volume of conclusive evidence to show that India is the home* of sugar cane, there is room for diversity of opinion as to when exactly the manufacture of sugar began in this country. These questions, however, are not, strictly speaking, germane to the primary aim of this monograph which is to discuss the problems pertaining to the modern sugar industry. It is of interest, however, to note that sugar cane has been known to India for over 2,000 years; and there are, besides, several indications that Northern India is the home of sugar cane.† The earliest reference to this in Western Countries dates back to 627 A. D. when sugar figures among the spoils taken by the Byzantines after their conquest of Dastagerd in Persia. It is also on record that the Chinese Government during the reign of

*It will be of interest to note that India is also the birth-place of Cotton and Cotton manufactures. Vide Author's "The Indian Cotton Textile Industry, Its Past, present and future," 1930, and "How to Compete with Foreign Cloth" 1931.

†Etymologically also sugar is of Indian origin, the earliest forms of the word being, *Sharkara* in Sanskrit, and *Sakkara* in Prakrit. Thence it can be traced through all the Aryan languages, as *Schakar* in Persian, *Sukkar* in Arabic, *Suicar* in Assyrian and Phœnician, *Saccharum* in Latin, *Azucar* in Spanish and Portuguese, *Zuchero* in Italian, *Sucre* in French, *Zucker* in German, etc.

Emperor Tai Tsung (627 to 650 A.D.) sent a batch of Chinese students of agriculture to Bihar to study the method of cultivation of sugar cane and manufacture of sugar. From the Mahommedan writers we learn that sugar cane was introduced by the Arabs into Sicilly about 703 A.D. and that it spread from there to other Western Countries, especially Spain, as early as 755 A.D.

2. INDIA BIRTH-PLACE OF SUGAR-MANUFACTURE.

It would thus be clear that India is the birth-place of the manufacture of sugar from sugar cane. Sugar (*Sharkara*) is mentioned in the *Shastras* as one of the five '*Amritas*', *i.e.*, celestial sweets. We learn from the testimony of the Mahommedan writers that first class white sugar was produced from '*Gur*' throughout Northern India, Burdwan and Murshidabad Divisions in Bengal up to Gorakhpore in Oudh before the advent of the British.

About the 13th century, sugar cane cultivation spread over all the countries round the Mediterranean; and these places became the sources of supplies of cane sugar to Europe and Africa. It also appears to be quite certain that, about the time of the second voyage of Columbus, cane was introduced into America; and it is extremely probable that the local type now used only as chewing cane in Brazil was the variety known as "*Puri*" in Bengal. Later, with the introduction of sugar cane cultivation in many parts of America by the Spanish, the Portuguese and Dutch, the production of sugar increased so rapidly that it became an article of common consumption.

The sugar industry in India throve fairly well up to the time of Napoleon, *i.e.*, up to the beginning of the 19th century, and a large quantity of sugar was exported to European countries even then.* But, when Napoleon was starved of sugar supplies from outside owing to the naval blockade, he engaged scientists to find out from the sweet vegetables growing in Europe a crop capable of producing sugar. This research and subsequent improvement in cultivation led to rapid expansion of sugar-beet cultivation which proved an obstacle to further growth of manufacture of cane sugar in India, but even at the end of the 19th century almost all the villages in India produced a sufficient quantity of crude sugar for their wants. With the spread of civilization, however, the people of India gave up their prejudice against imported sugar and started consuming it in preference to the indigenous sugar, which was more costly. The increasing importation of cheap refined sugar from abroad operated to the detriment of the sugar manufacturing industry of India.

The history of modern sugar may be said to begin from 1791, in which year, due to the massacre of almost all the white population in the black rebellion in Hayati and San Domingo, disappeared the largest producers and exporters. The price of sugar rose rapidly; and the East India Company took advantage of this rise to

*Up to the 17th century, cane-sugar was the only kind known in commerce. But in 1747, Margraf demonstrated the existence of about 6% sugar in beet-root; and in 1795, Achard manufactured beet sugar on his farm in Silesia, and presented leaves of refined sugar to Frederick William III of Prussia in 1799.

export sugar from India to England, not as producers but merely as merchants, buying in the open market and exporting. In 1791 four parcels were exported from Bengal to serve as loaf sugar for tea. This sugar was sold at Rs. 88-6-0 to Rs. 156-6-0 per cwt. Even then the East India Company lost money on the first parcel and gained only 6% on all the four.

The economic policy of the British Empire now began to influence the sugar industry in India. There were two groups of producers, the West Indian Merchants and Planters and the East India Company. The former seemed to have been more influential because the duties favouring the West Indian producers were in force for many years. An *ad valorem* duty of £37-16-3 was levied on sugar, being a manufactured article. This was much in excess of the duty specifically levied on West Indian Sugar. In 1821 there was a modification of Duty and in 1836 East and West Indian sugar entered England on equal terms.

Following on the emancipation of the Slaves, the West Indian Planters were faced with the dislocation of business and this change of policy naturally evoked a violent protest from that quarter. As a consequence of the equalization of duties, considerable capital was invested in India, and West Indians and Mauritian planters were attracted here. So much so that by 1846 the export of sugar from India to Britain had reached 60,000 tons. Factories started at Azizpore, Motihari, Belsund, Barachakia, Gorakhpore and Rosa in the West

Indian plain, aiming at producing sugar direct from sugar cane.

Enterprises depending on *Gur* Refinery were started in Bengal and of this, those at Doobah at Cossipore, Albion and Ballicoll seem to have been the largest. Doobah, which in one year turned out 7,000 tons of sugar, was believed to be the largest and the best equipped in the world. About this time enterprizes were started in Madras under Messrs. Parry and Company, which still exist and the Aska Factory which was started by Messrs. Binny and Company in 1865 developed into the first cane sugar diffusion factory.

In 1846, under pressure of the Manchester School, British tariff policy swung violently towards free trade. The slave-grown sugar was admitted into Great Britain on equal terms with that produced by free labour; and in a few years the industry in India entirely disappeared.* It took another 50 years for a revival of interest in the Sugar Industry of India. Modern Sugar Factories were started in Bihar, from about 1903. Since then there has

---

*The export of sugar during 1874-75 to 1878-79 was as follows:—

	Cwt.	Rs.
	(In thousand.)	
1874-75	498	31,92
1875-76	420	25,39
1876-77	1093	92,51
1877-78	844	74,58
1878-79	279	20,43

The sugar exported was of a very inferior quality used mostly in brewing in England.

been a slow and steady growth of the industry, although it must be said that no help was given by the Government either by a protective tariff or by any other means. The imports were increasing considerably from 1900 onwards and the only check that they suffered was in the War years when the import was reduced considerably, due to high prices. The imports in 1914-1918 averaged 531,713 tons valued at Rs. 13·48 crores as compared with an average of 723,915 tons valued at Rs. 12·71 crores during 1910-14. But the tendency to expansion began again in 1923-1924 and reached the highest figure 9,39,600 tons in 1929-30.

With these preliminary observations, we may now turn to the history of the Industry during the 20th century, to the tariff duty on the imports of sugar during this period, to the circumstances which led the Government to investigate into the possibility of the establishment of a sugar cane manufacturing industry in the country, to the advantages resulting to the country from the establishment of the industry, and to the future of the sugar industry in India.

3. Import Duty.

The import duty on sugar in India from 1894-1895 to 1915-1916 was only 5% and was a revenue duty. In March, 1916, the duty on sugar was increased to 10%; in March, 1921, it was again raised to 15% and in March, 1922, to 25%. In June, 1925, the Import Duty on sugar which was on an *ad valorem* basis was converted into a specific one and the rate was raised to Rs. 4-8-0 per cwt. This remained in force up to February, 1930. It was raised to Rs. 6 per cwt. in March, 1930, and to Rs. 9-1-0 from 1st September, 1931. Even to-day the duty is Rs. 9-1-0 per cwt. of which Rs. 7-4-0 is the protective duty, and Re. 1-13-0 constitutes the surcharge duty of 25%, imposed for revenue purposes. Table I shows the duty after April 1932.*

TABLE 1.

Sugar excluding Confectionery.	Duty from April, 1932
(1) Sugar, crystallized or soft 23 D. S. and above	Rs. 9-1-0 per cwt.
(2) Sugar, crystallized or soft inferior to 23 D. S. but not inferior to 8 D. S.	Rs. 9-1-0 per cwt.
(3) Sugar below 8 D .S. and Sugar-candy...	Rs. 9-1-0 per cwt.
(4) Molasses	*Ad valorem* 31¼%
Molasses	*Tariff values (From 1-1-1934).*
(1) Imported in bulk by tank steamer	Rs. 1-2-0 per cwt.
(2) Otherwise imported ...	Rs. 1-10-0 per cwt.

*This surcharge has an admittedly protectionist effect, and has greatly helped the development of the industry. In January 1934, the Bengal Chamber proposed a Resolution for discussion at the Annual Meeting of the Associated Chambers urging the abolition of the surcharge. The grave injury that would result to the country, in the event of the acceptance of this proposal by the Government, is pointed out in a note in Appendix 1.

4. Quantity and Value of imports of sugar and Import duties in various countries.

It should be observed here that from 1916 onwards sugar has been subjected to an increasingly heavy duty in India; and further it can be seen from Table No. 2 that the increase in the quantity of sugar imported from abroad has taken place in spite of a heavy Import duty ranging from 50 to over 100%. The duty on sugar has yielded a vast amount of money to the Government of India. The Import duty on sugar in 1900-1901 yielded only Rs. 53 lakhs whereas the amount produced in 1929-30 was Rs. 870 lakhs*. The imports show a rapidly declining tendency after 1929. It must be observed here, however, that the high duty on the import of sugar in India is by no means exceptional, as still higher duties are found in various other countries of the world. A statement has been given in Table No.3 showing the Import duty on sugar in several countries of the world. Recently, various countries have increased their duties, *e.g.*, United Kingdom, many of the Continental European States, Canada and China, while several others have adopted more far-reaching methods of regulation through State monopolies or the adoption of

---

*The yield from this source is now decreasing. During 1931-32, it only yielded Rs. 8,00 lakhs, in 1932-33, Rs. 684 lakhs, and the estimate for 1933-34 is Rs. 6,10 lakhs, but it is not likely to be realized, in view of the great reduction in import.

TABLE No. 2.

Showing the imports of sugar, all kinds (excluding molasses) in tons, and value thereof.

—	1913-14	1926-27	1927-28	1928-29	1929-30	1930-31	1931-32	1932-33	1933-34 (April to Oct.) (seven months).
	Pre-war year.								
United Kingdom ...	900	9,200	400	48,00	59,300	8,400	22,900	34,900	...
Ceylon ...	100	2,100	2,800	4,00	3,600	5,700	1,100	100	...
Java ...	583,000	611,700	692,200	850,800	781,100	809,700	366,800	294,800	...
Mauritius ...	139,600	100	...	...	...	...	...	...	...
Strait Settlements ...	2,900	1,100	1,200	900	600	500	400	200	...
China and Hongkong	1,500	3,100	3,100	2,100	6,100	5,100	5,000	2,200	...
Egypt ...	100	...	...	...	...	...	...	...	...
Japan ...	100	...	100	300	500	...	100	4,000	...
Germany ...	700	49,200	1,600	300	15,200	11,700	15,400	300	...
Austria ...	74,000	9,800	300	...	1,400	...	400	...	...
Hungary ...		26,000	2,300	2,100	36,500	13,800	600	...	...
Netherlands ...	...	3,700	700	1,600	2,500	600	600	500	...
Belgium ...	...	13,800	400	300	1,800	300	200	2,500	...
France ...	...	200	...	800	11,900	...	...	...	...
Czechoslovakia ...	...	28,800	1,100	400	9,700	600	1,100	500	...
Italy ...	...	3,700	200	...	...	...	...	...	...
United States ...	...	15,500	500	200	200	200	300	...	...
Other Countries ...	100	48,900	18,900	200	9,200	44,600	101,200	29,500	...
Total all countries									
Quantity in Tons ...	803,000	826,900	725,800	868,800	939,600	901,200	516,100	369,500	162,000
Value Rs. (lakhs) ...	14,29	18,36	14,50	15,86	15,51	10,54	6,01	4,12	1,70

TABLE

Comparative Table of Import Duties

Country.	Quality.	Country's Currency.	Duty Rate.
1. India ...	Sugar and Sugar Candy including confectionery.	Rs.	9 1 0
2. Germany ...	Sugar Refined ...	Reichsmarks	32 0 0
	Sugar Raw ...	„	27 0 0
3. Czechoslovakia...	Sugar, Raw or Refined.	Cr. or Cents	338 0 0 or 4·55 0 0
4. France ...	Sugar Refined ...	fcs.	170 0 0
5. United Kingdom (Duty for lower degrees of polarizing is correspondingly lower).	99° polarizing and higher.	£	0 11 8
	„ „ ...	£	0 4 10
	„ „ ...	£	0 4 8·2
	„ „ ...	£	0 3 6·5
6. Irish Free State	Sugar Refined ...	£	0 11 8
	„ „ ...	£	0 14 0
7. China ...	„ „ ...	Gold Units or Cents	5·80 or 1·74
8. United States ...	„ „ ...	Cents	2·65
	„ Raw ...	Cents	2·50
9. Canada ...	„ Refined over 98°	$	1·89
	„ „ „	$	1·09
10. Australia ...	...	...	...
11. South Africa ...	...	...	...

* This Table is based on the information given in the "Indian

No. 3.*

on Sugar in Principal Countries.

Rates. per	REMARKS.	Basis of conversion into Rupee per cwt.	Rupee equivalent at par per cwt. of 112 lbs.
cwt.	Rs. 7-4-0 Protective. Rs. 1-13-0 Surcharge from April 1932.	per cwt.	9 1 0
100 Kilos.	...	R. M. 102=Rs. 100.	15 15 0
100 Kilos.	...	"	13 7 0
100 Kilos.	...	Rs. 275=$ 100.	14 0 2
lb.	...	"	
lb.	...	fcs. 600=Rs. 100.	14 4 0
cwt.	General Tariff.	1s. 6d. par.	7 12 4
cwt.	Empire Tariff.	"	3 3 4
cwt.	Preferential Colonial.	"	3 1 10
cwt.	Certified Colonial.	"	2 5 9
cwt.	Gereral Tariff.	"	7 12 4
cwt.	United Kingdom.	"	9 5 4
Picul.	...	Rs. 275=$ 100.	5 5 8
lb.			
lb.	Ruling from 17th Jun 1930.	Rs. 275=$ 100.	8 2 6
lb.		"	7 11 2
100 lbs.	General Tariff.	Rs. 275=$ 100.	5 13 0
100 lbs.	Preferential Tariff.	"	3 10 6
...	Nominal: Complete embargo against imports for many years.	...	6 0 0
..	...	...	5 7 6

Trade Journal" and "Sugar Reference Book and Directory, 1932-33."

quota systems for the regulation of imports, *e.g.*, Soviet Union, Australia, Turkey and Latvia.†

5. APPOINTMENT OF THE INDIAN SUGAR COMMITTEE.

Although a high revenue duty existed on sugar, its effects on the Sugar manufacturing Industry of India were not examined by the Government before 1929. The National importance of sugar in the country was not paid any attention to until after the Great World War, when the desirability and possibility of ultilising the sugar resources of India were examined without any intangible result by the Government of India. In February, 1919, Mr. Wynne Sayer of the Indian Agricultural Service was appointed to compile relevant data, statistical and otherwise, as regards the best method exploiting the advantages which India possessed in respect of sugar cane. Immediately after that in 1920 the Governor-General-in-Council appointed the Indian Sugar Committee. The resolution of the Government dated 2nd October, 1919, in appointing this Committee stated that regarding the desirability of expansion of the sugar cane and sugar manufacturing industry, there could be no doubt, that the annual consumption had been increasing steadily for many years and in India no less than elsewhere. It was also recognised that the sugar cane was indigenous in India which until very recent years stood first of all countries in the world in the area under cane.

†Tables No. 2 and 3 will be found on pages 9 and 10.

It was also notorious that the yield both of cane and raw sugar per acre and the percentage of available sugar extracted from cane were depressingly low. While, therefore, India should be in a position, as she was in the past, to produce a surplus of sugar for export, she had, in fact, had to supplement her own supplies by imports, whose tendency to increase had been checked only by the War. The Government were also aware of the difficulties in extending the sugar industry, apart from the difficulties attending the cultivation and manufacture of cane sugar in all countries. There were several problems with which the Indian industry was confronted and which were peculiar to India. The systems of land tenure exhibited great variety and were complicated by the customary laws of inheritance and joint ownership. The bulk of the sugar produced in India was consumed in its crude state as *Gur* or Jaggery and this fact had an essential bearing on the prospects of a successful venture for the production of factory sugar in any particular locality. The Government of India felt that the time was opportune for the appointment of a representative Committee to investigate into the problem in all its bearings and to advise whether a definite and co-ordinated line of policy could be laid down for the promotion of further development and appointed a Committee under the Chairmanship of Mr. J. MacKenna, Agricultural Adviser to the Government of India, to examine the various sugar cane growing tracts of India with a view to determine the nature of the expansion possible in such tracts either by the development of a factory industry or by improvements in the existing indigenous methods; to review the position of India with regard to the world's sugar supply and to formulate recommendations for the improvement of that position, etc.

The Sugar Committee submitted a very favourable and comprehensive report laying great stress on the importance of sugar in the National Economy of India. It is a matter of great pity, however, that the recommendations of this Committee appointed by the Government were pigeon-holed for a few years.

The next stage in the progress of the Industry opened in 1929, due to the existence of the remarkably high revenue duties on sugar imports. The high Import Duty on Sugar subsisted for many years, but it must be observed that the Government never comprehended the full significance of the development of sugar-manufacturing industry in the agricultural, rural and industrial economy of the country. They did evince some interest in this matter spasmodically, but no sustained effort was made to raise the sugar-cane and the sugar industry to their legitimate place in the National Economy. As a result of several fortuitous circumstances, conditions were created which were propitious for the establishment of a sugar industry in the country. The Imperial Council of Agricultural Research deserves considerable credit for inviting the attention of the Government to the possibility and necessity of the establishment of this Industry in the country.

6. Imperial Council of Agricultural Research.

The establishment of the Imperial Council of Agricultural Research may well be regarded as an epoch-making event in the History of the Agricultural improvement in India. The inaugural meeting of the Council was held in June, 1929, and at this meeting representatives of the various provinces reported the progress made by the provincial governments in the preparation of a scheme for assisting the Sugar Committee. In this Committee the Council has a qualified and a representative body to which are referred all questions affecting the welfare of the sugar-cane industry in the country. The Sugar Committee* meets generally once a year, and has had six sittings till December, 1933. This committee has received a general mandate from the Council to examine and report on measures, necessary for the development of the sugar-cane industry in India. One of the recommendations of this Committee, which met for the first time in October, 1929, was that the Government should be asked to institute an enquiry through the Tariff Board in regard to the question whether protection should be given to the Indian sugar-cane industry. This recommendation was accepted by the Council, and its representations were successful in inducing the Government

*This Committee consists of 12 members, and includes representatives of manufacturers, agriculturists, and of Government. The Committee has also co-opted about 10 members to maintain its representative character. In 1933, the Committee co-opted two members representing the Indian Sugar Mills Association of Calcutta.

to order a Tariff Board enquiry into the question whether protection was required, and if so in what measure for the Sugar Industry in India. This enquiry was referred to the Tariff Board in May, 1930. In making this application, the Imperial Council of Agricultural Research had taken into consideration the fact that the three provincial governments, which were widely interested in the Sugar Industry, *viz.*, the United Provinces, the Punjab, and Bihar and Orissa, (representing 80 per cent. of the sugar cane area in British India) together with the Government of Bombay, had asked for a Tariff Board enquiry.

The Sugar Committee of the Imperial Council recognised in 1929 the fact that a steady increase in the import of White Sugar had occurred in the recent years in spite of the existence of a certain measure of protection which had been afforded by the existing specific duty on Sugar. Despite an increase in the cane area, and the yield per acre in some tracts and the amount of the White Sugar manufactured in the country, India was very little nearer to being self-supporting in 1929 in regard to sugar produced, than in 1919 when the Indian Sugar Committee reported. The magnitude of the issue will be clear from the fact that the area under sugar-cane in India in 1929 was 2¾ million acres or about 25% of the total area under sugar-cane in the world. The value of sugar-cane products produced in India in 1929, on the basis of the prices prevalent in that year was approximately Rs. 42 crores, while in addition, about Rs. 21 crores were paid annually for imported sugar.

The Sugar Committee also considered that the time had come when the Import Duty should definitely be made a protective duty instead of a revenue duty, and further that definite protection to the sugar-cane growing industry should be given for a period of 10 years or so in the first instance. They also felt that Indian Agriculture was passing through a period of reconstruction and the time was opportune for the development of the Indian sugar-cane industry. It was also pointed out that a good deal of the preliminary work, necessary for placing the Indian Sugar Industry on a sound foundation, had been carried out. As a result of the work of the Coimbatore Cane-Breeding Station, the Shahjahanpur Sugar Research Station, and the Sugar Bureau, Pusa, seedling canes of real merit have been produced, and distributed and are being grown on considerable areas. These improved varieties of canes covered nearly 18,14,000 acres, *i.e.*, more than half of the area under sugar-cane, in 1932-33, which has been estimated at 34,09,000 acres. The area under improved varieties of sugar cane was highest in the United Provinces, and next in Bihar and Orissa, the two provinces where the industry is chiefly concentrated.

7. THE INDIAN TARIFF BOARD, 1931.

The Tariff Board submitted a comprehensive report in the year 1931 recommending, *inter alia*, a grant of protection to the Industry for a period of 15 years and proposing that the protective duty on import of Sugar should be at Rs. 7-4-0 per cwt. for the first seven years and at Rs. 6-4-0 per cwt. for the remaining eight years.

8. SUGAR INDUSTRY (PROTECTION) ACT, 1932.*

The Government accepted the recommendations of the Tariff Board, and the Sugar Industry (Protection) Act, 1932, was passed by the Legislatures. This act provides for the fostering and development of the Sugar Industry and in accordance with its provisions, a protective duty at the rate of Rs. 7-4-0 per cwt. has been imposed on all classes of sugar until 31st March 1938, when a further enquiry will be made before the end of this period to ascertain if the protection to the sugar industry during the period from the 31st March, 1938 to the 31st March, 1946 should be continued to the same or to a greater or lesser extent. The Governor-General-in-Council has also been empowered to increase the duty imposed by the Act if he is satisfied after such an enquiry as he thinks fit that sugar is being imported into British India at a price which is likely to render insufficient the benefits intended to be conferred by the present duties.

Local Governments have also been empowered to make rules to provide that notices regarding the prices at which sugar cane is being bought at the factories should

*The text of the Act is given in Appendix II, along with a summary of the important recommendations of the Tariff Board, a summary of the *communique* issued by the Government of India on 30th January 1932, and the recommendations of the Select Committee of the Indian Legislative Assembly.

be affixed in conspicuous places near the entrances to the Sugar Factories.*

9. UNIQUE SUCCESS OF PROTECTION.

Over 100 factories of an average cane-crushing capacity of 600 tons per day have been established after the

---

*The U. P. Government published such rules in November 1933, by which it has been made compulsory for factories in the U. P. to publish, along with the price paid for purchase of cane, a figure of price of cane calculated according to the following formula ; $C = \frac{s \times p}{200}$ prescribed in the rules, on the assumption that the price of a maund of cane in annas shall be equal to half the price in annas of sugar made therefrom on the basis of the *highest wholesale price* of white sugar made in U. P. on an f. o. r. Cawnpore basis minus four annas, and the extraction percentage of sugar which has been fixed at 8·7 for the year 1933-34.

Although these rules do not fix the price of cane, they are definitely unfair to manufacturers. It is preposterous to take the maximum price of sugar of any factory in the province *i.e.* of only the best quality of sugar (leaving 2nd and 3rd qualities), and again not the ex-factory but Cawnpore price, with the addition of Railway freight, for calculating the minimum price of cane of all factories.

One result of the publication of the notices by the factories containing the theoretical price to be paid by them based on such fictitious data has been that a false impression has been created in the minds of the agriculturists that they are being cheated by the manufacturers who are paying them a smaller price than is due to them. The aim of the U. P. Government in making it compulsory for factories to publish such prices was to educate the cultivator but the result has been the creation of an unwarranted feeling of dissatisfaction towards the manufacturer, because of the wrong theoretical calculation of price of cane.

grant of protection to the Industry and it appears certain that by the year 1933-34 the Indian Sugar Industry will produce practically the full quantity of Sugar required in the country, if not more. If any import of sugar is necessary, it will be either of a class of sugar which is not made in the country or such as would be required to meet the fastidious taste of a certain class of the people who require highly refined and white-crystalled sugar.

10. SELF-SUFFICIENCY IN PRODUCTION.

The development of the industry has, indeed, been remarkable for its rapidity. Even the Government would not have expected that a stage would be reached, within only 2 years of the grant of protection when the industry would be in a position to supply the full requirements of the country for sugar, and be compelled to think of foreign markets for export of surplus production.

11. LARGE IMPORTS OF MACHINERY.

The value of Sugar machinery imported during the last six years, showing the chief countries from which it was imported, is given in Table No. 4 on page 21. The great increase in imports of machinery is visible. We do not expect large imports after 1934.

TABLE NO. 4.

Value of Sugar Machinery imported during the last six years.

(In thousand Rs.)

Year.	Whence imported.				
	U K.	Germany.	Belgium.	France.	Total.
1928-29 ...	16,30	23	...	61	17,51
1929-30 ...	8,49	8	3	30	9,21
1930-31 ...	10,82	23	...	2,30	13,68
1931-32 ...	26,22	1,18	22	2,22	30,14
1932-33 ...	91,48	...	...	...	1,53,11
1933-34 ... (April to October)	1,66,89	...	...	...	2,77,70

It will be seen from this that the value of the machinery supplied by United Kingdom has been more than half the total.*

12. MINIMUM BURDEN ON CONSUMER.

Incidentally this has also shown that if adequate protection is given to an industry, it is bound to be

*Of 27 plants ordered in 1932-33, 14 were British, 4 German, 2 Dutch. Of 47 ordered in 1933-34, 27 are British, 8 Dutch, 4 German, 2 French, 1 Belgian and 2 Czechoslovakian.

successful in rendering the country self-sufficient, and imposing the least burden on the consumer, due to internal competition which brings about a reduction in prices. As we will show later, this has happened in the case of the sugar industry in a remarkable manner. The price of Indian Sugar is about 2 rupees per maund lower than the price of imported sugar, (November 1933), as a result of the keen internal competition, and thus the burden on the consumer has been minimised,

13. PROBLEMS CONFRONTING THE INDUSTRY.

But the very rapid progress in the development of this industry which doubtless is a very satisfactory feature, has brought in its train, almost immediately, many problems which demand an immediate solution. These problems are manifold, *i.e.*, of excessive development of the industry in the United Provinces, and in Behar which are most advantageously situated, and the niggardly development in others like Bengal, Madras, Bombay, etc., of disposal of molasses, a by-product, the production of which has exceeded our requirements to such an extent that it fetches no price at all, as compared with about Rs. 1-8-0 a maund in 1929-30, the effect of the development of modern manufacture on the indigenous methods of production, *i.e.*, *Khandsari*, and manufacture of sugar from *Gur* in Refineries, manufacture of *Gur*, *Rab*, etc., location of factories, zoning, licensing, supply of cane, prices of cane, equitable distribution of profits derived from the industry between the manufacturers and cane-growers for whose benefit the protection has largely been granted, the problem of transport of sugar from the United Provinces and Behar & Orissa to distant markets like Madras, Karachi, Bombay, and resultant necessity of readjustment of Railway freights, the necessity of Standardized production, and of a Sales Organisation as in Java, etc., the urgent need of reduction in cost of production by utilisation of products like molasses in the manufacture of power alcohol for admixture with petrol as fuel for internal combustion engines, etc., and bagasse; by reduction in costs of agriculture by improvements in quality of cane, so as to yield a bigger percentage of sugar, and so as to extend the manufacturing season from 120 to 160 days or so, by growth of early ripening and late ripening canes; by researches for removing pests, and introduction of suitable varieties of cane so as to increase the crop per acre, by effecting economies in cost of manufacture, by increasing efficiency by chemical and engineering research, by suitable selection of efficient machinery, etc., by better method of distribution of markets between factories, by more rapid methods of supplying fresh cane to factories, by securing cheap railway and steamer freights, by economies in packing, by eliminating wasteful competition, and establishment of the necessary *espirit de corps*, by devising methods of finding an export market*, *e.g.*, in the

*No country has a soil or climate better adopted to the industry, or more abundant supplies of cheap labour, while the growth of a fresh great export trade would be of great importance and advantage to the country. In fact, it has been remarkable that India which can supply the whole world with sugar, actually does not produce enough for its requirements, and has to import sugar from abroad.

United Kingdom where we can get a preference in duty, by reduction of our cost of manufacture, in order to find an outlet for the surplus production (in excess of the normal consumption in the country) which is sure to come after the 1934 season,* etc. We will also refer to the consumption of sugar in India as well as other countries; and see what prospects there are for an increase in the consumption of sugar and *Gur* in India. We will treat these in the subsequent portions of this monograph.

We will also refer briefly to the manufacture of Sugar in other parts of the world, particularly Java, in view of its definite bearing on the Sugar trade and industry of India, and the restriction on output due to the decrease of consumption, during the last few years.

---

*The possibilities of India's ability to export are already being recognised. Vide the following extract from an article on "Sugar Technology in 1932" by Dr. O. W. Wilcox, published in "Sugar Reference Book and Directory, 1932-33". —"The Coimbatore canes are replacing the indigenous canes at a fairly rapid rate ; in consequence, the Indian ryot is developing considerable ability as a sugar producer, and there are some who visualise India as an exporting country in the not too distant future".

CHAPTER II.

Modern Developments in Sugar Industry and Cane Cultivation.

1. WASTAGE IN INDIGENOUS METHODS.

Before turning our attention to the various problems confronting the industry in regard to its manufacturing and agricultural sides, let us review the various methods employed at present for manufacturing sugar and *Gur*, the possibilities of their success in the future and also the statistical position of the growth of cane-cultivation and sugar manufacture up to the present time.

The occurrence of a very serious wastage of the sugar actually present in the cane, in the existing indigenous processes of extraction and conversion into both sugar and *Gur* is notorious. The Industrial Commission (vide page 80) roughly estimated, that of the sugar-cane grown in India *at least one third* was wasted owing to inefficient and primitive methods of extraction.

The Indian Sugar Committee, 1920, observed in their Report (page 260) that—

> "A thoroughly up-to-date factory can extract at least 96 per cent of the sugar actually present in the cane, and by an efficient control in the boiling house, 90 per cent of the sucrose in the juice can be recovered as manufactured sugar. In other words, about 86·4 per cent of the original sucrose in cane can be obtained as sugar".

In paragraph 336 of their Report, the Indian Sugar Committee remarked, in regard to the low recovery of sugar in India, as follows:—

> "We have assumed that cane in India contains on an average 12 per cent of sugar".* "If it were dealt with in a thoroughly efficient factory, it would be possible to obtain 9·5 per cent of marketable sugar from it. From cane with the same sugar content factories in Java recover 9·75 per cent of marketable sugar against an average of 6·85 per cent in Indian factories, the best of which obtain less than 8 per cent. There is thus a difference of almost 3 per cent between the results obtained by factories in Java and India".

2. IMPROVEMENT IN RECOVERY.

It will be shown elsewhere that the Indian factories have been alive to the possibilities of improvement in this direction, and have been trying to increase their efficiency. The percentage of recovery in India has been steadily increasing. From 7·45 in 1923-24, it reached 8·89 in 1931-32 as compared with 11·92 for Java, but has fallen slightly to 8·66 in 1932-33, due perhaps to a larger quantity of cane crushed, necessitating a prolongation of the season. The maximum recovery obtained in some of the old factories in 1932-33 was 11·1 *per cent*. The Khandsaris have also made improvement and are now able to recover about 5 per cent. of sugar. Further improvement in recovery percentage is possible, and

*The Indian Tariff Board (Sugar Industry Enquiry Report), 1931 assumed a sucrose content of 11·5 *per cent.*

vigorous efforts must be made by factories to recover a percentage which is at least equal to that of Java. But we will discuss this later.

3. Manufacture of *Gur*.

Let us first see what *Gur* is.

Gur may perhaps be best defined as cane juice in its natural state concentrated to its solidifying point without undergoing any material process of purification save the addition of a small amount of alkali or other clarifying ingredient, and the removal of the scum. It is a perfectly wholesome article of diet, and is very much in demand in this country, and is preferred to sugar by a large section of the people particularly in the village areas, and for some purposes, by all. Besides, *Gur* has an attractive flavour and delicious taste.

4. Method of manufacture of *Gur*.

Gur, it must be owned, is manufactured in an extremely wasteful, crude and primitive method. It is made in very small quantities. Its manufacture is a cottage industry, and is, as a rule, carried out by the cultivator in close proximity to his cane cultivation. The method of manufacture as well as the quality of *Gur* turned out varies from province to province. It is used either for eating, for refining, or for making sweetmeats and confectionery.

The best class of *Gur* is produced in Bombay and the Deccan, (the Bombay *Gur* has higher sucrose contents due to the richer canes used, and sells dearer) and in Meerut. However great the popularity of *Gur*, it must be admitted that there is a great and lamentable loss of sucrose in the present methods of manufacture of *Gur*, due to the poor strength of the bullocks (where bullocks are used) that run the crushing mills and to the fact that a large quantity of juice is left in the bagasse (or the residue of fibrous matter remaining after crushing the cane), the cane having been crushed once only, and the crude methods of boiling the juice in which inversion takes place from sucrose to glucose.* As a result, the recovery of the sucrose content of the cane works out to about 52 per cent. as against 86 per cent. obtained in a modern sugar factory.† The loss of efficiency due to the crude process of manufacture of *Gur*, thus works out to about 34 per cent. If we assume an average of 12 per cent. sucrose content for this cane, as has been done by the Indian Sugar Committee, the total recovery of sucrose from the 34,595,000 tons of cane used for the manufacture of *Gur* in 1932-33, would be 41,40,000 tons, out of which only 21,00,000 tons could be extracted by the present crude method, as against a possible extraction of over 35,30,000 tons of white sugar in the modern factory run

*This inversion is not, strictly speaking, a loss of sugar but it is a loss of crystallisable sugar which is of importance when the question of refining from *Gur* is considered. *Vide* Tariff Board's Report on the Sugar Industry, 1931, page 19.

†*Vide* Report of the Sugar Committee, 1920 (p. 262).

according to efficient lines. The total loss of sucrose thus entailed is tantamount to 15,00,000 lacs tons, which is equivalent to about as large a quantity of manufactured sugar.*

But the introduction of the power mill in place of the bullock mill, which happily is increasing, has made it possible to extract more sugar per maund of cane, and has considerably reduced the cost of production which however varies from province to province. According to the Director of Agriculture, Bengal, the extraction of juice per 100 maunds of cane is 62 per cent. from a bullock mill, and 68 per cent. from a power mill.

On this calculation, the loss of sucrose involved, as estimated in the preceding paragraph, by *Gur* manufactured in power mills, would be slightly lower.

5. SIZE OF THE *Gur* INDUSTRY.

Some idea of the size of the *Gur* industry in India can be had from Table No. 5 below, which gives the nett production of *Gur* from cane (and also palm) during the last ten years from 1923-24 to 1932-33, *available for direct consumption,* after allowing for the *Gur* equivalent of the cane used for other purposes (adopting the conversion factor of 10 tons of cane to 1 ton of *Gur*).

---

*The actual sucrose content of *Gur* varies considerably but may be placed at between 65 and 75 *per cent*, as compared with between 99 and 100 *per cent.* for white sugar (*Vide* Tariff Board's Report).

TABLE NO. 5.

Calculated nett production of gur in India for direct consumption.

Year.		Calculated nett production of *Gur*. Tons.
1923-24	...	... 2,400,000
1924-25	...	... 1,698,000
1925-26	...	... 2,089,000
1926-27	...	... 2,313,000
1927-28	...	... 2,276,000
1928-29	...	... 1,778,000
1929-30	...	... 1,837,000
1930-31	...	... 2,245,000
1931-32	...	... 2,772,000
1932-33	...	... 3,245,000
1933-34*	...	... 3,000,000

It will thus be seen that the consumption of *Gur*, which is roughly between 2½ and 3 million tons is on the increase. The total output of cane in India, excluding the quantity consumed in chewing, may, well be considered as potential raw material for *Gur* manufacture.

*This is our own estimate for 1933-34.

6. FUTURE OF *Gur* INDUSTRY.

Gur, which is the only form of sugar available in villages, is indispensable to agriculturists.* The cultivator does not ordinarily employ hired labour, and utilises the labour of the members of his own family, when they are otherwise idle, by growing cane.

The *Gur* Industry, we feel, will continue to flourish, if improvements are continually made in its methods of production, inasmuch as there is a strong bias in the minds of a large majority of the people for the use of *Gur*. We believe, however, that it is probable that as a result of the development of the white sugar industry in India, and as a result of the availability of *Swadeshi* sugar, many people will replace the use of *Gur* by sugar. To the extent that the white sugar industry gets an impetus on account of this reason, the market for *Gur* may decline. Any improvement in the economic condition of the people is also likely to have the effect of making them consumers of sugar in place of *Gur*, which a large number of people are unable to do at present, owing to the generally prevalent higher price of sugar, as compared with *Gur*. Notwithstanding this, if the *Gur* industry keeps abreast of the times, and introduces efficient methods of production by eliminating waste of cane-juice by introduction of heavier power-crushing mills, by introduction of improved boiling pans, improved furnaces, by provision

---

**Vide* The Indian Sugar Industry—By Khan Bahadur S. M. Hadi, Director of Agriculture, Bhopal State, P. 50.

of superior canes and by provision of skilled and technically qualified labour, it need have no apprehension about its continued existence.

7. Methods of Manufacture of Sugar.

The methods of manufacturing sugar from sugar-cane are:—

(A) Indigenous method.

(*i*) Open Pan process.

(*ii*) Manufacture of Raw sugar, *i.e.*, *Gur* and *Rab.*

and

(*iii*) Refining of raw sugar into white sugar by—

(*a*) either Bel-khanchi khandsaris,

(*b*) or Bel-centrifugal khandsaris,

(*c*) or Open Pan factories.

(B) Modern factory method.

(*a*) Refining of sugar from *Gur* or Jaggery in Refineries,

(*b*) Manufacture of sugar from sugar-cane direct.

8. Indigenous Methods—Raw Sugar, *i.e.*, *Gur* and *Rab*.

We have already described the manufacture of *Gur.* We will now describe the latter. *Rab* or *Massecuite* is different from *Gur* only in respect of its being of a thinner consistency. It is obtained by boiling the juice to a slightly lower degree of concentration than *Gur*. It is mainly used for the manufacture of crude sugar known as *Khand*. This process of manufacture of *Rab* is known as the *Bel* Process, and consists of boiling the juice obtained from the cane in bullock or small power mills in a series of open pans. This is prevalent largely in the Rohilkhand Division of the United Provinces. *Rab* is also prepared from *Gur* in the Eastern Districts of the United Provinces.

Rab is manufactured generally within easy reach of the cane supplies.

9. REFINING OF *Rab* INTO WHITE SUGAR.

The *Bel-khanchi* Khandsaris use no machinery. The cane-growers crush the cane in animal power crushers (which are generally taken on hire) and sell the juice (not the cane) to the Khandsaris who convert the same into *Rab* in direct-fired open pans. The *Rab* is placed in bags, and molasses is squeezed out by applying pressure. The brown sugar thus obtained is then treated with moistened weeds, and after it becomes almost white, it is dried in the sun.

The *Bel-centrifugal* Khandsaris adopt the same method as is adopted by the *Bel-khanchi* Khandsaris except that centrifugal machines which may be hand or power-driven are used for separating sugar from *rab*. In a modification of this process, the *rab*-boiler working in villages sells his *rab* to owners of centrifugal factories, that are generally located in towns.

The process of manufacture of sugar from the *rab* is accompanied by even more waste than is found in manufacturing sugar from *Gur*.

The open pan factories represent a further stage in the industrialisation of small-scale sugar manufacture. Such factories have generally got cane-crushers driven by oil or steam engines or by electric motors. *Rab* is boiled in open pans as before and power driven centrifugals are used for separating sugar from *rab*.

These factories differ from the modern sugar factories in size, and also in regard to the simplicity of the machinery and process employed. Most of these are large enough, however, to be classified as factories under the Indian Factories Act.

10. STATISTICS OF PRODUCTION OF KHANDSARIS.

It is a matter of great regret that statistics for the sugar produced by the various types of open pan concerns which may collectively (as also conveniently) be called *Khandsaris* are not available. It is a matter of pleasure however to find that the Imperial Council of Agricultural Research sanctioned a grant of Rs. 3,000 in November 1933, for taking a census of sugar production in villages and towns in the United Provinces by the Khandsari process. The Government of the United Provinces have undertaken the census of production for the year 1933-34, and has appointed a special staff of investigators for carrying on a detailed enquiry in the towns. For the rural areas, the information will be collected by Patwaris. The Punjab Government have also undertaken to compile the figures of production, etc., for Khandsari production in the Punjab.

As we have already observed, it is very necessary to have exact figures of production of sugar by this method, which is important from the agricultural point of view, consuming as it does a larger quantity of cane than the modern factories, at present.

The Indian Sugar Committee of 1920 (Paragraph 278) estimated the production of Khandsaris at 2,50,000 tons per annum.

The Tariff Board's estimate for 1927-28 amounted to 2,00,000 tons.

11. INCREASE IN KHANDSARI PRODUCTION.

Since the year 1931, the manufacture of sugar of the Khandsaris has increased, according to the opinion expressed by Mr. R. C. Srivastava, Sugar Technologist to the Imperial Council of Agricultural Research. Our private enquiries also point to an increase in Khandsari production. We therefore concur with this view. The system is not confined to Rohilkhand as before but is also spreading in the Punjab and there are indications of its adoption more and more in Madras, Bombay and Bengal also. It would be safe therefore if the production of khandsari sugar would be estimated at 2,75,000 tons in 1932-33. It is hoped that we would be able to get the actual figure of the production of khandsari sugar for the year 1933-34, as a result of the investigations undertaken by the United Provinces Government, and the Punjab Government.

We might observe, in passing, here that the recovery *percentage* of sugar by this method has increased since the Indian Sugar Committee reported in 1920, from 4 *per cent.* And although the Tariff Board's figure of 5·25 *per cent.* appears and is considered to be excessive, it would be safe if we assumed the average yield of sugar at 5 *per cent.* Thus a production of 2,75,000 tons of sugar for 1932-33 would mean a consumption of 5,50,000 tons of cane.

12. FUTURE OF KHANDSARI PROCESS OF PRODUCTION.

Although one is naturally inclined to feel doubtful about the sucess of this form of manufacture of sugar which is very wasteful and uneconomic as compared with the modern factory, its importance in the transitional stage of the industry cannot be mimimized as it can be undertaken in the interior parts of the country, where owing to lack of communications or scattered nature of cane areas, it would not be worth while for modern factories to be established.

The Indian Sugar Committee condemned the khandsari industry, largely on the ground of its inefficiency. Since then, as a result of the imposition of the protective tariff on Sugar, the industry has made some progress as estimated above, due, *inter alia*, to the advantages it has in purchasing cane at a rate, which is considerably lower than the market rate, and the increase in the recovery percentage by improvement in methods of manufacture, and the low overhead charges, etc. The Tariff Board expressed the opinion that the industry must undoubtedly play an important part in providing an outlet for surplus cane. The Report also stated that these khandsari factories are easily and quickly established, and their capital cost of crushing cane is estimated at 6·79 annas per maund, against that of Re. 1 in case of central factories. The industry, as seen above, is of a great magnitude, giving employment to thousands of people at a time when their labour is running to waste and holds an important position in the agricultural system of the United Provinces. A set-back to this industry would therefore be a very great hardship to the cultivators, particularly in Rohilkhand where the area under cane is about one-tenth of the total area in India, and where the cane is almost entirely sold for white sugar making by the *Bel* process. The only way of saving it or of prolonging its existence, is to increase its efficiency, by carrying on vigorous research, by the adoption of the improved *Bel* system known as *Hadi* or *Bhopal* method, or by the modified Rohilkhand *Bel*,* as was tried by the Sugar Technologist in 1932-33, and which yielded larger quantity of *rab*, by the provision of technical assistance, and skilled labour, and by a whole-hearted co-operation of cultivators, zemindars, the khandsari and the Government.

The Imperial Council of Agricultural Research* should continue to help this industry which gives employment to a large number of people and which is of so great importance in the agricultural economy of the country, by undertaking researches for effecting economy in methods of manufacture, and by eliminating waste, wherever possible, by the assistance of efficient machinery.

Mere sentiment alone however will not be of help in saving the industry from sinking, with which it is

---

*This was tried at the Nagalia farm, Bilari, belonging to Lala Har Sahai Gupta, in 1932-33. The Imperial Council gave a grant of Rs. 4,000 for the purpose. For a description of the *Bel*, *vide* "The Open Pan System of White Sugar Manufacture" by R. C. Srivastava, page 114.

*In November 1933, the Imperial Council sanctioned a scheme of Rs. 1,50,000 prepared by the Sugar Technologist for establishment of a Research Station for making improvements in Khandsari method of sugar Manufacture and indigenous process of making *Gur*.

threatened by the efficient factory production on a large scale.*

The industry, if it wishes to survive, has an up-hill task before it. Its future will depend considerably on its own efforts. It will have to make earnest endeavours for deriving a better percentage of sucrose, and improving the quality of sugar turned out by it.

13. Modern Gur Refineries.

One modern method is to refine sugar from *Gur*.

As we have already seen, and we shall see later, between 2 to 3 per cent. of the cane crop in India is used in manufacture of sugar from *Gur* in refineries, during the last two years. The cane equivalent of *Gur* used in refineries computed on the assumption of one ton of *Gur* representing 10 tons of cane, was 16,20,000 tons of cane in 1932-33. The total production of sugar in modern factories in India showing the percentage recovery, number of factories and the quantity of *Gur* melted during the last ten years from 1923-24 to 1932-33 is given in Table No. 6, below.

---

*Even the Tariff Board which showed such great interest in the Khandsari industry, could not help observing that the Khandsari system of manufacture, if the scheme of protection is successful, should to a considerable extent give place to a system of central factories, (*vide* para 81).

TABLE NO. 6.

Production of Sugar from Gur in Modern Factories in India.

Year.	No. of factories working with *gur*.	*Gur* melted. (tons.)	Sugar produced (tons.)	Per cent. recovery.
1923-24 ...	22	120,301	56,406	46·88
1924-25 ...	13	68,451	33,593	49·07
1925-26 ...	19	73,914	38,409	51·96
1926-27 ...	22	112,671	58,085	51·55
1927-28 ...	19	101,466	52,055	51·30
1928-29 ...	14	58,472	31,038	53·08
1929-30 ...	11	37,476	21,150	56·43
1930-31 ...	10	57,738	31,791	55·44
1931-32 ...	17	126,159	69,539	55·12
1932-33 (estimated) ...	22	162,000	91,000	56·17

It will be seen from this that the total production of sugar in 1932-33 was 91,000 tons, from 162,000 maunds of *Gur* melted in refineries, and the percentage recovery was 56·17. The total production of sugar from cane, from *Gur*, and from indigenous processes is given in Table No. 13.

14. FUTURE OF REFINERIES, ONLY MANUFACTURING SUGAR FROM *Gur*.

It will thus be seen that the return from 100 maunds of cane manufactured into *Gur* and then refined into sugar is $5\frac{1}{2}$ maunds of sugar as against 9 maunds obtained by manufacture of sugar directly from cane, the quantity of molasses being the same in each case. Thus, clearly, sugar made from *Gur*, besides being a little brown, is more expensive, as compared with the white sugar manufactured direct from cane.

This uneconomical method of manufacture of sugar from *Gur* is doomed to die out in course of time. It is clear that such a wasteful system of manufacture of sugar cannot continue and it is probable that unless the price of *Gur* is very low and that of sugar very high, this industry will be extinct in the immediate future. It is thus impossible to take a hopeful view of the future of the *Gur* refining industry.*

15. MODERN CANE-FACTORIES.

We may now turn our attention to the modern industry manufacturing sugar direct from cane.

The modern Sugar Factories started from the beginning of the 20th Century. In 1919-20, the number of modern factories was 19, but the number began to

* *Vide* para **274** of the Report of the Indian Sugar Committee, and para **20** of the Report of the Tariff Board.

increase slowly. The total quantity of sugar produced by factories direct from cane since 1919-20 to 1932-33, the number of factories producing sugar direct from cane and our estimate of the production in 1933-34 and 1934-35 are given in Table No. 7 below. Figures of the percentage recovery of sugar in India and in Java are also given for the sake of comparison.

TABLE No. 7.

Production of Sugar direct from cane in modern factories.

Year.		No. of Factories.	Quantity of Sugar produced direct from cane (in tons).	Per cent. Recovery for India.	Per cent. Recovery for Java.
1919-20	...	19	23,300	...	...
1921-22	...	20	28,250	...	...
1922-23	...	20	23,620	...	...
1923-24	...	23	38,312	7·45	11·44
1924-25	...	23	33,805	7·79	12·38
1925-26	...	23	52,990	8·03	12·38
1926-27	...	25	62,941	8·47	10·85
1927-28	...	26	67,684	8·60	11·62
1928-29	..	24	68,050	8·59	12·16
1929-30	...	27	89,768	9·07	12·42
1930-31	...	29	119,859	9·09	11·43
1931-32	...	32	158,581	8·89	11·92
1932-33	...	57	290,177	8·66	...
1933-34*	...	135	700,000 (estimated)	8·90	...
1934-35†	...	155	875,000	9·10	...

*The earthquake on 15th January 1934, damaged several mills in Bihar, and it is apprehended, production will go down considerably in 1933-34.

†These are our estimates.

The considerably increased production estimated for 1933-34 by us is due to the following reasons. During 1932-33, the production of sugar from 32 old factories was 187,685 tons, which represents an increase of 18% over their production for 1931-32. The output of 26 new factories which worked during 1932-33 was 102,492 tons. It is probable that owing to further extensions the same rate of increase will be maintained by the old factories during 1933-34. Besides, several of the 32 new factories started in 1932-33 commenced crushing very late in the season. A large number of these new factories also have put up extensions. It is therefore very likely that the production from factories which started crushing in 1932-33 will also increase considerably. Due to these factors, and the addition of over 75 new factories which have started crushing in 1933-34, and which are of a higher capacity than the average 600 ton factories, and the extension of the average crushing season from 120 to 150 days, (the maximum was 184 days), the production of sugar from cane-factories will, according to our estimate, be not less than 7,00,000 tons, during 1933-34.

We confidently hope that during the season 1933-34 the modern factories will produce a quantity of sugar, which coupled with the Khandsari production will be more than the normal annual consumption in the country during the last few years (estimated at 9,40,000 tons). There would thus seem to be no need of any import of sugar at all. A few modern factories are projected for working in 1934-35 and it is definitely certain that by

1934-35 India will produce a quantity of sugar, which will be more than the estimated present figure of the demand (9,40,000 tons).

16. Future of Cane-Factories in India.

The consummation of the seven-year plan inaugurated by the Government in April 1932 for the establishment of the Sugar Industry in India materialized within only two years. This is a feature for which the Government may well congratulate themselves, and those responsible for the development of the industry may legitimately feel proud. But they cannot afford to rest on their laurels. They have before them the uphill task of stabilizing the industry.

It is hoped that the industry will carry on vigorous research in regard to its agricultural, manufacturing, and commercial aspects, with a view to decrease the cost of production, as before long it will be faced with the necessity of finding an outlet for its surplus produce in foreign markets, and of standing competition with them in the home market, and these would only be possible if the cost of production is appreciably reduced.

We are convinced that modern cane-factories in India have a bright future before them, and it is their duty to go on increasing their efficiency by emulating the example of the Java and Hawaiian industry and bring their working to such a pitch of perfection that India might well become an envy of the world. For this purpose, the industry will doubtless have to keep abreast of the times by carrying on vigorous research, not only in the direction of effecting greater efficiency by cheapening the cost of agriculture, by growing a larger quantity of cane per acre, by growing a better quality of cane, by introduction of early and late ripening varieties, etc., but also by reducing manufacturing costs by increasing efficiency, by prevention of loss of sucrose from deterioration of cane mill juices due to bacterial action, by use of efficient antiseptics, like Electrolytic Chlorogen,* by research in Chemistry and Engineering, and also by a better utilisation of its by-products like molasses and bagasse. Then alone the industry will be in a position to export its products to other markets.

17. Cane-Factories working as refineries.

It would also perhaps be possible for cane-sugar factories to refine sugar from *Gur*, during the off season, from June to September, when cane is not available, in order to reduce their overhead costs, but the possibility of their success in this direction depends considerably on the price, at which *Gur* is available in every district, being low, and the price of sugar being comparatively higher. This possibility of reduction of overhead costs, and of giving employment to a few people during the off-season, by engaging themselves in refining sugar from *Gur*, should be carefully investigated.

**Vide* International Sugar Journal, July 1927,—an informative article by Dr. J. H. Haldane.

18. Statistics of Production and consumption of Cane, Sugar, etc.

Having dealt with the progress and the potentialities of the sugar industry in India, it would be of great interest to turn to the statistics of the area under sugar-cane, area under improved varieties, both in the provinces, and in the whole country, of the uses of cane, of the production of sugar from various sources, of the consumption of sugar in India (as also in different countries of the world for the sake of comparison and estimation of the possibilities of increase in consumption in India), etc.

19. No reliable statistics of cane-crop.

At the outset it must be observed that the official statistics pertaining to the sugar cane crop give the area under cane and the yield of *Gur* only. No figures are given for the tonnage of cane. At the present time all the crop cutting experiments on which these official returns are based, end in the weighment of *Gur*, and not of cane. The Sugar Committee of 1920 drew attention to this defect (*vide* page 353), and recommended that the results of these experiments should be reported in terms of weight of cane and not of *Gur*. It is a matter of regret that the old system condemned by the Indian Sugar Committee still continues and it is not at all surprising if the forecast based on such methods is far from true. The absence of reliable information in regard to the actual cane crop would hamper our work in many ways and may lead us to incorrect conclusions, and consequently a false step, which cannot be too much regretted.

20. Case for the Economic Survey Committee.

The Government of India have just initiated a comprehensive economic review, and have appointed an Economic Survey Committee. The Imperial Council of Agricultural Research have decided to co-operate with it. I hope that this matter will be put up for consideration, before the Economic Survey Committee, and that a way will be found for compiling reliable statistics in regard to the actual cane-crop in the country, in appreciation of its great importance.

21. Present statistics of cane-crop an unsatisfactory basis.

With the statistics that are now available, it is not possible for us to find out the actual quantity of production of cane each year, as the weight of the cane produced per acre varies with the locality and also the variety of the cane. Likewise, the weight of cane required for manufacturing a unit of weight of *Gur*, also varies with the variety of cane. It is clear therefore that neither of the two official figures of acreage and yield of *Gur* can be used by themselves for making an accurate estimate of the yield of cane. In all cases where accuracy is necessary, the forecast figures for *Gur* only have to be made use of as a basis.

22. ACREAGE OF CANE-CROP OF 1933-34.

The area under sugar-cane during the year 1933-34, which is given from the Final estimate of the Sugarcane crop of 1933-34, (published on 15th February 1934) which is based on reports received from Provinces and States containing on an average 96 per cent. of the total area under sugarcane in India, shows that out of the total acreage of 33,05,000 under cane, 17,31,000 were in the United Provinces, 4,67,000 in the Punjab, 4,18,000 in Bihar and Orissa, 2,57,000 in Bengal, 1,20,000 in Madras and 1,02,000 in Bombay. The percentage of the acreage based on the average percentage of sugar cane area in each province and the total area under sugarcane in India based on the figures for the five years ending 1931-32 was as follows:—

51·8% in the United Provinces,	14·6% in the Punjab
9·9% in Bihar & Orissa	7·2% in Bengal
3·6% in Madras	3·3% in Bombay.

23. ESTIMATED PRODUCTION OF SUGARCANE.

In Table No. 8 given below, the official figures for area under sugar cane and total or gross production of

Gur are given from 1923-24 to 1932-33. In the last column of the table *calculated* figures of the production of sugarcane have been given. It may be explained here that the calculation has been made on the following assumptions:—

(1) that of the total production of *Gur* in a year, the quantities produced from improved and indigenous varieties of cane are in proportion to the areas under these varieties. (The figures for the area under improved varieties are taken from the next Table, (*i.e.*, No.9)

(2) that the factor of converting *Gur* per acre into cane per acre is 11 for the indigenous varieties, and 10 for the improved varieties, corresponding to the yields of 9 and 10% *Gur* on cane respectively.

The former factor of 11 was accepted by the Indian Sugar Committee (vide paragraph 274), and appears to be correct still as far as the indigenous varieties of cane are concerned. The factor of 10 was adopted by the Tariff Board in view of the increasing production of improved varieties. We feel that in view of the continued increase in the cultivation of improved varieties since 1931-32, it would not be wrong to accept the factor of 9 for the future years, *i.e.*, after 1935

TABLE NO. 8.

*Area under Sugar-cane and estimated production of Sugar-cane in India.**

Year.		Area under Sugar cane. 1,000 acres.	Gross production of *Gur.* 1,000 tons.	Calculated production of Sugar cane 10 and 11 factors. 1,000 tons.
1923-24	...	3,105	3,502	38,455
1924-25	...	2,704	2,722	29,866
1925-26	...	1,806	3,143	34,382
1926-27	...	3,075	3,420	37,392
1927-28	...	3,105	3,376	36,842
1928-29	...	2,650	2,827	30,669
1929-30	...	2,677	2,885	30,961
1930-31	...	2,902	3,359	35,780
1931-32	...	3,076	4,116	43,316
1932-33	...	3,321	4,684	50,000
1933-34	...	3,305	5,067	55,000 (Estimated)

*It will be observed from the above table that while the area under cane has increased from 3·1 million acres in 1923-24 to 3·3 million acres in 1932-33, (an increase of 9·7 per cent), the production of cane has increased during the same period from 38 million tons to 55 million tons or by 45 per cent. This correspondingly greater increase in the production of cane is due to the greater yield of high-tonnage improved varieties of cane.

24. Area under Improved varieties of Cane in India.

We give in Table No 9 below, figures showing the improved varieties of cane in India from 1923-24 to 1932-33.

TABLE NO. 9.

Area under improved varieties of Cane in India from 1923-24 to 1932-33.

Year.	Acres.
1923-24	60,604
1924-25	75,334
1925-26	171,808
1926-27	207,989
1927-28	268,688
1928-29	301,098
1929-30	549,025
1930-31	817,094
1931-32	1,170,479
1932-33 (estimated)	1,814,388

It will be observed from here that the improved varieties of cane now cover more than half of the total acreage under cane in India. This tendency of sowing improved varieties is greatly on the increase.

25. AREA OF IMPROVED VARIETIES OF CANE IN THE PROVINCES.

In Table No. 10 below, we give figures for each province showing the acreage under improved varieties of sugar cane from 1929-30 to 1932-33.

TABLE NO. 10.

Area under improved varieties of Sugar-cane in different provinces from 1929-30 to 1932-33.

(In thousand acres.)

Province.	1929-30	1930-31	1931-32	1932-33
U. P. ...	281	514	678	1,187
Punjab ...	79	70	120	172
B. & O. ...	81	70	189	236
Bengal ...	74	100	100	100 (estimated)
Madras ...	22	10	26	52
Bombay ...	nominal	nominal	nominal	6
N. W. F. P. ...	...	40	38	38 (estimated)
Assam ...	6	6	7	8
C. P. ...	1	4	7	8
Burma ...	1	...	2	3
TOTAL (in Thousand acres) ...	549	817	1,170	1,814 (estimated)

26. Utilization of the Cane-Crop.

Let us now see how this cane-crop is utilized. The cane-crop is used for five main purposes:—

(a) For sugar-manufacture in modern cane factories. Exact figures for cane crushed in these are available.

(b) For sugar-manufacture in modern *Gur* Refineries. Exact figures for the quantity of *gur* melted are available, and the equivalent quantity of cane is calculated from this on the assumption that one ton of *gur* represents 10 tons of cane.

(c) For sugar manufacture by the Open Pan Process, (referred to in paragraph 9 of this chapter). The figures for cane crushed are estimated from the *Khandsari* production, on an assumption of an average yield of 5 per cent.

(d) For planting sets and chewing. Accepting the figure of the Indian Sugar Committee, the amount of cane required for chewing has been taken as 4·5 million tons. For planting sets, 2 per cent. of the crop has been added.

(e) The manufacture of *Gur* (excluding *gur* used for refining). This represents the net quantity of *gur* available for direct consumption. The quantity of cane required for this purpose is the balance of the total cane crop (as shown in Table No. 8), after allowing for the quantities used up for purposes stated in (*a*) to (*d*) above.

The quantity of cane used for manufacture of *gur*, and sugar and for other purposes, from 1923-24 to 1932-33, and the percentage of its uses for different purposes, are shown in Table No. 11 and 12 respectively.

TABLE NO. 11.

Quantity of cane (in thousand tons) used for sugar and Gur manufacture and for other purposes.

Year.	Cane used in factories.	Cane equivalent of *Gur* used in refineries.	Cane used in indigenous processes. (Estimated)	Cane used for sets and chewing purposes. (Estimated)	Cane used for *Gur* manufacture. (Estimated)	Total cane crop (Estimated)
1923-24 ...	514	1,203	4,000	5,300	27,448	38,455
1924-25 ...	434	685	4,000	5,120	19,627	29,866
1925-26 ...	659	739	4,000	5,140	23,844	34,382
1926-27 ...	742	1,127	4,000	5.200	26,323	37,392
1927-28 ...	786	1,015	4,000	5,200	25,841	36,842
1928-29 ...	791	585	4,000	5,110	20,183	30,669
1929-30 ...	990	375	4,000	5,120	20,476	30,961
1930-31 ...	1,317	577	4,000	5,250	24,636	35,780
1931-32 ...	1,783	1,262	5,000	5,400	29,871	43,316
1932-33* ...	3,350	1,620	5,500	5,500	34,595	50,000
1933-34* ...	5.500*	...	...	...	...	55,000

*Estimated.

TABLE NO. 12.

Proportion (per cent.) of cane crop used for sugar and Gur making and for other purposes.

Year.	Cane used in factories.	Cane equivalent of *Gur* used in refineries.	Cane used in indigenous processes.	Cane used for sets and chewing purposes.	Cane used for Gur manufacture.	Total cane crop.
1923-24 ...	1·3	3·1	10·4	13·8	71·4	100
1924-25 ...	1·5	2·3	13·4	17·1	65·7	100
1925-26 ...	1·9	2·1	11·6	14·9	69·5	100
1926 27 ...	1·9	3·0	10·7	13·9	70·5	100
1927-28 ...	2·1	2·7	10·8	14·1	70·3	100
1928-29 ...	2·6	1·9	13·0	16·7	65·8	100
1929-30 ...	3·2	1·2	13·0	16·5	66·1	100
1930-31 ...	3·7	1·6	11·2	14·7	68·8	100
1931-32 ...	4·1	2·9	11·7	12·4	68·9	100
1932-33 ...	6·6	3·2	11·0	11·0	69·0	100
1933-34* ...	10	...	...	...	...	...

*Our estimate.

It will be noted that the quantity of cane used in modern factories is only a small fraction of the total cane-crop of India. The manufacture of *Gur* still takes up by far the largest part of the cane-crop, representing, during 1932-33, over 11 times the cane used in modern factories. The Khandsari industry was estimated to take approximately double the quantity required by modern factories, but it is certain that in view of the great increase in production of sugar factories in 1932-33, which went up to 2,90,000 tons, the proportion must have decreased, and in future years, it will be smaller than the factory consumption. At the present time, however, it must be observed that from the agricultural point of view, the *gur* industry, as also the Khandsari industry, occupies a very important position.

27. TOTAL PRODUCTION OF SUGAR.

Let us now turn our attention to the figures of the total production of sugar in India, from various sources.

It will be seen that the percentage of the increase in production of *cane-sugar*, as compared with 1930-31, has been 33% in 1931-32, and 142% in 1932-33.

The figures of nett production of *Gur*, and of Sugar from *Gur* along with the percentage of recovery have been given in Tables Nos. 5 and 6.

Table No. 13 gives the total production of sugar from 1923-24 to 1932-33, and our estimates for 1933-34 and 1934-35.

TABLE NO. 13.

Total production of Sugar in India in tons.

Year.	Central Factory Sugar from Cane.	Central Factory Sugar from Gur.	Khandsari sugar (estimated).	Total production.
1923-24 ...	38,312	56,406	200,000	294,718
1924-25 ...	33,805	33,593	200,000	267,398
1925-26 ...	52,990	38,409	200,000	291,399
1926-27 ...	62,941	58,085	200,000	321,026
1927-28 ...	67,684	52,055	200,000	319,739
1928-29 ...	68,050	31,038	200,000	299,088
1929-30 ...	89,768	21,150	200,000	310,918
1930-31 ...	119,859	31,791	200,000	351,650
1931-32 ...	158,581	69,539	250,000	478,120
1932-33 (estimated)	290,000	91,000	275,000	656,000
1933-34* ,, ...	700,000	90,000	260,000	1,100,000
1934-35* ,, .	875,000	75,000	200,000	1,150,000

28. FORECAST OF PRODUCTION OF SUGAR IN INDIA.

It must be explained here that our estimate of the total production of sugar in the country in 1933-34, and 1934-35 differs considerably from the Forecast of the Annual Production and Consumption of Sugar in India made by the Sugar Technologist to the Imperial Council, which was published in the Indian Trade Journal in May 1933. His forecast is given in Table No. 14.

* These are our estimates.

The terrible earthquake which took place in Bihar on the 15th January 1934 caused appalling damage to life, property and crops. Several Sugar Mills were damaged. It is apprehended that the factory production will go down by about 50,000 tons in 1933-34.

TABLE NO. 14.

Sugar Technologist's forecast of Annual Production and consumption of sugar in India upto 1934-35 (from Cane and Gur.)

Particulars.	Actual 1931-32.	Estimated 1932-33.	Estimated 1933-34.	Estimated 1934-35.
	Tons.	Tons.	Tons.	Tons.
1. Production from existing capacity of old factories.	228,0C0	228,000	351,000	586,000
2. Production due to increase in capacity of old factories (at 10% of previous season's capacity).	...	23,000	35,000	60,000
3. Production from new factories commencing manufacturing operations during the season.	...	100,000	200,000	nil
4. Total production of factory Sugar.	228,000	351,000	586,000	646,000
5. Estimated production of Khandsari Sugar.	250,000	275,000	300,000	300,000
6. Total production of all kinds of Sugar	478,000	626,0C0	886,000	946,000
7. Consumption of Sugar.	982,540	940,000	940,000	940,000
8. Difference between consumption and production representing margin for imported Sugar.	5,04,540	3,14,000	54,000	—6,000

Mr. Srivastava, in our opinion, has greatly underestimated the production. The cane-crushing capacity of factories is very much greater than that assumed by him, the number of factories started has also been larger than calculated by him, the production due to the increase in the capacity of old factories has also been greater than the 10 per cent assumed by him (during the year 1932-33, 18·4 per cent. more sugar was produced by old factories, as compared with 1931-32), and the duration of the crushing season has also been greater.

The estimate of the sugar Technologist has gone far wrong even for 1932-33 and will turn out still more incorrect in 1933-34 and 1934-35 as a result of the large extensions in plants, and the large number of mills (over 75) with over 600 tons daily cane-crushing capacity, the extension of the duration of the crushing season, the probable increase in recovery of sugar due to the efficiency of the machinery built according to the latest scientific advancement (during 1932-33 also, it was found that the average recovery in the new factories in the United Provinces was higher than in the old ones, being 8·61 and 8·48 per cent. respectively), to the availability of larger supplies of improved cane, and to the increase in the number of factories (not less than 20), projected for working in 1934-35.

We estimate the total production* of sugar in India to be 11,00,000 tons in 1933-34, and 11,50,000 tons in 1934-35, as against 8,86,000 tons in 1933-34 and 9,40,000 in 1934-35 as estimated by the Sugar Technologist.

---

* As a result of the damage caused by the Earthquake on the 15th January, 1934, we expect the factory production to decrease by about 50,000 tons in 1933-34.

The Sugar Technologist estimated the total consumption of sugar in India for 1932-33, 1933-34, and 1934-35 at 940,000 tons, and drew the inevitable conclusion that the home production of sugar from cane and *Gur* during *1934-35* should *fully come up to the home consumption.*

The Sugar Technologist also gave the following "further word of warning" in conclusion, which deserves careful attention.

'The rate at which the sugar industry has been developing during the last two years has recently become too fast to be healthy. In view of the statistical position disclosed in the table (*vide* Table No. 14), considerable caution and restraint are necessary in connection with any further extension of the industry, if it is to be saved the fate of jute, rubber and a number of other industries which are now suffering from the ill-effects of overproduction.'

29. FORECAST OF CONSUMPTION OF SUGAR IN INDIA.

In giving the above warning, The Sugar Technologist has assumed that the demand for sugar will remain at its present level, and that by *1934-35*, India will produce 6,000 tons more than her consumption which has been estimated at 9,40,000 tons. As stated above, we believe that the stage when India will produce more sugar than she now needs for consumption will come in *1933-34*, when the production will be *considerably* greater than her normal consumption. But we do not share the opinion of the Sugar Technologist that the consumption of sugar will remain steadily at the same level. We believe that consumption of sugar will increase on account of several factors.

Firstly, as a result of an improvement in the economic conditions, and the lifting of the present depression.

Secondly, as a result of the fall in the price of sugar because consumption will be stimulated owing to the cheapness.

The price level and the purchasing power of the people are important factors affecting the consumption of sugar. In Table No. 15 below, we give the yearly average price for Java White Sugar in Calcutta and the annual consumption of sugar (excluding *gur*) for the last 10 years from 1923-24 to 1932-33.

TABLE NO. 15.

Price Level and consumption of Sugar in India.

Year.	Yearly average price of Java Sugar in Calcutta. (Rs. per md.)	Consumption of Sugar in India. (Tons.)
1923-24	18 0 0	678,081
1924-25	14 4 0	859,057
1925-26	10 15 0	1,011,488
1926-27	11 14 0	999,302
1927-28	10 7 0	1,101,524
1928-29	9 13 0	1,164,805
1929-30	9 0 0	1,324,923
1930-31	8 11 0	1,215,585
1931-32	10 1 0	982,540
1932-33	10 10 0	928,095

From this, it can be seen that the consumption of sugar reached the highest point during 1929-30 and 1930-31, when the prices were the lowest. We can therefore safely conclude that if prices of Indian sugar go down, as they are likely to do, owing to keen internal competition, inspite of the high tariff on foreign sugar, there is every likelihood of an increase in consumption. The prices of Indian sugar have already lost their parity with Java Sugar, and there is a prospect of a further decline in prices of Indian Sugar, during the 1934-35 season, as compared with the present price of about Rs. 8-8-0 per maund.

Besides, as we will show in Table no. 17, the *per capita* consumption of sugar is notoriously low, as compared with other countries of the world. The *per capita* consumption of sugar in 1929-30, 1930-31 and 1931-32 was 8·6, 7·8, 6·0 lbs., while the consumption of *Gur* during those years was 11·9, 14·4, and 17·6 lbs., respectively. The total *per capita* consumption of both sugar and *gur* was thus 20·5, 22·2, and 23·6 lbs., in 1929-30, 1930-31, and 1931-32 respectively. This is remarkably very low, as compared with the *per capita* consumption in 1930-31 of 55 lbs. in Germany, 60 lbs. in Czechoslovakia, 107 lbs. in the United States, 107 lbs. in Australia, 57 lbs. in France, and 94 lbs. in Canada. The consumption is high in advanced countries, and particularly in countries producing sugar. There is thus a great potentiality of increased consumption, if there is an improvement in the economic condition of the people.

Thirdly, as a result of the replacement of *gur* by sugar, in consequence of a change in the taste of people.

This is sure to happen to a certain extent. It is difficult to forecast with exactitude the extent of such replacement of *gur* by sugar. That there will be such a tendency is however undoubted. As far as we can visualise, the demand of *gur* will undergo a considerable decline, with the increase in the indigenous production of sugar and the spread of civilization, and of the use of beverages, like tea, coffee, etc. There will thus be scope for the Indian factories not only for meeting the present requirements but for an increased demand arising from a decline in use of *gur*. Besides, this potentiality is sure to materialize to a greater extent if the price of sugar is not much higher than *gur*.

Fouthly, by use of sugar as an industrial raw material.*

---

*By treatment of sugar with acid at high temperatures. For example, a substance called levulinic acid is produced and when in turn this is combined with certain alcohols, fragrant esters are formed that have useful solvent powers. The investigation of the practice of mixing sugar in *lime-sand mortar* is of greater interest. Controlled tests have shown that, if as little sugar as 6 per cent. of the quicklime is included in mortar, the tensile strength is increased about 60 per cent. The addition of about 5 lbs. of sugar for each 100 lbs. of lime would add very little to the cost of laying bricks or plastering walls. The sugar is added, dissolved in water, after the lime has been slaked.

Intensive study for the use of sugar in various ways is being done in Mellon Institute of Industrial Research, Pittsburgh, U. S. A. Such researches should also be carried on in India.

30. INCREASE IN FACTORY PRODUCTION *vss.* KHANDSARI PRODUCTION.

The price of Indian Sugar has gone down considerably since July 1933 and therefore the khandsari production must have also declined considerably. The factories will therefore necessarily replace a portion of the khandsari production. We would like to point out here that we do not believe that the khandsari production will ever come up to 300,000 tons as was forecasted by the Sugar Technologist for the years 1933-34 and 1934-35. The observation made by the Hon'ble Mr. J. P. Srivastava, Minister of Education, United Provinces in the Sugar conference held at Simla on 10th July 1933 is significant and will bear quotation: "We have actually found that white sugar is taking the place of khandsari sugar and even of *Gur*. In Rohilkand, a lot of khandsaris have gone out and people are using white sugar. We also know that at the present price of sugar it does not pay the khandsaris to work and as long as this low level is maintained, there will be greater and greater opening for white sugar. Although therefore we should proceed with caution in the matter of the establishment of new factories, I will not quite say that the limit has been reached for all times."

31. EXPORT OF SUGAR POSSIBLE.

There is thus ample scope for the modern factories, and, as stated above, there are possibilities of increase in India's consumption also. And in addition to this, it would be possible to export sugar from India to foreign countries, if our cost of production is reduced to about Rs. 3 per maund, which can be achieved by increase in efficiency of mills, larger recovery of sugar, cheaper supplies of cane, by increasing the yield of cane from 13 tons per acre in some places to about 50 tons per acre as in Java, etc., etc.

The comparative inefficiency of our production can be seen from the fact that whereas Java produces 6 tons of sugar from every acre of cultivation, we produce only 1·7 ton of sugar taking the official figure of 13 tons of cane per acre and 9 per cent. yield of sugar extraction. If we improve our efficiency it should not be difficult for us to export our sugar to the United Kingdom on account of the Empire Preference in the import duty, (*vide* Table No. 3, giving the schedule of duties on sugar).

Let us also see the figures of *Per Capita* consumption of sugar in India and other countries in the world, for the sake of comparison.

India, it must be stated, consumes a very remarkably small quantity of sugar, at the present time. Her consumption of sugar, as we saw in Table No. 15, has been practically stationary since 1925-26, the variation being small.

In Table No. 16 given below, we give the *per capita* consumption of sugar, of *Gur* and of both sugar and *Gur*, in India, during the last 10 years.

TABLE NO. 16.

Per capita consumption of Sugar and Gur in India.

Year.	Consumption in lbs. *per capita.*		
	Sugar.	*Gur.*	Sugar and *Gur.*
1923-24	4·7	16·5	21·2
1924-25	5·8	11·5	17·3
1925-26	8·6	14·0	20·8
1926-27	6·7	15·4	22·1
1927-28	7·3	15·0	22·3
1928-29	7·6	11·6	19·2
1929-30	8·6	11·9	20·5
1930-31	7·8	14·4	22·2
1931-32	6·0	17·6	23·6
1932-33 (estimated) ...	5·8	20·4	26·2

32. FIGURES OF *Per Capita* CONSUMPTION OF SUGAR IN INDIA AND OTHER COUNTRIES.

In Table No. 17 below, we give a list of various other countries consuming sugar, showing their *per capita* consumption in 1929-30 and 1930-31. This Table is based on the authority of Dr. Gustav Mikusch of Vienna.

TABLE NO. 17.

Per capita consumption of Sugar in different countries.

Country.	Consumption of Sugar (lbs. *per capita* raw value.)	
	1929-30.	1930-31.
Europe.		
Germany	55·8	55·6
Czechoslovakia	61·1	60·2
Austria	72·1	64·4
Switzerland	93·7	98·5
France	55·3	57·3
Belgium	61·9	61·7
United Kingdom	96·8	108·5
Denmark	115·7	119·3
Average Europe ...	39·5	42·1
Asia.		
China and Hongkong	4·9	4·0
British India	20·5	22·2
Japan and Formosa (Saipan included)	28·2	27·8
Persia	24·7	22·0
Average Asia ...	15·4	15·9

Per capita consumption of Sugar in different countries—contd.

Country.	Consumption of Sugar (lbs. *per capita* raw value.)	
	1929-30.	1930-31.
Africa.		
South African Union	44·8	41·2
Mauritius	54·0	53·8
Average Africa ...	13·0	12·3
America.		
United States	113·8	107·1
Hawaii	119·3	115·5
Cuba	93·5	82·0
Canada	97·9	94·1
Brazil	44·3	43·2
Average America ...	79·1	74·8
Australia (continent)	111·1	107·8
Average Australia ...	89·3	88·4
World	30·4	30·8

33. PROVINCIAL DISTRIBUTION OF THE INDUSTRY.

Let us now see the distribution of the Sugar industry and supply of cane in the various provinces and consider whether the development of the industry in all provinces has been satisfactory.

CHAPTER III.

Provincial Distribution of Cane-cultivation, Cane-factories, and Provincial Production.

1. ALL-INDIA DEVELOPMENT OF INDUSTRY SATISFACTORY.

In the preceding pages, we have seen that so far as the country as a whole is concerned, the development of cane cultivation and of factories has been satisfactory, in that within only two years of the grant of protection to the industry, a stage of self-sufficiency in production of sugar has been reached, and indeed, what is more, export markets will have to be thought of before long.

The establishment of sugar factories, it need hardly be stated, depends on the availability of the requisite supply of cane, and the production of cane depends on suitable land, climatic conditions, etc. Let us see the development of cane-cultivation and factories in various provinces.

2. DISTRIBUTION OF CANE-AREAS IN PROVINCES.

We have shown in the previous chapter that the United Provinces furnish more than half of the total acreage under cane in India. The percentage of acreage under cane in the various provinces, as compared with the area under cane in All-India acreage which was 33,05,000 in 1933-34, is shown below.

51·8% in the United Provinces; 14·6% in the Punjab; 9·9% in Bihar and Orissa; 7·2% in Bengal; 3·6% in Madras; 3·3% in Bombay. In table No. 10 we also showed the area under improved canes, during the last few years.

3. Agricultural Improvements in the United Provinces.

The United Provinces of Agra and Oudh lie between 23°52′ and 31°18′ N. and thus fall *entirely outside the tropics.* The acreage under cane is more than half of the total acreage under cane in India.

It will be seen from Table No. 10 that the progress made by the United Provinces in extending the cultivation of improved varieties is remarkable. The United Provinces which possess more than half the acreage under cane in India and about three-fourths of that acreage under improved varieties, hold an important position in the manufacture of sugar.

The work done at the Coimbatore Research Station for improving the quality of cane and for breeding new canes is noteworthy. Hitherto, the attention of the station has been focussed, as is natural, chiefly upon producing improved canes which will be suitable for conditions in the main sugar belt of India, *i.e.*, in the

United Provinces and Bihar and Orissa. The United Provinces Government stated before the Tariff Board that whereas indigenous varieties may be expected to yield 350 maunds of cane per acre, Coimbatore varieties cultivated in the same system would yield 600 maunds and cultivated extensively on the Java system would yield up to 1,000 maunds per acre. The United Provinces are also endeavouring to cultivate special kinds of cane, *e.g.*, Co. 214, which ripens early, and cane which ripens late, to enable the factories to extend the crushing season.

The Report of the Administration of the Department of Agriculture of the United Provinces for the year ending June 1932 states that Co. 213 is still the most widely grown of the newer canes. It is high yielding and capable of doing well under normal crop conditions but has shown itself unduly susceptible to mosaic disease. Co. 200 and Co. 244, it is observed, have considerable vogue in the west of the province. The former appears to yield better in the west than eleswhere and the latter does well on less highly manured lands.

The total area under improved and ordinary varieties of cane in the United Provinces during 1932-33 was 16,52,000 acres out of which 11,87,778 were under improved varieties and about 500,000 acres under ordinary varieties. Considering that the area in 1926-27 under improved varieties of cane was less than 1 lakh of acres, the advance is remarkable. Merrut, Rohilkhand

and Gorakhpur Divisions had the largest area under cane in 1931-32:—

—	Ordinary.	Improved.	Total.
	Acres.	Acres.	Acres.
Meerut ...	66,357	3,11,653	3,78,010
Rohilkhand ...	1,05,915	2,51,013	3,56,928
Gorakhpur ...	1,04,163	1,36,321	2,40,484

The percentage under improved cane in the United Provinces in 1931-32, was 61% of the whole crop, while in Meerut and Rohilkhand it is as high as 82% and 71%. Research work in the direction of improvement of canes is going on at Shahjahanpur.

While the yield from indigenous varieties of cane is about 13 tons per acre, the yield from Coimbatore varieties is nearly 36 tons.

The cost of growing cane, the Tariff Board observed in 1931, was estimated at between 4 and 5 annas a maund. We have not been able to verify this figure.

4. IMPROVEMENTS IN BIHAR AND ORISSA.

The Province of Bihar and Orissa lies between 19°3′ and 27°31′ N. Orissa occupies the most southerly position in the Province and is thus entirely within the tropics, whereas Bihar proper is *entirely sub-tropical.*

The special features of Bihar are that its climatic conditions are transitional between the tropical and the sub-tropical, that much of its cane is grown without irrigation, and that it was till lately the chief centre for the manufacture of sugar direct from cane in India.

Orissa however is essentially a rice-tract and offers hardly any prospect of cane.

The spread of Coimbatore varieties of sugar cane has been phenomenal during the last 5 years. Out of a total of nearly 2,50,000 acres under improved canes, nearly 2,00,000 acres are in Bihar proper, according to the Report of the Agricultural Department for 1931-32. The spread is increasing so rapidly that it is felt that in one or two years, local varieties will be completely ousted.

The total acreage under sugar cane in Bihar was about 3,02,000 in 1932-33, and 418,000 in 1933-34.

The yield from indigenous canes in Bihar is about 13 tons per acre, while the yield from Coimbatore variety is about 18 to 20 tons.

The Tariff Board remarked that the cost of cultivation of cane worked out at between 4 and 5 annas a maund. We have not been able to verify this.*

* The Director of Agriculture of the Bihar Government stated in reply to a question put at the Bihar Sugar Conference held at Patna in January 1934, that the cost of production worked out to 0-2-6 in North Bihar, and 0-3-0 in South Bihar.

5. IMPROVEMENTS IN THE PUNJAB.

The Punjab lies between 27°39′ and 34°2′ N. It is *well outside the tropics*, but stands second in point of acreage amongst the cane-growing provinces of India. Although Punjab grows about 5 lakhs acres of sugar cane, the prospects of manufacture of white sugar are limited to a small proportion of that acreage, due to the short monsoon period and the extremes of temperature which are serious handicaps. The short duration of the crushing season, and the danger of frost are the limiting factors. The possibility of establishment of sugar-factories, therefore, is confined to the south of the Punjab where conditions are similar to those of the United Provinces.

The yield of cane in the Punjab from indigenous varieties is about 13 tons per acre, while from Coimbatore varieties it is about 15 tons.

The Tariff Board remarked that the cost of cultivation of cane was estimated at about 5½ annas per maund.

We have not been able to verify this.

6. IMPROVEMENTS IN MADRAS.

The Madras Presidency lies between 8°4′ and 20°26′ N and is *entirely within the tropics*. Although nowhere in India are the climatic conditions more favourable for the successful cultivation of cane than they are on irrigated lands in Madras, the area under sugar-cane in Madras is both small and scattered. The acreage under cane in 1932-33 was a little over 1 lakh. Inspite of its tropical advantage Madras offers limited prospects for cane, due largely to the widespread preference for rice wherever supplies of irrigation water are assured, and to the very scattered area on which cane is now grown. Madras has not benefited from the Coimbatore Research Station, as the experiments conducted there have so far been directed to production of cane suitable for subtropical conditions. The average size of a holding in Madras is extremely small and the difficulties in the way of sugar factories obtaining control over a sufficiently large area of cane are very great. But these difficulties are now being overcome. The yield of cane has improved to 35 tons per acre, and the cost of cultivation of cane has now come down to above 4 to 6 annas per maund, due to fall in prices, chiefly of manures, fall in wages, etc.

The cost of production of cane, according to the Tariff Board, was estimated at from 7 to 12 annas per maund.

We have not been able to verify this.

7. IMPROVEMENTS IN BOMBAY.

The Bombay Presidency proper lies between 13°53′ and 24°43′ N and is thus almost *entirely within the tropics.* The area under cane was 1,05,000 acres in 1932-33 and 1,02,000 acres in 1933-34.

The Deccan lands and their projected extension afford the brightest prospects for the extension of cane in Bombay. Bombay is also capable of producing a higher yield of cane per acre perhaps than any other part of India. The Tariff Board were informed that in certain fields at the Belapur estate a yield of 40 tons or more of cane had actually been realised. This represents about 1,080 Maunds per acre and compares well with the Java production. The actual average for the Belapur estate was about 24·69 tons, *i.e.*, 676 maunds in 1929-30.

The cost of cane was estimated to be about 12 annas per maund by the Tariff Board, but we have not been able to verify the figures.

8. Improvements in Bengal.

The Presidency of Bengal lies between 20°35′ and 27°13′ N. and is *almost entirely sub-tropical.* In point of acreage in India, Bengal stands fourth now, although in the early years of the 20th centuary, it was second. Cane is grown in every district of the province, but the crop is of small importance. The total area under sugar-cane in Bengal was 2,33,000 acres in 1932-33, and 2,57,000 acres in 1933-34.

The province appears to afford suitable facilities for the development of cane-manufacturing industry, particularly in view of the decline in the demand and price of Jute, which is the crop of greatest importance to this province.

The cost of cultivation per maund of cane, the Tariff Board were informed was about 7 annas. The Bengal Government now believe that the cost has come down to about 3 annas per maund. We have not been able to verify this.

9. PROVINCIAL DISTRIBUTION OF FACTORIES.

Having seen the developments in the cultivation of cane, and the possibilities therein, let us now turn our attention to the progress of the cane-manufacturing industry, and see its relative position and development in the various provinces, during the last three years. We will compare the production of sugar and Molasses in the chief provinces during the last two years, the recovery percentage of sugar, the duration of the crushing season, etc., and consider the possibilities of the development of the industry in various provinces. Table No. 18, below, shows the number of ftactories operating from 1931-32 to 1933-34 in the various provinces.

A complete list of factories in India, with their names, capacity, and location is given in Appendix III.

TABLE NO. 18.†

Provincial distribution of Cane-Factories‡ in 1931-32 to 1934-35.

Province.	No. of factories* operating in.			
	1931-32.	1932-33.	1933-34.	1934-35 estimated.
United Provinces...	14	33	70	75
Bihar & Orissa ...	12	19	34	37
Punjab ...	1	1	9	12
Madras ...	2	2	11(*a*)	13
Bombay ...	1	1	8(*b*)	10
Burma ...	1	1	1	2
Bengal ...	...	...	2	6
Total for India ...	31	57	135	155

†In addition to these cane factories, there were 12 *Gur* Refineries, *i e.*, factories working with Raw Sugar alone, 1 being in Bihar and Orissa, 5 in United Provinces, 4 in Madras and 2 in Punjab.

‡ While a majority of these factories have a capacity of crushing over 500 tons of cane per day, there are several which have very small capacity. For the list of factories, province by province, See App. III.

*Out of these factories 12 in United Provinces, 8 in Bihar, 1 in Punjab and 1 in Madras had refining plants also.

(*a*) 1 in Travancore, 1 in Mysore.

(*b*) 1 in Kathiawar.

The number of factories in the United Provinces in 1933-34 is more than double the factories in Bihar and more than half the number of factories in India. Bihar stands a good second, Madras, Bombay and Punjab are third, fourth, and fifth respectively, while Bengal is very much behind so far. More than hundred factories have been established after the grant of protection, and plants of several old factories have been considerably extended. Let us now see the figures of production of sugar in these provinces.

10. PRODUCTION OF SUGAR AND MOLASSES IN THE VARIOUS PROVINCES.

The production of sugar and molasses in 1932, by the factories, both old and new, in the United Provinces, Bihar and Orissa, Bombay, Madras, the Punjab and Burma, as compared with 1931, can be seen from table No. 19, 20 and 21, given below. The tables also give statistics of the quantity of cane crushed, molasses produced, the recovery percent of cane, recovery of molasses percent of cane.

TABLE NO. 19.

Production of Sugar and Molasses by Factories in the United Provinces.

Particulars.		1932-33.			1931-32.
		Old Factories.	New Factories.	Total.	Total.
Cane crushed	Tons	871,613	769,881	1,641,494	774,926
Sugar produced	,,	73,998	66,346	140,344	66,312
Molasses produced	,,	32,535	32,055	64,590	30,340
Recovery of Sugar per cent. cane...	...	8·48	8·61	8·55	8·59
Recovery of Molasses per cent. cane...	...	3·8	4·1	3·9	3·9

TABLE NO. 20.

Production of Sugar and Molasses by Factories in Bihar and Orissa.

Particulars.		1932-33			1931-32.
		Old Factories.	New Factories.	Total.	Total.
Cane crushed	Tons	1,066,230	428,297	1,494,527	829,624
Sugar produced	,,	92,464	36,146	128,610	75,091
Molasses produced	,,	41,196	16,672	57,868	31,883
Recovery of Sugar per cent. cane...	...	8·67	8·44	8·60	9·06
Recovery of Molasses per cent. cane	...	3·9	3·9	3·9	3·8

TABLE NO. 21.

Production of Sugar and Molasses by Factories in Bombay, Madras, the Punjab and Burma.

Particulars.	1932-33.			1931-32.
	Old Factories.	New Factories.	Total.	Total.
Cane crushed ... Tons	214,210	...	214,210	178,949
Sugar produced ... „	21,223	...	21,223	17,178
Molasses produced ... „	7,961	...	7,961	6,985
Recovery of Sugar per cent. cane... ...	9·90	...	9·90	9·60
Recovery of Molasses per cent. cane ...	3·7	...	3·7	3·9

11. TOTAL PRODUCTION OF SUGAR AND MOLASSES IN INDIA.

Table No. 22 below gives the figures for production of sugar, molasses, etc., from cane-factories, both old and new, for the year 1932 whole of India as compared with 1931-32.

TABLE NO. 22.

Total Production of Sugar and Molasses by Factories in India.

Particulars.		1932-33.			1931-32.
		New Factories.	Old Factories.	Total.	Total.
Cane crushed	Tons	21,52,053	11,98,178	3,350,231	17,83,499
Sugar produced	„	1,87,685	1,02,492	290 177	1,58,581
Molasses produced	„	81,692	48,727	1,30,419	69,208
Recovery of Sugar per cent. cane	...	8·72	8·55	8·66	8·89
Recovery of Molasses per cent. cane	...	3·8	4·1	3·9	3·9

It will be seen therefrom that the quantity of sugar produced in 1932-33 as compared with 1931-32 was 83 per cent. more, of molasses 88% more, and of cane crushed 87% more.

12. RECOVERY OF SUGAR FROM CANE.

In Table No. 23, below, are shown the figures of the average percentage recovery of sugar in the various Provinces, and for All-India, during the last 5 years.

TABLE NO. 23

Recovery of Sugar from Cane during the Five Seasons 1928-29 to 1932-33.

Provinces.	Recovery of Sugar per cent. cane.				
	1928-29.	1929-30.	1930-31.	1931-32.	1932-33.
United Provinces ...	8·37	9·00	8·88	8·59	8·55
Bihar and Orissa ...	8·61	8·90	9·17	9·06	8·60
Bombay, Madras, Punjab and Burma ...	9·93	10·12	9·84	9·60	9·90
All-India	8·59	9·07	8·09	8·89	8·66

It will be seen from this that the average for All-India has decreased slightly, due partly to the larger quantity of cane crushed, necessitating a prolongation of the season. The recovery in factories which worked for the first time during the season 1932-33 was 8·55 per cent. In United Provinces the recovery in New Factories was actually higher than the old factories, the figure being 8·61 per cent. and 8·48 per cent. respectively.

It is also interesting to see that of the 33 Factories working in the United Provinces in 1932--33, the extraction percentage for 10 factories was between 9·0 and 9·5 while it was between 9·0 and 9·2 per cent. for only 4 out of 19 factories in Bihar and Orissa.

The highest recovery for the season 1932-33 was 11·1 per cent. as against 11·3 per cent. during the preceding season.

13. Is development of the industry in provinces satisfactory?

It is difficult to answer this question categorically. It is easy to see from Table No. 18, that the development of the factories in United Provinces and Bihar and Orissa can be considered satisfactory. But the development in other provinces when the industry can be developed, has been very niggardly so far. This question was discussed thoroughly at the sugar conference held by the Government of India at Simla on the 10th, 11th and 12th July 1933. The discussion gave rise to a sharp conflict of opinions.

14. Madras says "No".

The representatives from Madras, Punjab, Bombay, Mysore and Hyderabad felt that their provinces were yet lagging behind in the development of the industry, while United Provinces and Bihar had forged ahead, and they could not accept the Resolution moved by the Hon'ble Khan Bahadur Saiyid Muhammed Hussain, Minister-in-charge of Education and Development Departments, Bihar and Orissa, which appeared to suggest that there should be no more factories than the existing ones. In fact it was pointed out, that Madras consumed sugar to the extent of 100,000 tons a year, out of which 55,000 tons was imported by sea in 1932-33. Madras therefore had need of more factories unless it desired to remain dependent upon Java or Northern India. It was also pointed out that the Tariff Board had emphasized that the strongest aspect of the case for protection of the industry was that based upon the national importance of promoting the cultivation of sugar-cane, and that from that point of view there was need of promoting sugar factories in Madras.

It was further stated that hitherto it was thought that canes produced in Coimbatore had been suitable only for the Northern Provinces. But recently in one of the Government farms Co. 213 had been raised and it had been found very suitable with a yield of about 35 to 40 tons and the cost of cultivation of one ton came down to only Rs. 2-8-0.

15. PUNJAB SAYS "NO".

The Minister for the Punjab also supported the Minister for Madras, and observed that while the Punjab had increased its cane cultivation from 3 lacs to 5 lacs acres, they had only two factories. They had great need of expansion.

16. BOMBAY SAYS "NO".

The Director of Industries from Bombay also expressed himself in opposition to the Resolution moved by the Minister from Bihar. He pointed out that conditions in Bombay were somewhat different from those prevailing in the United Provinces and Bihar. In the Bombay Presidency factories were established on the basis that they must grow their own cane; they could not easily buy cane. The acreage in Bombay under cane was 100,000 but they were distributed. They had only one factory working up to 1931-32. The Bombay Government were considering how best facilities could be given to capitalists to enable them to obtain suitable lands on lease so that they might be able to start factories.

Bombay was fortunate in regard to the yield of cane. The Belapur factory grew cane which yielded 37 tons per acre, and the percentage of recovery of sugar was 11 which, he pointed out, was the highest figure in the whole of India.

It was also pointed out that the Bombay Government had invested about 10 crores of rupees on irrigation in Deccan, and it was felt that it would be difficult to make those canals financially successful unless the white sugar industry was established in that area. The Government of Bombay were therefore keen on promoting the development of more factories, and they therefore could not agree to the Resolution proposed by the Minister from Bihar.

17. Development of the Industry in India Considered "Satisfactory"?

The Resolution moved by the Minister from Bihar was however accepted by a majority of votes (18 votes to 11), at the Sugar Conference. The Resolution reads as under:—

"Whereas the recent development of the sugar industry in India has been rapid, although it cannot be said to have been excessive, and whereas, owing to the general fall in prices of agricultural produce there has been a natural tendency towards an increase in the area under sugar-cane, the Conference is of opinion—

(*i*) that when the modern factories now under construction are working at full capacity, it is likely that these and existing factories will produce sufficient white sugar to meet the existing demand for white sugar,

(*ii*) that in view of the consideration that whilst the potential supply of raw material is very large, the demand for sugar in India is limited, further extensions should be carefully watched in the interests of the establishment of a sound industry, and

(*iii*) that if the production of sugar-cane expands beyond the actual requirements it would be extremely difficult, and indeed almost impossible, for any reasonable level of prices for *Gur* to be maintained."

18. Bengal's Niggardly development and apprehensions against restriction.

The Hon'ble Nawab K. G. M. Faroqui, Minister for Bengal pointed out his apprehension that if the Resolution were passed by the Conference, the United Provinces and Bihar Governments might approach the Government of India with definite proposals for restricting the starting of new factories elsewhere by legislation. He was however assured by the Chairman of the Conference Sir Fazl-I-Hussain, Member of the Executive Council of the Governor-General-in-charge of the Department of Education, Health and Lands, that the passing of the Resolution would in no way help any of the provinces to come to the Government of India and ask for any particular legislation.

Mr. D. P. Khaitan, representative of the Indian Sugar Mills Association, nominated by the Government of Bihar and Orissa to this Conference, took up the brief on behalf of Bengal in absence of any non-official representative from Bengal at the conference. He pointed out his firm conviction that in order that India may prosper, it is desirable that each province should as far as possible prosper along parallel lines.

19. Development in various provinces helpful and desirable.

It will thus be seen that the various provinces which have not yet been able to develop the sugar industry so far, are anxious to do so. We are of opinion that there are clear advantages in the development of the industry in various provinces. To wit, the advantages of protection would be better distributed; the cultivators of cane in the various provinces may share the benefit of protection; inter-provincial jealousies could be avoided; it would be possible to compete more easily with Java sugar if the industry was spread all over the country, by avoiding transport of sugar over long distances, and consequent high freight charges, etc.

We would only suggest that the provinces should not enter upon a cut-throat competition amongst themselves. and thus jeopardise the chances of the establishment of an efficient industry in the country, able to stand competition with foreign countries.

We propose to examine closely in the next Chapter the prospects and possibilities of the successful establishment of the sugar industry in Bengal, as we are of the opinion that the development there has been very niggardly so far, although the province appears to have suitable facilities for the cultivation of cane and development of sugar factories.

CHAPTER IV.

Possibilities of Development of the Industry in Bengal.

1. SUGAR-CANE, A SUITABLE ALTERNATIVE CROP.

We have seen in the previous chapter that the development of the sugar industry in this province has been very niggardly although her soil and climate are exceptionally favourable for the cultivation of this crop. Bengal has always grown a certain amount of sugar-cane and was once a sugar producing country. In point of area under cultivation of cane Bengal now stands fourth in India, but it is well-known that in the early years of the 20th century Bengal took the second place. This decline in the cultivation of the cane crop in this province has been due largely to the spread of the jute crop in which Bengal enjoys a monopoly in the whole world. The question of the development of the sugar industry has now assumed a great importance in this province as a result of the decline in the demand of jute and the precipitous fall in the price of jute due to excessive production during the last four years. The necessity of having some other crop in place of the jute crop is exceptionally great at the present moment. If the deterioration in the economic condition of the province is to be arrested, some alternative crop has got to be thought of and sugar-cane would seem to answer this purpose best.

2. QUALITY OF CANE AVAILABLE.

It is gratifying to find that the Department of Agriculture in Bengal has introduced a Mauritius variety of cane called 'Yellow Tanna'. This is a very hardy and drought-resisting cane, but its juice and *gur* produced from it leave much to be desired. Its other good qualities and heavy yield led to a great expansion of its cultivation throughout the province. Some ten years ago the Department of Agriculture introduced new Coimbatore varieties of cane. These were very hardy canes and were heavy yielders with very rich juice. Of these Co.213 has proved the best, and is now spreading very rapidly in most parts of the province. It is a matter for satisfaction that experiments are being continually made for finding out a quality of cane even better than Co.213. The present position is that the area under Coimbatore cane is spreading rapidly, but so far in only a few localities there is sufficient area under this crop to supply large factories. If the Department of Agriculture take a keener interest in this question it would not be at all difficult to make still greater improvements in the quality of cane.

The total area under cane was 2,33,000 acres in 1932-33 and 2,57,000 acres in 1933-34. Of this about one lac acres are under improved variety and it is gratifying to find that the recent crop-cutting experiments indicate that the normal yield of *gur* which was 37 maunds per acre has now increased to over 50 maunds per acre, due largely to the introduction of the improved varieties of cane by the Agricultural Department. Taking even the lower figure of 37 maunds of *gur* per acre the total production of cane *gur* comes to about 92,50,000 maunds. In addition to this date-palm juice yields *gur* estimated at about 27,50,000 maunds making a total of 1,20,00,000 maunds.

3. BENGAL, SUITABLE FOR CANE-CULTIVATION.

Is it not then surprising that although there are such large areas of cultivation under cane, and great possibilities of the development of the industry in Bengal, she has only two modern cane-crushing large sized factories, and she has to remain dependent upon the imports from Java or from other provinces? Bengal is eminently suited for the development of this industry. I hope that by 1934 she will have at least 10 factories of a daily 400-ton cane-crushing capacity. What is lacking is merely a spirit of enterprise and organised efforts on the part of the people as also the Government. The situation in regard to the jute industry which is in a deplorable state, and the necessity of a restriction of output of jute, if a fall in price is to be averted, have brought to the forefront the question of the cultivation of an alternative crop in place of jute. Sugar-cane appears to be in our opinion the best alternative crop suitable for the purpose. His Excellency Sir Stanley Jackson Governor of Bengal, also observed in the course of a speech delivered at the Annual Meeting of the Associated Chambers of Commerce in Calcutta on the 14th December 1931 as follows:—

"Large areas in four out of five divisions in Bengal are eminently suited for growing sugar-cane.

also be observed that the introduction of Co. 213 which is not only rich in purity but also produces heavy outturn, and its extension over the sugar-cane growing areas of Bengal make it possible to manufacture sugar direct from cane on a large scale.

5. ADVANTAGES IN ESTABLISHMENT OF THE INDUSTRY IN BENGAL.

There are several advantages in the development of the sugar industry in Bengal from the point of view of the whole country. Firstly it would be better to distribute the profits of protection over the various provinces, particularly when conditions are favourable, and thus eliminate provincial jealousy and feelings. Secondly, the cultivation of the sugar-cane crop would give a great relief to the cultivators of jute who are in dire distress. Thirdly, it will be possible to engage the middle-class people of this province suitably in the manufacture of sugar. Fourthly, it will enrich the province as a whole and be of help in utilising the national resources with which the province is endowed. Fifthly, it will provide excellent avenue for investment of money by small capitalists in this province, without taking any great or undue risk in view of the fact that the industry has been assured of protection by the Government for the next few years.

6. 14 POINTS IN FAVOUR OF BENGAL.

1. Climatic conditions in Bengal quite favourable for the growth of sugar-cane.

2. The grey-silt areas, too, usually consist of fairly rich soil which makes it possible to produce a heavier yielding crop than any other province.

3. Irrigation, too, usually an expensive proposition is generally not required over the major part of the province, as rainfall, both in incidence and amount, is sufficient for the needs of the crop.

4. It should also be noted that Co. 213 variety of sugar-cane is capable of standing water-logging; in fact it has been found to grow in a foot of water, for one or two months during the monsoon without any serious deterioration.

5. The Bengal Government are of opinion that the sugar factories should be more profitable in Bengal than in any other province as the cost of production of cane is comparatively low (*Vide* "Sugar in Bengal" page 5).

6. Increase in area near some places makes it possible to establish sugar factories on a large scale.

7. Raiyats will also be benefited by the establishment of sugar factories, for while they will undoubtedly still continue to make *gur*, it would almost certainly be not more than the quantity required for themselves and their immediate neighbours, and their excess cane can thus be sold to

factorics. They will thus free their bullocks at a time when they require them for land preparation for *kharif* crops and will relieve them from the exacting work of cane-crushing.

8. The *Bhadralog* class will find an excellent avenue for employment in large scale cane-factories, and this will be welcomed at the present time, particularly as their condition is very pitiable.

9. The development of the cane factories will also be instrumental in preventing the wastage of cane in refining sugar from *gur* and this will be a national advantage.

10. The establishment of the cane sugar factories in Bengal will be a blessing in another way, *viz.*, effective competition, which the factories in Bengal will be able to offer, with the imported sugar at the port of Calcutta and the neighbouring places, owing to the great reduction in the cost of transport, as compared with factories situated, for instance, in Bihar, selling sugar to Bengal after paying high freight charges.

11. The advantage in freight, which the mills in Bengal will have over the mills in other provinces in supplying the large demand of sugar in Bengal, as also in the provinces of Burma and Assam, will be a compensating factor, which would counteract the disadvantage which Bengal may have as compared to other provinces in

regard to a higher cost of production (*vide* Tariff Board's Report) due to the inferior quality of cane, shorter duration of the working season, etc.

12. The realisation of some price for molasses required for consumption in Bengal will be another compensating factor in favour of mills situated in Bengal.

13. Another incidental advantage of the establishment of sugar factories in Bengal will be a better distribution of the profits arising from the protected industry in the various provinces and the elimination of any feeling about a disproportionate burden of protection being felt by consuming provinces for the sake of manufacturing provinces.

14. The efficiency of the Bengali cane-grower is on the whole fairly high (*Vide* Indian Sugar Committee's Report, p. 117).

We hope that earnest efforts will be made by the public for starting cane-sugar factories in suitable areas in Bengal in order that more employment may be created for the people; the distress of the cultivators may be remedied to some extent, by furnishing of an alternative crop to Jute, by a higher realisation of price from the cane crop, and in order that improvement may be brought about in economic conditions in the province which has suffered a great deal more than other provinces due to the calamitous fall in prices of primary products during the last five years*. It is to the interest of other provinces also to look with favour on the development of this industry in this province, as then alone will it be possible to offer competition with imported sugar at the Port and in the neighbouring areas in Bengal which consume large quantities of sugar, and to do away with the importation of sugar completely from foreign countries. We hope that the people of the province will seize the opportunity that has offered before it is too late, and that the Government of Bengal will spare no pains in carrying on research work for the development of better qualities of cane by carrying out a botanical and chemical survey of the canes now grown; by making trials of superior exotic varieties, by conducting experiments for proper application of manure for each variety of cane-grown, etc., and will offer suitable inducements to the people to start large scale cane-factories on the most modern and up-to-date methods.

---

*The Bengal Jute Enquiry Committee have also observed in their Report (published in February 1934) that Bengal can grow excellent sugarcane, and that sugarcane is a suitable alternative crop to jute.

CHAPTER V.

Utilisation of By-products, (Molasses and Bagasse)

(a) Molasses.

1. MOLASSES, MOST IMPORTANT BY-PRODUCT.

The proper utilisation of the by-products of an industry plays an important part in determining the margin of profits in the industry and its future development.

Molasses is the most important by-product of the Sugar Industry, from the point of view of the factories as also of indigenous small-scale manufactures. Molasses is that liquid substance or syrup which remains after the massecuite has been cured. It is often boiled again for making lower qualities of sugar, and the molasses finally obtained is exhausted and contains very little sucrose. The other by-product is bagasse or as it is sometimes called megasse. This bagasse is the residue of fibrous matter which remains after the cane is crushed. Out of 100 maunds of cane about 9% of sugar and 4% of molasses are recovered by the factories and about 5·2% of sugar and 4·5% of molasses are recovered by the Khandsaris.

2. PRECIPITOUS FALL IN PRICE OF MOLASSES.

The molasses produced by the factories and khandsaris in the past was consumed largely in the tobacco industry and in the manufacture of plain country spirits. The consumption of molasses in both these ways has fallen by more than 75% at the present time. While there has been such a heavy fall in the consumption of molasses its production has naturally increased considerably since 1931, as a result of the establishment of a very large number of factories. The production of molasses in India was estimated at 269,000 tons in 1930-31 and 366,000 tons in 1931-32. In 1933-34 it will be over 500,000 tons. The molasses obtained in the *Khandsari* sugar factories which is richer in sucrose than factory molasses is either sold direct to the consumers or made into second class eating *gur*. The sudden increase in the production of molasses with a concomitant decrease in its consumption has created a problem of first rate importance and should engage the anxious attention of all sugar manufacturers. It is not possible to realise even one anna per maund for the molasses in view of its great overproduction and absence of demand as compared with the price of Rs. 2-12-0 which was obtained in the year 1930-31. When the Tariff Board reported they assumed in their calculations that the factories will be able to realise about Rs. 1-8-0 per maund for their molasses. The opinion of the Indian Sugar Committee that "the time is remote, therefore, when the sugar manufacturer in India need anticipate any difficulty in disposing of his molasses", has also gone wrong, as stated above.

3. Impossibility of throwing away molasses.

It is really unfortunate that a situation has developed whereby not only can this most important product of the sugar industry not be profitably utilised, but involves expenditure in its disposal. If the molasses are thrown in the adjacent river or watercourse, there is no doubt that the water will be polluted. If it runs into pits a serious nuisance will arise in the neighbourhood to such an extent that it would ruin the public health and may cause closing down of the factory.

The problem of molasses consists in its disposal at a profit. In the Philippines some manufacturers have given up all the benefits by throwing it away to the nearest river or sea. In India too, such a situation might arise in the near future, if suitable methods are not devised for utilisation of molasses.

4. Outlets for molasses.

The problem is therefore one which should be examined very closely in order to remove the great handicap that has beset the industry almost during the very first year of its existence under the regime of protection. The quantity used in curing tobacco will decline further, owing to the increasing use of *biris* and cigarettes, and decrease of *hookah and chilam.* We must therefore think of other outlets for disposal of molasses. These are:—

(*i*) Methylated Spirit.
(*ii*) Cattle food.
(*iii*) Production of the yeast as a source of food.
(*iv*) Fertiliser.
(*v*) Road-surfacer.
(*vi*) Cheap confectionery.
(*vii*) Fuel.
(*viii*) Alcohol for power in partial substitution of petrol.

5. Methylated (Denatured) Spirit, and potable spirit.

At the present time about a million gallons of methylated or denatured spirit are imported annually from Java. During the year 1932-33 the import was 8,56,800 gallons, valued at Rs. 8 lakhs, as compared with 10,52,400 gallons, valued at Rs. 10 lakhs in 1931-32. This latter represents the produce of about 4,25,090 maunds of molasses. An increase in the duty from 7½ per cent. *ad valorem* to about 25 per cent. would make it possible to shut out its import completely and to substitute the same from this country. A partial solution of the difficulty in finding an outlet for molasses can thus be found in the development of the Indian Spirit Industry. Spirit can be manufactured from molasses. A large quantity of spirit is used bv the various industries, *e.g.*, Lac Industry, Varnish Industry, Paint and Furniture-polishing Industries. As a result of the great fall in the price of molasses it would be possible to encourage the distilling industry in the country without affecting in any way the industries consuming spirit, and to supply the country's requirements from internal production cheaply owing to the tremendous fall in price of molasses. The loss to Government's revenue will be only about Rs. 75,000 per year. The possibilities of this should be carefully examined.

The production of country spirits in India has decreased considerably, during the last 12 years. About 1920, the quantity of molasses consumed for making potable spirit was 4 times the quantity used to-day. But excessive excise duty has resulted in the consumption being scarcely large enough to justify the operation of distilleries. At present the distilleries suffer due to lack of an outlet and have work hardly enough for 6-7 months in a year. This is partly due to the Government's policy of reducing the consumption of potable spirituous liquor, and of deriving maximum revenue from minimum consumption. One result of the excessive taxation has also been an increase in the practice of illicit distillation of liquors by the poorer classes.

We would like to see the production and consumption of liquor in India brought down to a minimum, as soon as possible, and therefore suggest that other avenues should be explored for utilisation of molasses.

6. CATTLE FOOD.

The scope for the use of molasses as cattle food does not appear to be great due to the difficulty in marketing combined with a traditional conservatism of owners of most of the cattles in India, as they are used to free grazing with hardly any expenditure on other food-stuffs. But now that molasses can be given away without cost by factories, a certain amount can thus be consumed. This may solve the problem of disposal to a certain extent.

7. YEAST.

The use of molasses as a source of yeast is new to Indian ideas, and is not likely to develop very much.

8. FERTILISER.

It is possible to use molasses as a fertiliser in its raw state, but our cultivators will have to be educated to its use and ample supplies of water would have to be provided in order to dilute the molasses before it could be put on the land.

Used in a small quantity, it tends to improve the land. Sir Vijayaraghavachariar recently observed that he had seen molasses being used as manure. This avenue of use of molasses should therefore be explored and the Agricultural Departments should carry on research in regard to the same. It is also possible, we are informed, by using a particular Plant to recover the potash from molasses and to produce ash with a high content of potash therefrom.

Potash is necessary to plant-life in order to enable starch, sugar cellulose and carbo-hydrates to be produced. Potash plays a large part in the development of leaves and woody parts of the stems of plants and gives the plant more resistance to attacks on fungous diseases or the like.

Sugarcane on an average extracts from the soil about 100 to 150 pounds of potash per acre and its is desirable that this should be replaced either by potash recovered from molasses or from fresh sources, if the land is not to be impoverished and the yield of crop not to be lowered. It is possible to return the available potassic content of molasses in an easily assimilable form to the land and to use it for the fertilisation of sugarcane or other crops.

one object of this invention is to produce a furnace to burn molasses at the lowest temperature and recover the highest possible yield of potash. The invention also includes a plant for burning waste molasses from cane sugar factories or *gur* refineries comprising a furnace into which the said waste product suitably preheated is introduced into or upon a revolving drum from which it falls as drops or threads to be burned as it falls. It has been estimated that the working cost based on dealing with 12,000 maunds of molasses in 24 hours works out to 1½ annas per maund of molasses. Taking the average ash contents of molasses to be about 9%, 100 maunds of molasses will yield 9 maunds of ash which may have an approximate potash content of 34% or 3% of valuable fertilizer value. Such a product based upon other potash product will have a value of Rs. 2-12-0 per maund at the factory. Reduced to one maund of molasses the estimated value of the product will come to about 4 annas from which the cost of treatment will take away 1½ annas. The estimated profit will therefore be at least 2 annas per maund of molasses thus treated. For the whole season this will give a substantial profit. This is a direction well worth investigating by the factories.

9. Road Surfacer.

Another use though comparatively insignificant, to which molasses can be turned, is for road surfacing, by mixing it with a certain amount of Pitch. Experiments in this direction should be carried on, with a view to see how far this can be a commercial success, in competition with other products.

10. CONFECTIONERY.

Molasses were used for cheap confectionery in the villages, but since the decline in the price of *gur* and sugar, its consumption has considerably decreased.

11. FUEL.

Molasses can also be used as fuel. Some experiments were carried out in Java, and a few factories burnt a mixture of bagasse and molasses. In Australia several mills burnt molasses as a fuel in their furnaces. Molasses mixed in small proportion to bagasse burns well and produces profitable calories. This practice is followed in many centres in the Philippine Islands when there is a shortage of bagasse or when this has only a small calorific power, which happens at the beginning of the milling season, but the requisite quantity of molasses is too small for this purpose to solve the problem of its disposal.

A countless number of furnaces have been proposed for the burning of molasses alone in the Philippine Islands, but none of them to our knowledge has given satisfactory results. Besides, the construction of special furnaces, its repair and maintenance entail heavy expenses for which no compensating benefit is received. The possibilities of this however should be investigated in India.

In some factories the press-cakes are mixed with slack coal and brickets are manufactured. These bricks are used for burning.

12. POWER ALCOHOL.

It is certain however that the best and most promising outlet in India for the molasses would be in its manufacture as power alcohol.

13. STUDY OF ALCOHOL AS FUEL.

The entire scientific world unanimously recognizes the fact that the fuel of the future for engines of internal combustion is alcohol. This can be produced from vegetable materials with which nature provides us generously and there is no danger that they will be exhausted in the course of time. The development of this industry is of considerable importance in the industrial development of this country; it is vital because of the possibility of providing the country with a motor fuel which is both cheap and easily obtainable. Alcohol has many advantages over gasoline. One of these is the fact that the raw material is produced annually, and alcohol is the only fuel which can be produced without danger that its existing natural source of supply will be exhausted.

The manufacturer of sugar finds in molasses first class material for the production of alcohol.* The future

* "Molasses is the cheapest raw material in common use for the production of alcohol for industrial purposes, the price being governed by supply and demand". *Vide*, Report of the Imperial Sugar-cane Research Conference, London, 1931.

development of the alcohol industry can easily go beyond the limits of the imagination of the greatest enthusiasts, not because its growth can be achieved easily but because of the constant and increasing demand for motor fuel at low prices. It must be admitted that *alcohol is the most economical fuel manufactured at the present time.*

The value of alcohol as a fuel for internal combustion engines has been recognised in various countries, *e.g.* France, Germany and America. In Germany alcohol was used during the last World War in very great quantities by the army for motor transport, for which purpose it was mixed with benzol. The importance of alcohol as a fuel depends on its possibilities in the future as a substitute for kerosene or petroleum.

Alcohol has a lower caloric power than kerosene or benzol or benzine; but since it requires less air to effect combustion, less caloric power is lost, and since its resistance to compression is greater, it is of more value as a fuel than the other two substances. Kerosene or petroleum is not a chemically pure substance but a mixture of great number of substances. Its properties cannot be determined definitely, since they vary as the grade of petroleum varies. While alcohol is low in caloric power, it possesses an ignition temperature around 270 degrees and can be used only with a pressure of from 70 to 90 pounds per square inch. Due to this, the thermic efficiency can be increased from 22% to 30%.

The start of engines burning alcohol offers no difficulty, and engines burning alcohol develop 20% more power than the same engines when they burn gasoline. The combustion of alcohol is perfect and the escaping gases do not have an offensive smell. Pure alcohol offers great advantages. Since alcohol contains oxygen in molecules, it requires less air for combustion than gasoline does. Another outstanding feature in favour of alcohol which should not be lost sight of, is its clean combustion. The carbon formation is practically nothing. The cleanliness of alcohol as fuel, compared with gasoline, can be demonstrated by burning a small quantity of gasoline and a small quantity of alcohol and holding a cold piece of metal or a glass object over the flames of each product. Alcohol which is of uniform compression and contains one-third of its weight in oxygen, burns completely and does not leave any deposit or residue.

Alcohol also does not produce violent explosions such as gasoline and other motor spirits produce. As a result the motor runs smoothly, thus reducing the amount of wear and tear. The engine is not overheated as in the case of gasoline or other fuels. It keeps the spark plugs clean, thus assuring more efficient ignition. Alcohol, it is also recognised, is a good "anti-knock" fuel.

As alcohol generates less heat in the combustion process, it needs less water for cooling. Alcohol is less disagreeable to work with and the danger of poisoning due to inadequate supply of air does not exist when alcohol is used in an engine in a closed place. Medical authorities claim that the rapid increase in cases of neurosis or hysteria in big cities is due to the fact that the air is poisoned by carbon monoxide. This could be prevented with the use of alcohol as fuel instead of gasoline.

Even if the cost of production of alcohol is high due to the necessity of using denaturants which are very costly and of little use but whose use is imposed by legislation coupled with taxes which must be paid to the Government, the manufacturer of alcohol can still put his product on the market at low prices. If the manufacturers of alcohol can succeed in getting the Government of India to abolish the use of costly denaturants and substitute less costly ones for them such as petroleum and gasoline for motor alcohol and exempt alcohol from any excise duty as on petrol, the immediate success of the industry would be assured, and it can compete safely with petroleum industry. It must be observed that 95°-96° alcohol mixed with gasoline or ether will prove unsuitable for use as the continuous evaporation produced in the carburator will make the temperature go down to a limit which will give way to the separation of alcohol, then the gasoline or ether, more volatile, evaporates, leaving alone the alcohol which will hinder normal operation of the motor. Pure alcohol, however, mixed with gasoline in fixed proportions improves the quality of the former. It is mixible at all temperatures, never reaching a point of separation. The best way therefore of having an outlet for the production of alcohol is to make the distilleries manufacture pure alcohol. This fact must not be lost sight of.

14. ASSISTANCE TO POWER ALCOHOL MANUFACTURING INDUSTRY, COMPULSORY USE OF ALCOHOL WITH PETROL.

Power alcohol can be produced in India and mixed with petrol in the proportion of one part of alcohol and three parts of petrol or 20% alcohol and 80% petrol. Several countries have in fact passed legislation making it imperative for petrol companies to use a certain percentage of alcohol with petrol. I give below a statement showing the form in which assistance might be given to the industry and what is done in other countries.

Australia—A mixture of 17 per cent. alcohol and 83 per cent. petrol is used on a small scale—legislation contemplated.

Austria—(1) The law provides that mixing shall be compulsory if the (duty paid) price of petrol exceeds the price of alcohol--not operative.

(2) The petrol *cartel* takes over the alcohol from the State Alcohol and arranges disposal. During 1933 it is expected that they will take over about 250,000 gallons.

Brazil—Petrol companies are required by law to purchase power alcohol equivalent to 5% of their petrol imports. The law is suspended as most of the alcohol produced is only of 94% strength and the concentrating plant is of insufficient capacity.

Czechoslovakia—The addition of 20—25 per cent. of alcohol to motor fuel is compulsory and 98½ of the petrol sold is this mixture. The amount of alcohol so used is about 11 million gallons.

France—(1) Importers of petrol are under a legal obligation to take from Government a quantity of alcohol equivalent to 8—10 per cent. of their petrol imports.

(2) The State buys alcohol from the refineries up to a certain limit of quantity at £41 per ton (Rs. 1-15-3 per gallon) and sells it to the petrol distributors at a much lower price corresponding roughly to the (internal) price of commercial motor spirit, *viz.*, £17 per ton (13 annas per gallon) the loss being partly made by a special additional import duty of 1*s*. 3*d*. per gallon on all imported petrol and kerosene. The amount of alcohol to be allocated for motor fuel for 1933 is estimated at 45 million gallons.

(3) All "heavy" petrol must be mixed with 20-25 per cent. of alcohol, this is sold at 2½*d*. per gallon cheaper than "light" petrol. A mixture of 20 per cent. alcohol is permitted without a declaration in fuel grade petrol.

(4) The cost of these subsidies to the State is estimated at 206 million francs or say 3½ crores of rupees.

Germany—The oil importers and indigenous producers are required to purchase from the alcohol monopoly a quantity of power alcohol corresponding to 10 per cent. by weight of their imports of petrol and Benzol plus 6 per cent. of their imports and/or production of kerosene at a control price of £45 per ton. The amount of alcohol taken over is estimated at 42 million gallons. The mixtures permitted range from 10 per cent. to 30 per cent. alcohol.

Greece.—(1) It is proposed to standardize a mixture of 78 per cent. petrol with 22 per cent. alcohol but also to permit the use of unmixed petrol.

(2) To fix annually the quantity of mixture to be made. It is estimated that 1½ million gallons of alcohol would be so used.

Hungary—(1) Petrol over ·735 S. G. must be mixed with 20 per cent. alcohol (unless used for agricultural purpose) about 90 per cent. of the motor fuel used is this 'Motalco'.

(2) The duty on light petrol (below ·735 S. G.) is 4*d*. per gallon higher than that on 'Motalco'.

Italy—A definite allocation of the total production of industrial alcohol is made to the motor industry—at present 2¼ million gallons which is less than 3 per cent. of the total consumption of motor spirit. This is taken over at a control price (Rs. 1-6-10 per gallon) but does not pay the petrol duty.

Latvia—The mixture of 25 per cent. alcohol with 75 per cent. petrol is compulsory. The alcohol is a state monopoly.

Sweden—There is no legal regulation but power alcohol is free of all duty. The mixture used is 25: 75. The quantity of alcohol used for motor fuel is about 2 million gallons.

Yugo-Slavia—The mixture of 80 per cent. petrol with 20 per cent. alcohol is compulsory except for aeroplanes.

It can be seen from these statements that whereas in several countries the use of a specified mixture has been made compulsory, in others, the principle has been adopted of requiring the oil companies, by legislation, to purchase annually a quantity of Power Alcohol corresponding to a certain percentage of their imports and production of petrol and benzol; and in some countries even of their kerosene. The adoption of this method leaves certain amount of latitude to the petrol distributing companies in distribution, and in practice the mixture is sold at a price somewhat lower than pure "light" petrol inspite of the fact that it actually costs more. A more positive method of promoting the use of alcohol as a motor fuel is its exemption from duty as in Sweden, but the Government of India will, we are afraid, necessarily plead inability in accepting this suggestion on the ground of financial stringency and loss of revenue from import duty on sugar.*

*With the proposal of an excise duty, the Government will not be able to complain about lack of funds.

15. Modification in Denaturing Rules in India essential.

Several countries have been experimenting for years with power alcohol in order to make it a commercial success for the use in internal combustion engines. The United States of America, South Africa and Philippine Islands have succeeded considerably with mixtures of alcohol and ether, *e.g.*, Natalite—but these countries are fortunate enough to have received the full support of their governments. The greatest drawback in this country however to any experiments in this direction materialising lies in the present Excise Rules relative to denaturation. The Government insists upon the use of *Caoutchoucine* as an ingredient for denaturation. This substance which is obtained from the destructive distillation of rubber is not suitable for denaturing alcohol intended for use in internal combustion engines as it leaves a gummy residue which clogs valves and fuel jets. True, Government have of late relaxed to some extent the use of *Caoutchoucine* for denaturation in special cases, *e.g.*, manufacture of high grade soap and have permitted in its place the addition of 5% Wood Naphtha, but the price of this ingredient is prohibitive. It seems to us that the use of *Caoutchoucine* or Wood Naptha is not imperative as a denaturant so long as *Pyridine*, the other ingredient insisted upon, is used. *Pyridine* in itself renders alcohol unfit for human consumption and if denaturation be permitted with *Pyridine* alone—in increased proportion of 1% instead of ½% as at present—the difficulties regarding the denaturation of Commercial Spirit will be immediately overcome and power alcohol could then be produced to sell considerably below the current price of petrol in moffussil.

16. Government *Vs.* Power producers' interest.

It is realised however that this current price of petrol includes heavy duties paid to Government and it is apprehended that the Government may not be willing, if only for this reason, to encourage the production of a substitute for petrol which would no longer bring to them the same amount of money from the Duty. This therefore naturally brings to the forefront an unfortunate but inevitable clash between the interest of the Government in search of revenue and the interest of Power producers in search of a cheap and efficient fuel. The duty of the Government in this respect is clear, *viz.*, to sacrifice their revenue for giving the much-needed aid to the sugar industry. Besides, the production of power-alchol would only represent a small percentage of the total consumption of petrol, and as such would not cause a material loss of revenue to the Government.

17. Government Interest to develop the industry.

The possibility of petroleum companies with colossal capital being able to reduce their price so as to make it impossible for competitors to market Power Alcohol is no legitimate and sound argument against the proposal of accepting the project. On the contrary if Power Alcohol can keep down the price of petrol, it must result in an enormous economic saving to the country. The fact should never be lost sight of by the Government that in view of the tremendous increase in the output of sugar in India, the production of an increasing quantity of molasses is inevitable, and unless some suitable outlet is found for the utilisation of molasses, the development of the sugar industry will be considerably retarded. It need hardly be pointed out that the Government are not likely to lose any revenue ultimately, because if the sugar industry is successful, as it promises to be, it will contribute to the Government in a variety of ways, *e.g.*, income tax, super-tax, etc. Experiments should therefore be carried out by the Research Institutes, Government Experts, as well as the sugar industry to produce Power Alcohol suited to the requirements of internal combustion engines.

18. EXPERIMENTAL FACTORIES.

We are glad to find that the Sugar Committee of the Imperial Council of Agricultural Research have just recommended (in November 1933) a scheme under which two distilleries—one at Cawnpore and the other perhaps at Amritsar would be selected and apparatus would be added on to produce absolute alcohol for making experiments on the production of motor fuel. It is further satisfactory to learn that if these experiments are found successful, the Council will—following the law in other countries like France—recommend to the Government for introduction of a law by which it would be made compulsory for all petrol sold in the country to be mixed with a specified proportion of a solution of alcohol made from molasses. We hope the experiments will be carried on.

with zeal and expediency, in appreciation of the urgent nature of the necessity of a solution of the problem.

19. Cost of production of Power Alcohol.

In connection with this question of utilisation of molasses in the manufacture of Power Alcohol the question of cost of production of Power Alcohol from Indian molasses is of fundamental importance and before undertaking legislation for its compulsory admixture as fuel for internal combustion engines, a fuller study of its economies is essential. A control of its price would be desirable for the protection of the consumer. A study should also be undertaken of the technical difficulties that would confront us in regard to this question. The question of distribution arrangements and costs also requires study. The sugar factories, and thus to a considerable extent the distilleries, are remote from the ports and thus from the centres from which petrol is distributed and where mixing could best be done. Technical difficulties which have been found in other countries but which have been got over may be indicated below:—

20. Technical Difficulties.

(1) For successful admixture with petrol alcohol must be of at least 99½ per cent. purity; 98 per cent. spirit will not do (this is clearly shown by Brazil and Cuban experience as well as by experiment) Modern plant for the production of anhydrous alcohol can produce

by this distillation a purity of 99·8 to 99·9 per cent.

(2) Mixtures of alcohol and petrol for successfull commercial use must be between comparatively close limits. Mixtures containing less than about 15 per cent. alcohol are unworkable for several reasons whilst mixtures containing above 20-25 per cent. call for special engine adjustments and the fuel consumption is higher.

(3) Alcohol absorbs water readily and the addition of quite small quantities of water to an alcohol-petrol mixture results in separation and cloudiness. Fortunately these difficulties are mainly met with at low temperatures and percentage of water required to produce separation is higher with increased alcohol content; this is illustrated by the following figures:—

Composition of Mixtures.		Percentage of water sufficient to cause separation.	
		At 0°C.	At 10°C.
Alcohol 10%	Petrol 90%	0·25%	0·20%
15%	85%	0·50%	0·40%
20%	80%	0·60%	0·48%

Figures are also required for +10°C and for mixtures up to 25 per cent. alcohol—these determinations could easily be made.

It is clear that the degree of concentration of the alcohol used is of very great importance as the separation of a watery layer, *e.g.*, at pumps would mean the loss of a considerable proportion of the added alcohol. For example, at 24°C. with a 20/80 mixture once separation has begun 1 per cent. of water would cause about 12 per cent. of alcohol to separate out.

(1) Information is required as to the rate at which different petrol-alcohol mixtures will absorb moisture under Indian conditions of storage, temperature and humidity. These data would be essential to the formulation of a distribution scheme.

(2) For a given power output more alcohol is necessary than petrol due to the lower calorific value of the former. In practice the addition of 15 per cent. alcohol leads to no noticeable increase in fuel consumption an addition of 30 per cent. alcohol means an increase in consumption of about 10 per cent. This would not be a serious consideration with a 20/80 mixture since alcohol is a good "anti-knock" fuel.

21. Anhydrous Alcohol and Cost of Production.—

Whatever may be the form which legislation might take it would be advisable for the Government to fix the sale price of Power Alcohol and if possible also the price of the mixture. The cost to the consumer must be determined by a thorough enquiry before undertaking legislation. For that purpose the Government should obtain accurate figures of the cost of production of anhydrous alcohol in India. It should be remembered that alcohol after mixing with Petrol must be about 99½% absolute at least, *i.e., practically anhydrous*, otherwise difficulties due to water separation would arise. The estimate of the cost of manufacture *omitting the cost of raw material* for a modern installation in America is given below :—

		Per American gallon.
Manufacture of 90 Spirit	...	8 cents.
To anhydrous ...	...	2 ,,
Total	...	10 ,,

At normal exchange it is six pence or Rs. 0-5-4 per Imperial gallon. The sub-committee appointed by the Sugar Committee of the Imperial Council of Agricultural Research calculated that with molasses at nine annas per maund Power Alcohol would cost annas 14 per gallon, and with no value for molasses, at about 6 annas.

Working on the basis of figures supplied to the Tariff Board (which assumes an output of 33,063·4 gallons of rectified spirit from 15,322 maunds of molasses) the cost of production has been calculated as follows :—

TABLE NO. 24.

Cost of Production of rectified spirit from molasses.

	Per gallon spirit. R.	A.	P.
Cost of Molasses at 6 as. per maund Freight on molasses @ 0-4-3 per maund	0	4	9
Works cost	0	2	9·6
Cost of denaturant	0	1	4·4
Depreciation on drums	0	0	7·7
Cost per gallon rectified spirit ...	0	9	6·7
Cost of concentration (American figure)	0	1	2
	0	10	8·7

This is about 11 annas per gallon at the distillery. If no freight has to be paid on molasses, cost would be reduced to say 9 annas per gallon but the above includes nothing for overhead charges or for freight on spirit to concentrating and distributing centres. The C. I. F. price of petrol at ports with which the above figure has to be compared may be taken at some 0-5-0 per galllon—this is exclusive of all storage and distribution costs.

The real cost of power alcohol at the distilleries under favourable circumstances is several times the cost of petrol at ports. The transport of alcohol and petrol is expensive and distribution cost high due mainly to evaporation losses.

22. Consumption of petrol in provinces, and India.

The figures of the consumption of petrol in various provinces for 1929, 1930, 1931, as also in India are given in the Table (Nos. 25 and 26.)

TABLE NO. 25.

Consumption of Petrol in Provinces.

Statement showing the petrol sales in the various provinces for the year 1929, 1930 and 1931.

Province.	GALLONS.		
	1929.	1930	1931
Madras	10,331,000	11,248,000	10,696,000
Bombay	11,936,000	12,971,000	13,182,000
Bengal	9,913,000	10,976,000	10,782,000
United Provinces ...	3,753,000	4,476,000	4,553,000
Burma	7,623,000	7,756,000	7,137,000
Shan State ...	550,000	663,000	621,000
Punjab	4,602,000	5,397,000	5,560,000
Bihar & Orissa ...	2,537,000	2,940,000	2,736,000
Central Provinces ...	2,317,000	2,660,000	2,247,000
Assam	1,285,000	1,599,000	1,764,000
North West Frontier Provinces ...	1,263,000	1,514,000	1,660,000
Rest of Br. India & Indian States ...	9,767,000	11,460,000	11,723,000
Total ...	65,877,000	73,660,000	72,661,000

TABLE NO. 26.

Consumption of Petrol in India from 1926-27 to 1932-33.

Year	Petrol (million gallons).	Year	Petrol (million gallons)
1926-27 ...	... 36·3	1929-30 ...	... 79·2
1927-28 ...	... 48·6	1930-31 ...	... 79·4
1928-29 ...	... 61·2	1931-32 ...	... 75·5
		1932-33 (Esti.)	... 69·5

(Import duty on petrol is 10 annas per gallon, from 1932).

The consumption of three principal sugar-producing provinces—the United Provinces, Bihar and Orissa, and the Punjab, was less than 13 million gallons. If a 20/80 mixture were adopted, Upper India will account for only 3 million gallons of alcohol, while an outlet is desired for 10 million to 20 million gallons. Making due allowance for present and future molasses—production in Madras, Bengal and in Bombay, it is still clear that power alcohol would have to be used even in the ports.

23. Railway freight on petrol.

The railway freight in India on petrol in bulk works out approximately as shown in Table No. 27 below.

TABLE NO. 27.

Railway freight on Petrol.

Freight per tank wagon of 5,000 gallons—Approximate.

Distance.	On E. I. Railway.	On N. W. Railway.	On B. B & C. I. Rly. from Bombay.	Per gallon annas and pies.
300 miles ...	560	600	475	1-5 to 1-9
600 miles ...	840	890	805	2-5 to 2-8
1,000 miles ...	1,040	1,100	920	2-9 to 3-5
Calcutta-Delhi ...	850 to 900	...	...	2-9

The freights on power alcohol would thus have to be considerably reduced, particularly for long distances, *e.g.*, at the various ports, in order that the mixtures can sell at reasonable prices at the various consuming centres.

24. EXPERIMENTAL FACTORIES FOR STUDYING PLANTS, COSTS, ETC.

It would be of great help if experimental factories would be set up at suitable places in India where various details can be settled and data obtained, *viz.*, cost of production of *Anhydrous* alcohol, information regarding the type of plant required and most suitable to Indian conditions, etc. We also understand that the Petroleum companies are now not opposed (as they were once) and are willing to co-operate in the distribution of power alcohol if a workable scheme is devised. Thus one more obstacle is removed in the way of the Government. We fervently trust that the Government of India will explore this avenue of helping the sugar industry with the utmost zeal, and expediency, even at the risk of loss of some revenue, for the ultimate benefit to the country.

There is no doubt that with the price of molasses at about 0-2-0 per maund the cost of production of alcohol will be very low, and the possibilities of successful manufacture of power alcohol should be very closely examined. On the successful production of power alcohol a great deal of the success of the sugar industry hinges. The potentiality of exporting sugar would depend still more on the success achieved in this direction, as then alone will it be possible to bring down the cost of production to the level of other countries like Java, Cuba, Philippines and Hawaiian islands.

The results of the experiments which will be conducted under the auspices of the Imperial Council of Agricultural Research, will be very anxiously awaited.

25. PRICE OF MOLASSES.

The average market price per maund of molasses in India was Rs. 1-8-0 in 1931, 0-10-0 in 1932, 0-4-0 in 1933 and about nothing in 1934.

26. PRODUCTION AND IMPORT OF JAVA MOLASSES.

Let us now see the total production of molasses in India from cane-factories, refineries and khandsaris, and the import of molasses (in tons) during the last four years. The figures are given in table No. 28 below.

TABLE NO. 28.

Production and import of molasses (in tons).

—	Cane factories.	Refineries.	Khandsaris.	Total Indian production.	Imports.
1929-30	35,393	12,899	200,000	248,292	71,761
1930-31	48,187	20,458	200,000	268,945	102,024
1931-32	69,208	22,042	250,000	341,250	40,191
1932-33	130,419	...	...	420,000 (estimated)	31,991
1933-34	300,000 (estimated)	...	...	5,00,000 (estimated)	2,401 (April to December.)

27. IMPORT OF MOLASSES MUST BE STOPPED.

The value of the import of molasses was Rs. 42,63,995 in 1930-31, Rs. 15,82,250 in 1931-32 and Rs. 10,66,648 in 1932-33. The value of the import in the year 1933 was Rs. 69,000 only. Even so the Government must keep a close watch, and if imports show an increasing tendency, the duty should be raised and imports stopped for the sake of the Indian industry, for it must be remembered that Java is prepared to reduce the price till a level is reached which will not give her the price of the cost of production and freights. The reason why Java can afford to consider the molasses of no value, and throw it into the sea, if necessary, is due to her efficient state of the industry, aided by Government for a long period. The duty on molasses must be made specific, and high, to guard against any imports from outside. The consumer will not suffer at all due to this, as a result of the internal competition.

28. Facilities for Sale of Molasses

There ought to be a better organization of sale of molasses in India. The Railways should also help by providing tank wagons for transport in bulk; they ought also to lower the freights from manufacturing centres to consuming markets. It is a matter of regret to state that practically no reduction has been made by railways although the price has fallen from Rs. 2-8-0 to 0-2-0 per maund. The Railway freights ought to be considerably lowered, in order to enable molasses to move, and the freights must be charged on the principle of "charging what the traffic will bear."

The Indian factories ought also to produce better molasses, like the Java molasses, by improving the colour and density which are its chief defects.

29. Use of Bagasse, as fuel, costly.

Bagasse (or megasse) which is the residue of fibrous matter remaining after the cane is crushed is another important by-product of this industry. The bulk of bagasse obtained by crushing cane in the factory is burnt as fuel for generating steam, and for boiling the juice in rab or *gur* making. As a rule almost all the power required in factories is obtained from bagasse and occasionally it is supplemented by coal or fire-wood. Various sugar factories require only a small amount of outside fuel to supplement the use of bagasse. In the International Sugar Journal for the month of August 1929, Mr. E. L. Squires observes "Apparently bagasse is a very high-priced fuel and it might be better to burn the sugar." The high railway rates of freight on coal, and the absence of a demand for bagasse for other purposes are probably responsible for the general practice of its consumption as fuel.

30. Production of paper.

Investigations made in the past on bagasse indicate possibilities of its being put to various profitable uses, the most important of which are its utilisation for the production of papers, purified cellulose and fibre boards.

The cellulose content in bagasse is always 40 to 50 per cent. A portion of it is lost however in the mechanical and chemical process and the yield of bleached cellulose is very low, being on the average about 25 to 28 per cent. Due to this low yield and of the harsh and "rattly" texture of paper prepared from bagasse cellulose, it has not been found practicable to make use of it for the manufacture of high grades of paper. However, it appears to be possible to obtain from the bagasse 31 to 32 per cent. of bleached cellulose by adopting slightly less chemical process. This however not being very clean is suitable, in admixture with bamboo or grass cellulose for the production of inferior grades of paper (badami and bleached) which are consumed in the country in large quantities.

31. MANUFACTURE OF ARTIFICIAL SILK.

Experiments carried out at the Imperial Institute, London, serve to show that cellulose suitable for artificial silk can also be prepared from bagasse. So far as we are aware, however, commercial success has not yet been obtained in its utilisation for this purpose, although it is known that in 1928 a firm in Cuba had put on the market a cellulose which was claimed to be suitable for use in the manufacture of paper and in the artificial silk industry. The question is still being investigated by the Hawaiian Sugar Planters' Association. As other suitable raw materials, *e.g.*, bamboo, grass, etc., are available in plenty in this country and which may be utilised for papers and cellulose for artificial silk, the utilisation of bagasse for these products may be ruled out of consideration.

32. Packing Papers, and Fibre-boards manufacture, a possibility.

During the last decade the production of packing papers and fibre-boards from bagasse has been developed considerably in the United States of America and in other sugarcane producing countries. The Celotex Coy., Louisiana, uses enormous quantity of bagasse obtained from Cuba for the manufacture of insulation and structural boards, panel boards, corrugated boards and wrapping papers, etc.

The uses to which bagasse can be put in this country are:—

1. In the manufacture of inferior grades of paper, and

2. In the manufacture of packing papers and fibre boards.

The market for the latter products and the price at which bagasse can be available will, however, determine the possibility of employing the material on a commercial scale for these uses.

A large production of imported old newspapers is used for packing purposes by the retail trade. The figures of the imports of packing papers, old newspapers, paste boards, etc., into this country in1931-32 and 1932-33 are given in Tables 29 and 30 below.

TABLE NO. 29.

Import of packing papers, old newspapers, etc., for the years 1931-32 and 1932-1933.

	Quantity in tons.	
	1931-32	1932-33.
Packing paper ...	10,241	16,244
Old Newspaper ...	41,866	47,369
Straw Boards ...	9,872	14,989
Paste Boards, Mill Boards etc.	372	356

TABLE NO. 30.

Import of packing papers, old newspapers, etc., for the years 1931-32 and 1932-33.

	Value in Rupees.	
	1931-32.	1932-33.
Packing paper ...	31,31,016	45,35,100
Old Newspaper ...	34,51,608	42,38,556
Straw Boards ...	11,68,054	18,41,067
Paste Boards etc. ...	3,30,330	2,52,838

The total consumption of packing papers (for which purpose newspapers are also largely used) may therefore be taken at about 60,000 tons a year valued at about Rs. 87 lakhs. Doubtless old newspapers are cheaper than packing papers but their use for wrapping foodstuffs is unhygienic.

33. Use of Packing paper in substitution of old newspapers.

The retail trade is however, slowly taking to the use of packing paper for wrapping and packing purposes. With some propaganda work it is possible to induce the trade to use cleaner packing papers in place of old newspapers. Further the sugar industry itself can consume a large quantity of packing papers in the form of paper bags. The present practice in sugar industry is to pack and despatch sugar in gunny bags. Short fibre and dirt from this bag get mixed up with sugar, and these are not only a great nuisance to the consumers but they also lower the value of sugar. The gunny bags can therefore be lined with paper bags at a very small additional cost. This will have the advantage of keeping the sugar clean and protect it at the same time from atmospheric moisture. For the retail trade, small quantity of sugar can be sold in paper bags instead of more expensive cloth bags as it is sometimes done at present.

34. Experiment in manufacture of packing paper promises success.

An experiment recently carried out at the Forest Research Institute, Dehra-Dun, is reported to have indicated that a packing paper with satisfactory tensile bursting strengths can be produced from bagasse particularly if a small percentage (15 to 20%) of bamboo or some other long fibre is mixed with it. A market for packing paper already exists in the country, as shown above, and promises to increase in the future. At the present time packing paper is not manufactured at all in the country; there is thus a promising field for the utilisation of bagasse for this new industry.

35. Large potential market for fibre boards.

The use of fibre boards for structural, insulation and other purposes has grown rapidly in Western Countries. It does not appear, however, likely that the use of boards will be equally extensive in this country for various reasons, climatic and otherwise. It is likely however that a fairly large demand for fibre boards (pressed and insulated) may grow up in this country for certain special requirements, *e.g.*

1. In large office buildings, on floors and ceilings for sound and heat insulation.
2. In theatre and cinema halls, on walls, floors and ceilings to obtain perfect acoustics or to correct defective acoustics.
3. In factories for sound proofing or vibration proofing of machinery.

4. In the construction of cool chambers, ice-chests refrigerators, refrigerating railway cars, etc.

5. In the construction of motor car bodies and similar constructional work where strength and ability to withstand vibration, combined with lightness is required.

6. In the manufacture of boxes, *e.g.*, fibre board trunks, suitcases, attache cases, cardboard boxes of various shapes and sizes for medical phials, soaps, scents, stationery, hosiery, glass-ware, laboratory apparatus, chemicals, etc., etc.

For some of the above uses straw board is at present used. In view of the fact, however, that cereal straws are not available at cheap prices in this country, except in a few localities, it is likely that boards made from bagasse may successfully compete with and replace straw boards in many of the above uses. It appears therefore, that there is a large potential market for fibre boards also in this country.

36. PRICE OF BAGASSE.

The calorific value of dry bagasse, a bulk of which is burnt as fuel in the factories, is about 8,000 B. T. U., while that of average anthracite coal is 12,000—14,000 B. T. U. Roughly speaking about $1\frac{1}{2}$ tons of dry bagasse is equivalent in heat value to 1 ton of coal. Taking Rs. 10 to 12 as the average cost of coal in the localities where a large number of sugar factories are situated (eastern parts of the United Provinces and Bihar and Orissa) the minimum price at which sugar factories may part with the bagasse is about Rs. 7 to 8 per ton of dry bagasse. To this we must add the cost of handling and transporting bagasse from the sugar factories to the paper board mills. As bagasse it a very bulky material, it would be economic to locate the paper or board mill as near as possible to the sugar factories in order to minimise the transportation charges. Taking on the average Rs. 4 to 5 per ton as the cost of handling and transporting bagasse from factories to the paper mills, the minimum price of dry bagasse may be taken at about Rs. 12 per ton.

Considering the current price of bamboo, grass or straw it appears that at the above price bagasse may compete favourably with them as a raw material for the production of packing papers or for the utilization in the manufacture of inferior grades of papers from bamboos and grasses. An approximate estimate of the cost of production of packing papers based on the results of an experiment carried out at the Forest Research Institute, Dehra-Dun by Mr. M. P. Bhargava, Officer-in-charge of the Paper Pulp Section, shows that the manufacture of these papers from bagasse at Rs. 12 per ton may be as remunerative as the production of ordinary grades of writing and printing papers from bamboo or grass. The commercial possibility of this industry which promises success, should therefore be carefully examined.

37. Paper and Board Mill's Future—Imperial Council's Duty.

With the development of industries in the country and a rise in the standard of living, consumption of packing papers and boards is bound to increase considerably in the near future. The possibility of utilising bagasse for the manufacture of these products has been shown above, the two important conditions necessary for success being (*i*) that bagasse should be available at prices which bear the same relation to the cost of coal (f.o.r. sugar factories) as the calorific values of the two materials bear to each other and (*ii*) that paper or board mills should be situated in the vicinity of sugar factories so that the handling and transportation charges may be reduced to the minimum. The application of bagasse to the manufacture of papers and boards will, we feel, make a more economic use of the material than burning it as fuel, encourage the growth of a new industry and render the country independent of imports of these products from foreign countries. The Imperial Council of Agricultural Research should therefore also direct their attention to this matter. It would be helpful if it may set up one or two experimental factories at convenient centres.

38. Advantageous position of paper and Board Mills near Coal-fields.

There will be a considerable reduction in the price of bagasse in factories which are situated nearer to the coal-fields, due to the lower freight charges on coal, and consequently a lower price for coal—an alternative fuel. The success of manufacture of paper near sugar factories, situated, for instance, in Bengal and Bihar nearer the coal-fields, would thus be assured due to the comparative cheapness of the raw material.

39. Better utilisation of bagasse would increase Country's Coal consumption.

The utilisation of bagasse for paper-making, board-making, etc., will stimulate the demand for coal, and will give a fillip to the coal industry also. Thus the development of the sugar industry will benefit the coal industry also in asmuch as demand for coal in the sugar factories will increase considerably.

40. Other by-products.

Other by-products like bagasse ashes, filter press mud cakes, etc., can be used as manure for the lands. But these are very insignificant.

Let us now turn our attention to other problems of the industry.

CHAPTER VI.

Regulation of the Industry, Distribution of Benefits, and relations between Cane-growers and Sugar Manufacturers.

1. The problems stated.

We propose to discuss in this chapter various problems pertaining to the industry, *e.g.*, whether (1) either cane-growers or sugar-manufacturers are being unduly benefited at the expense of the consumers, and whether the benefits of the industry are being fairly distributed between different interests, whether (2) it is desirable and practicable to regulate the relations between cane-growers and sugar-manufacturers by zoning, licensing, fixing of cane prices, or other means, and whether (3) it is necessary to introduce legislation for the better regulation of the industry.

2. Why protection granted to the industry.

Protection was recommended for the sugar industry by the Tariff Board, and granted by the Government, as it fulfilled the three conditions laid down by the Fiscal Commission, and established its claim for State assistance. The Tariff Board emphasized however, that although this was so, the strongest aspect of the case of protection was that based upon the national importance of the cultivation of cane. The Tariff Board also considered that the expansion of the sugar industry was an indispensable adjunct to the agricultural development. In chapter IV of their Report, the Tariff Board observed :—

"It will be useful here to summarise our conclusions regarding the importance of cane cultivation in the agricultural system of India. Sugarcane occupies a definite place in the crop rotation of this country which it would be difficult to fill if any considerable reduction in the area occurred. Its cultivation is followed by increased yields of other crops sown in rotation with it, partly as a result of the residual effect of the manure used in cane cultivation but largely also on account of the thorough stirring up and aeration of the soil which is a feature of the intensive cultivation required if heavy crops are to be obtained. It is also of great importance as a source of cattle fodder at a time when the supply of grass has begun to decline. At all times it occupies a prominent position in agricultural economy as being one of the few crops on which the cultivator relies to meet his cash requirements and at the present time, when the prices of other agricultural products have fallen to very low levels, the importance of maintaining the area under cane and its prices cannot be overestimated. The payment of rent and irrigation dues depends to no small extent on this crop and any serious setback to its cultivation would not be without effect on the finances of at least some of the local Governments. The development of well irrigation as a condition precedent to intensive cultivation would present serious difficulties if no cane were grown and in the heavily populated tracts its cultivation may be regarded as essential to agricultural improvement. Finally it is the one crop for which, if it can be utilized for the manufacture of white sugar, the home market is more than sufficient. While it is beyond the power of Government to control the prices of other agricultural products, since these depend on world conditions, in the case of cane it is possible to ensure the maintenance of a reasonable price level by protecting the *gur* market against foreign competition and by providing an outlet for any surplus cane produced by the development of the white sugar industry."

The Tariff Board, while discussing the question of the period of protection, made the observation that if any real development in the sugar industry is to be secured, if new factories are to be established, land improvement and irrigation undertaken with a view to cane cultivation, it is essential that both the agriculturist and the industrialist should be assured of protection for a lengthy period and in their view no period of less than 15 years would suffice.

3. PROGRESS OF THE INDUSTRY.

We have seen in chapter II, that the industry has progressed very rapidly, and a stage has practically come when we need no import of sugar, and have to think of foreign exports. The latter depends on our ability to reduce our cost of production. Let us see now whether the profits of the industry have been fairly distributed.

4. FALL IN PRICE OF SUGAR.

The Tariff Board estimated that there will be a progressive decrease in the cost of production of sugar in India, and in order to establish the industry successfully in India recommended a higher import duty for the first seven years, (Rs. 7-4-0 per cwt.) and Rs. 6-4-0 per cwt. for the next 8 years). The total amount of duty in force has been even higher, *i.e.*, Rs. 9-1-0 per cwt., (including the revenue surcharge of 25%). The Tariff Board estimated the basic fair selling price of sugar at Rs. 9-5-9 per maund, during the first few years after the grant of protection, and Rs. 7-12-5 per maund, at the end of the protective period of 15 years. This took account of 0-10-8 as the realisation of the price for molasses, during the first few years, and 0-6-9 at the end of the period. If we deduct this, no value being realised at present for molasses, the basic fair selling price of Indian sugar, on the calculation of the Tariff Board, would be Rs. 10-0-5 at present, and Rs. 8-3-2 at the end of 15 years.. The price at which Indian sugar has been selling is very much lower than these prices, calculated by the Tariff Board, although there has been no return for molasses. This has been due to the internal competition, which has been brought into play, as a result of the establishment of a large number of factories. Although therefore the sugar manufactured in India can sell at a little higher price in parity with the price of imported sugar, the Indian sugar manufacturers have not taken advantage of that, and the consumer has benefited to that extent. With the increasing competition, it is certain that there will be a further fall in the price of Indian Sugar, irrespective of the price at which imported sugar may sell. The price of Indian sugar (1st quality) has been about Rs. 2 per maund lower than the price of imported sugar, during the last few months of the year 1933, and the early part of the year 1934, and indeed, it must be emphasised, is not determined by prices of imported sugar.

5. PRICE OF CANE--FAIR OR LOW?

The fall in the price of sugar has necessarily meant the payment of a slightly smaller price to the agriculturist for his cane. The cultivator of cane has, however, we are happy to state, been well off due to the fair price he has realised for his cane, as compared with prices of other crops, which have undergone a precipitous decline. The fact that the area under cane cultivation has gone up so rapidly and that there is an increase of cultivation of the high-crop yielding improved variety points to the fact that he is reaping larger benefit from this crop than from others. The fall in the price of sugar has certainly been responsible for a smaller price being paid to him for cane, but he has no valid reason to complain, as he is realising far higher prices of cane from the factories than from others to whom he sells his cane, and the price realised by him is well above his cost of production and as he has been doing well in a period of general distress, and this has also resulted in consumers' interests being safeguarded. The salvation of the industry, as also of agriculture, lies in improving the outturn of cane per acre, and the quality of the cane. The manufacturer is also aware of his responsibility in the matter of payment of a fair price to the cultivator to encourage him to grow cane, on which the working of his factory depends. Indeed even in self-interest, he will pay him a fair price. His interests are not opposed to that of the cultivator, on whose co-operation he depends. Besides, it cannot be disputed that although the factories consume hardly 10% of the total cane grown in India, the factories have paid prices for their cane which are far higher than the price realised by the cultivators when they sold their cane to *gur* manufacturers, khandsaris, and others.

6. Benefits fairly distributed.

We are of the opinion that the benefits of the industry have been on the whole, distributed fairly, between various interests affected, and there is no cause for feeling otherwise. What is more, we fervently believe that the energies of those having the interest of the industry at heart should be directed to researches in the direction of improving cultivation, and hence the outturn and quality, as then the cultivator will receive more money per acre of cultivation than at present, without increasing the cost to the manufacturer. The cost of production as has been indicated elsewhere, must be brought down, as no export of sugar is possible until the costs of production are materially reduced, and India will necessarily have to think of export markets in a year or two.

Even the Tariff Board observed: "The future of the Sugar Industry depends mainly on the cost of producing the primary material, *viz.*, cane, and the problem is, therefore, one of protecting a particular branch of agriculture until such time as improvements in methods of cultivation and developments in research enable the agriculturist to increase his yields per acre and thereby effect a substantial decrease in the cost of cane, while maintaining or increasing his own profits."

At the Sugar Conference held at Simla, in July 1933, there was a considerable discussion on this subject. The Hon'ble Dr. Gocul Chand Narang, Minister for Local Self Government (in Charge of the Industries Department), Punjab, averred that the price of about 6 annas being paid for the cane was an economic price. He stated that he had calculated that the cultivator was getting cent per cent profit on his investment, and that he was convinced that the cultivator was not being unfairly dealt with. He also stated that it was wrong to penalise the factories consuming only 5% of the total quantity of canes. The Khandsaris were known to be paying only 0-3-0 or even less per maund of cane to the cultivator.

Mr. H. C. Prior, Revenue Secretary of Bihar Government also suggested that in the opinion of the Bihar Government distribution of profits was not unfair. In fact he stated that the factories had paid for cane about three times the price paid by the indigenous *gur* manufacturer. He cited an instance that the average price of *gur* made from cane in South Bihar was Rs. 2 a maund, and that it represented a price of about $1\frac{1}{2}$ annas per maund of cane, as against about 0-5-0 per maund paid by factories.

Mr. D. P. Khaitan, representative of the Indian Sugar Mills Association speaking at the Simla Conference enquired what the position of the sugarcane grower would have been, if it had not been for the capitalists who had sunk their money and taken all the trouble they had in setting up the sugar factories. He further pointed out that even in areas where sugar cane had been planted, and grown for the factories and factories had not been able to buy these supplies, the sugar cane grower had not been able to get in the very same locality, more than 0-1-6 per maund for the cane which had been converted into *gur*, or had been used in khandsari factories. He observed that the fact remained that as a result of the development of this industry, the sugar cane grower has benefited to that extent that instead of getting one anna six pies or so, he has been getting over five annas per maund for his cane. Besides, he has improved his quality of cane, thus giving him a better return per acre, and he would not have gone in for the improvement of the quality but for the establishment of the factories. Nobody can contradict the position that as a result of the establishment of sugar factories the sugar cane growers had benefited considerably.

Although it is possible, that the factories in some places may have paid very low price for cane, the fact cannot be denied that on the whole the cultivators, as also the consumers have benefited from the production. If a minimum price was fixed for cane as is suggested by some, it would also be necessary to fix a minimum price for sugar and then the interest of the consumer would be left in the lurch. Nothing of this kind has been done and should be done. The problem of cane-price fixing bristles with difficulties. We would suggest that the Economic Laws of Demand and Supply should be allowed to operate, and the matter should be left to be solved without any interference from outside, both because such intervention is impracticable and unlikely to serve the purpose, and also because the factories realise that in their own interest it is desirable to pay a price which would induce the cultivator to grow requisite supplies of cane, and to effect improvements therein.

8. REGULATION OF RELATIONS.

Let us now consider whether it is desirable or practicable to regulate the relations between cane growers and sugar manufacturers whether by zoning, licensing, fixing of cane prices or other means.

We have already stated that in our opinion there is no serious cause for genuine complaint that the interests of any sections of the people interested in the industry *viz.*, manufacturers, cane-growers and consumers have been neglected or disregarded, and we believe that the benefits have been fairly distributed. If there are any factories which have paid too low prices of cane we believe that the force of public opinion will set things right, and what is more, if associations of cane-growers are formed, they will be of great use.

The sugarcane manufacturers deserve a word of praise for their enterprise in investing capital in this industry, the cultivators for having increased and improved the cultivation of cane and the consumers for having agreed to bear the burden of protection for the sake of the country's interests. The latter will find relief when they realise that their burden has been made somewhat smaller, as a result of the internal competition which has brought about a fall in the price of sugar.

9. Are Cane-price fixing, Zoning, and Licensing, practicable or desirable?

These questions were discussed at the Simla Conference. The Chairman of the Conference pointed out that any intervention by the Government in any of the above matters must involve legislation. The present position, the Chairman described, was that a man could establish any factory when he liked, where he liked and could buy cane whereform he liked and pay what price he liked. Similarly, the Sugarcane producer could bring under sugarcane such area as he liked, give up producing sugar cane if he liked, and sell it at whatever price he could get. That is, the policy of *Laissez Faire* prevailed on both sides, and things were left to adjust themselves.

The protagonists of the cultivators who feel however that the cultivators have been robbed of their legitimate profits and are being paid too low price for their cane, and have the feeling that the manufacturers are reaping rich harvests of profits, suggest that in order to increase the price of cane, minimum cane prices should be fixed, by legislation, as then alone the interests of the cultivators can be safeguarded.

Others suggest that it is unwise for the Government to intervene in the interplay of economic forces and that if things are left to themselves, they will adjust themselves in the course of time.

The Government of the United Provinces are strongly inclined to favour legislation for zoning factories and fixing a minimum price of cane. Mr. J. P. Srivastava, Minister for Education, United Provinces, observed at the Simla Conference that inspite of the well-known defects of zoning, he felt that zoning would be an advantage to the cultivator and the factory, and along with zoning, he suggested that there should be a minimum price of cane which should be arrived at with the help of a suitable formula, and further that there should also be a system of licensed contractors from whom alone the factories could purchase their cane, in order to guard against evasion of prices by factories. He observed, and with considerable truth, that there are numerous factories which even to-day pay a fair price, but which does not reach the cultivators, and that the middleman who is a parasite gets a big share out of it.

10. Is Fixation of Cane-Prices in cultivator's interest?

The Indian Sugar Committee discussed the system of the scales of payment for cane, and came to the conclusion that in Indian conditions, a sliding scale based on a price of cane equal to half the price of sugar manufactured from it subject to a minimum of 6 annas per maund would be suitable.

The proposal for fixing cane prices is made for the protection of the agriculturists. The Tariff Board also considered the proposai but came to the conclusion: "It is clear that no direct measures can be taken to ensure that a definite rate of cane is paid to producers". They further observed "Conditions differ so widely in India, as regards the output of cane per acre, the cost of cultivation and the sucrose content of the cane that no one scale of payment would be suitable to all conditions."

The Tariff Board also remarked that even if a scale could be devised which would be suitable for the very varied conditions of cane cultivation in different parts of India, the methods of evasion are so numerous that it is improbable that this could be successfully enforced. The Tariff Board concluded:

"But we must leave it to the good sense of factory owners and to their realisation that eventually the interests of the factory and of the cultivators are inseparably connected, to ensure adequate payment to the agriculturist for his cane."

11. U. P. Government in favour of fixing minimum prices.

In a memorandum circulated at the Simla Conference by Mr. J. P. Srivastava, Member for Education, United Provinces, it was suggested that there was no difficulty in the United Provinces about laying down what the minimum price to be paid for sugar cane should be. The generally accepted formula laying down that the price of cane in annas per maund should be $\frac{s \times p}{200}$ where p is the price of sugar in annas per maund, and s the average extraction of sugar from sugar cane of all vacuum pan factories in the province during the previous year, would be, he observed, suitable for the province, and there is perhaps no objection to laying down a uniform price for the whole province and that if necessary the figures could be varied with the time of the year at which the cane is delivered, though a uniform rate throughout the season would be better. The real point however, he observed, was not in laying down the rate but enforcing it. The danger was that still the price may not reach the growers, and therefore he suggested the system of licensed contractors who should, by legislation, be compelled to pay at least 90% of the price they received, to the actual growers. He further stated that the fixation of a minimum price was a complicated matter, and lent itself to numerous abuses.

It is clear therefore that even the U. P. Government who sponsored this proposal, are doubtful in their own minds about its practicability. Besides, it is clear that if any legislation fixing minimum prices for cane is adopted, it can only be for the whole of India, and not for any particular district or province, as that would place the factories situated within the area to which the legislation is made applicable, in a disadvantageous position as compared with other factories, and this handicap would be intolerable.

12. VARIOUS OTHER PROVINCES AGAINST LEGISLATION OF MINIMUM PRICE-FIXING.

We are entirely opposed to this proposal of cane price fixing as we are convinced that it will not be to the interest of the cultivators for whose benefit it is sought to be introduced.

First, let us see how this proposal was viewed by the representatives from various provinces, and by the different interests represented at the Simla Conference.

Mr. H. C. Prior, speaking on behalf of the Government of Bihar and Orissa said: "The view of my Government is that any legislation for zoning, licensing of factories, or fixation of cane prices is *impracticable and will go against the interests both of the cane growers and of the development of the industry*". He also added "The Sugar cane was then the most profitable crop for the raiyat to grow." He also observed that a fair price was generally paid for cane and it seemed likely that in North

Bihar the ordinary rules of supply and demand will result in a fair price being paid in the future. He concluded by saying that the Bihar Government considered that it would be *absolutely impracticable to enforce by legislation* the payment of any minimum price.

Dr. G. P. Hector, Director of Agriculture, Bengal, observed that the Bengal Government's view was that legislation was not necessary. All that they were anxious about was that nothing should be said or done at this stage of the industry to frighten away capital.

The Hon'ble Diwan Bahadur Kumaraswami Reddiar, Minister of Education and Excise, (In charge of Industries) Madras, remarked that so far as the Madras Government were concerned, they had at that time no intention of introducing legislation in the local legislature.

Mr. V. V. Gadgil, speaking on behalf of the Bombay Government said that they had not so far considered, nor had they under contemplation, any Bill for fixing of prices, or zoning or licensing.

13. INSUPERABLE PRACTICAL DIFFICULTIES IN FIXING PRICE OF CANE.

The representatives of manufacturing interests were also opposed to the proposal of legislation. We will now discuss the practical difficulties in enforcing legislation for fixing minimum price of cane.

(*a*) It would be difficult to determine a standard quality for which the price is to be paid. For instance, should a factory buy cane giving a smaller yield of sugar at the same rate as cane giving a larger yield? How are the quality disputes to be settled? What will the grower of the inferior cane do with it if he cannot sell it to the factory at a lower rate?

(*b*) Is the price of cane to be fixed for dry cane or fresh cane? What will the cultivator do with his dry cane?

(*c*) Is the cost of carriage to the factory gate to be deducted or not? Otherwise why should the factory get cane from a distance? What should the grower of that cane do with it?

(*d*) What is to be done when sellers of cane of their own accord compete with each other and insist on selling their cane at lower rates? This is not imaginary but has actually happened. Is it desirable to utilise the cane or let it rot?

(*e*) If a price is fixed, there will be hardly any impetus to improve the quality of cane.

(*f*) Is the law to apply only to factories or contractors also?

(*g*) Is the law to apply to people who buy cane to make *Gur* or manufacture sugar as khandsaris? How can it be discovered whether a middleman bought cane to sell it to a factory or a *Gur* maker or khandsari?

(*h*) Such a law would hinder the bringing about of a direct contact between the factory and the cultivator which is so desirable, and increase the number of middlemen, a situation which will adversely affect the interests of the cultivator.

(*i*) What would happen in a case where the cultivators grew types of cane which were unsuitable, as happened, for instance, in Bihar, where the cultivators grew Co. 205?

(*j*) What would happen when there is an excess of cane? The cane will fetch no price until it is carried over long hauls to other factories.

(*k*) What price will be fixed for the cane in the month of May, when the sugar content is extremely low?

(*l*) Can the legislaiton be made applicable only to factories which consume less than 10% of the total cane crop?

(*m*) Will the Government agree to neutralise the disadvantages suffered by some factories, in comparison with others, in the matter of railway freights? In some cases, the difference in railway freight between two factories amounts to six annas per maund of sugar, which is equivalent to a difference of half an anna in the price of sugarcane. Is it not unjust that a mill which is subjected to the handicap of a higher railway freight should have to pay compulsorily the same rate for cane as a factory more advantageously situated in this respect?

(*n*) Besides it will not be possible to ensure that the cultivator actually receives the minimum price fixed.

(*o*) It is difficult to visualise what would happen when there is an overproduction of cane, if a minimum price is fixed.

(*p*) Various difficulties will also present themselves in the case of unbonded cane brought to the factory for sale by a cultivator.

(*q*) The difficulties as to what variations should be permitted in regard to quality or variety of cane or season of supply, and as to what might be done when the minimum price fixed is in excess of the price of disposal of cane in any other manner, are serious, and it is difficult to devise a solution. In fact it is difficult to believe how a minimum price can be fixed. The fixation of a minimum price would be prejudicial to the interests of the grower as also the manufacturer.

(*r*) While the Government may think of fixing a minimum price of cane will they be able to assure the manufacturer of a minimum price for his sugar?

Thus there are very formidable difficulties in the fixation of minimum prices. The natural operation of the laws of supply and demand should be allowed to have its play and no artificial restriction should be brought in as that would be of no use in achieving the object. For instance, it may perhaps suit a cultivator to sell his cane at a reduced price, even at a moment when it is not wanted by the factory owner or the *Gur* manufacturer, or the khandsari rather than allow it to dry up or throw it away for want of a buyer. The best method of ensuring the payment of a proper price to the cultivator, if the Government are convinced that in any particular case the manufacturer is not doing so, is to bring into existence co-operative societies, which, as an organised body, might be able to deal better with the sugar manufacturers than a single individual.

14. BIHAR SUGAR CONFERENCE POINTS OUT DIFFICULTIES OF FIXATION OF PRICES.

At the Sugar Conference held at Patna, on the 4th January 1934, the representatives of the Bihar Government as also of Manufacturers hinted at several administrative and practical difficulties in regard to fixation of minimum or fair prices for cane. His Excellency the Governor of Bihar also pointed out clearly a few practical objections with regard to the fixation of prices or minimum price of cane, in his address in opening the Conference, and said that he was diffident. He observed that a fair price for cane in one locality was not necessarily a fair price in another, and a common formula might work out most inequitably for both the contracting parties. Moreover, he added that if a factory was prohibited from buying cane below a certain price, there was no compulsion, either moral or material, for it to continue to work for a single day after the season ceased to be profitable, and it might be that the unsaleable surplus for the cultivator would be increased and be turned unprofitably into *gur*, fed to the cattle, or used as field manure. He also pointed out that by fixing a minimum price (provided that it could be operative) a cultivator might get better paid for a part of the crop, but, on the whole, might find himself worse off on account of the large waste involved by early closing down of the factory. He concluded by saying that the problem of ensuring that a minimum price fixed by Government should reach the actual grower of cane was one of the most difficult in the present situation.

15. MODES OF PAYMENT OF CANE IN VARIOUS COUNTRIES.

Methods of payment of cane vary from country to country in accordance with its peculiar conditions.* A system found suitable in one country may be utterly unsuitable in other countries, due to differences in conditions of production, etc. Cane is raised in one of the three ways:—

(1) Entirely by independent cultivators (as in India).

(2) Entirely by mills themselves.

(3) Partly by the mill and partly by cultivators.

It is hardly necessary to add that the most economic method will be found where cultivation of cane and manu-

*Vide Economic Aspects of Cane Sugar Production Maxwell, pp. 59 to 75. Also see Chapter X.

facture of sugar are controlled by the same hands as in Java, because the smooth and efficient working of a mill depends on a well-regulated supply of cane of suitable quality. But that system, as we have observed elsewhere, is not practicable in India to-day.

Methods of payment must necessarily depend on the peculiar circumstances of each country, and it would be foolish to attempt to adopt any system prevalent in another country, without considering the differences in conditions. For example, we cannot adopt the practice in Java where 50 per cent. of the sugar recovered is paid to the planter for his cane, because sugar factories in Java do not buy cane from planters, and plant, cultivate, and harvest their own cane on land temporarily hired for the purpose; nor can we adopt the method of Queensland, where the price of cane is fixed by the Cane Prices Board, and the price of sugar is controlled by the Government and fixed at a very high level; nor of the Hawaiian Islands, where also the great bulk of the cane is raised by plantation companies. In Mauritius, where there are a great number of small planters, the cane is bought at so much per ton. The rate paid varies according to the quality of the canes, the locality, and other circumstances. There is also a system in vogue in which the planter is paid on the extraction of first grade white sugar or alternatively on all sugars, per ton of cane delivered. The actual quantity of sugar paid to the planter under this system varies form 60 to 72 kilos according to the factory, its location, and its efficiency.

In this country cane is purchased by factories at economic rates from growers, either direct or through contractors, according to the natural operation of Laws of Demand and Supply. The rate of purchase of cane varies from factory to factory, from province to province, and according to the period of season. It can be said generally however that the rate has been about 0-5-6 per maund, in the United Provinces and Bihar. No minimum prices are fixed for the purchase of cane, so far by any Provincial Government.*

16. SOME METHODS OF FIXING PRICES OF CANE IN INDIA.

Various systems have been proposed in this country for fixing the minimum price that should be paid by the manufacturer for the cane to the agriculturists†, but they have not found general support. We do not intend to examine minutely all these various methods as we are convinced for various reasons, of the impracticability of any system of enforcing payment, by legislation, of a fixed price of cane, as also because they have not been found generally acceptable.

Most of these systems have, however, one common feature, *viz.*, to vary the price of cane with the extraction percentage obtained by a particular factory or a group of factories. It was felt that this would act as an incentive for improving factory efficiency as the factory which paid

---

*In March 1934, the Government of India introduced an Enabling Bill for Regulating cane-prices. See Appendix 3(c).

†*Vide* Indian Sugar Committee's Report 1920, para 305 to 313. Also Indian Tariff Board's Report, 1929 p. 100.

a higher price of cane would be assured of improved supplies of cane in its vicinity. At the same time this system is open to the serious objection that it places a premium on inefficiency by enabling an inefficient factory to purchase its cane more cheaply, although it may be of the same quality. This feature would be noticeable particularly when there is a tendency, as appears at present, of increasing the production, even though a slightly less extraction may result (which would also mean a smaller payment for cane), because the aggregate profit would be enhanced thereby.

17. SLIDING SCALE OF PRICES FOR CANE.

To meet this objection the Sugar Technologist to the Imperial Council has suggested a formula of sliding scale of cane prices based on the assumption that the price paid for a maund of cane should be equal to half the price of sugar made therefrom.

The formula suggested by him and to which we will refer in detail, is $C = \frac{S \times P}{200}$ where

C = Price of cane (in annas per maund)
S = Extraction of sugar per cent
and P = Price of sugar (in annas per maund)

The extraction percentage can be fixed for each province every year or for five years in advance, and may represent the anticipated average extraction during each year. Thus the figure of 8·7 has been fixed for percentage of extraction of sugar for 1933-34 by the United Provinces

Government in accordance with the Rules published by them in November 1933. Similarly, if the fomula is acceptable to other provinces, they can fix a percentage for their own province. The percentage may vary, from province to province, and from year to year, according to the average extraction. For instance, it might be about 9·5 in Bombay and Madras, and 8·5 in Bihar.

For the sake of illustration, we give below a table showing the price of cane of standard quality in annas per maund, corresponding to different prices of sugar and different extraction percentages, calculated according to the formula $C = \frac{S \times P}{200}$.

TABLE NO. 31.

Price of cane corresponding to different extraction percentages.

Price of sugar (Rupees.)	Price of cane (Annas per maund).				
	Extraction 8·5	Extraction 8·75	Extraction 9·0	Extraction 9·25	Extraction 9·50
8 0 0	5.44	5·60	5·75	5·92	6·08
8 8 0	5·78	5·95	6·12	6·29	6·46
9 0 0	6·12	6·30	6·48	6·66	6·84
9 8 0	6·46	6·65	6·84	7·03	7·22
10 0 0	6·80	7·00	7·20	7·40	7·60
10 8 0	7·14	7·35	7·56	7·77	7·98
11 0 0	7·48	7·70	7·92	8·14	8·36

The advantage claimed for this formula is that it has only one variable *viz.*, "P", *i.e.*, the price of sugar, and can therefore be understood even by the grower. It is also claimed that it would give some advantage to an efficient factory with a higher extraction percentage.

The price of sugar, it is suggested, should be fixed periodically by some suitable authority, who would issue a statement showing the average wholesale price for factory delivery of first grade white sugar manufactured in India, during the preceding fortnight.

The price paid by the factory for cane would then be calculated on the basis of the average price of sugar ruling in the nearest or most repesentative market for which official figures are published.

The price of cane (value of "C") for purposes of sliding scale should, it is suggested be for cane delivered at the factory gate, including transport charges, dryage, commission, supervision charges, all being taken at their actual figures, subject to a maximum, in the aggregate, of one anna per maund.

It has also been observed by the Sugar Techonologist that the difficulties, on the score of methods of evasion which are easy and numerous in regard to the enforcement of any scale of prices fixed by law, are not serious. (We are not in agreement with this view). He has also stated that the real sanction will be the knowledge by the grower that he is entitled to a certain price for his cane. Hence, he suggests that the factories should post notices at all places where cane is being purchased, by or for them, giving full particulars of the price calculated according to the prescribed sliding scale, as well as of the charges on account of cartage, Railway freight, etc. Any disputes might be refered to Cane Marketing Boards set up for groups of 5 or 6 factories.

18. INIQUITY OF BASIS FOR CALCULATING PRICE OF SUGAR.

Although we are in general agreement with the adoption of the formula $C = \frac{S \times P}{200}$ for calculating the price of cane, as it gives a fair ratio between the price of cane and the price of sugar manufactured therefrom, we feel that (i) the adoption of an assumed figure of extraction would penalise factories which have a lesser efficiency as they would have to pay a comparatively higher price of cane, and (ii) that the fixation of a fornightly price of sugar in the nearest or most representative market based on the wholesale price quotation for first grade white sugar manufactured in India would constitute an utterly wrong and fictitious basis for the calculation of the price of cane. We suggest that it *would be fair if the fixation of price of sugar would be based on average wholesale ex-factory price of sugar of first as well as second qualities.*

19. UNITED PROVINCES SUGAR INDUSTRY (PROTECTION) RULES, 1933.

Let us consider here the effect of the revised Rules published by the United Provinces Government, under the Sugar Industry (Protection) Act 1932 and brought into operation from 1st December 1933.

The United Provinces Government have stated in a press communique that these rules do not enforce the payment of any prescribed prices or fix the rates which factories should pay for the cane purchased by them. They are intended primarily to educate public opinion and provide to cane growers data which may enable them to ascertain what a fair price for cane should ordinarly be.

These Rules* regulate the affixation of notices at conspicuous places near the entrances to the sugar factories, on the 1st and 16th of every month in Nagri and Urdu scripts, containing information as to (*i*) the rates at which cane is being purchased (either by new contracts or under previous contracts) at the factory (including its several purchasing centres) together with transportation and other charges, and (*ii*) price of cane worked out according to the formula $C = \frac{S \times P}{200}$, where

C = the price in annas per maund of cane delivered at the factory gate, including charges or allowances for transport, dryage, commission and supervision;

* Any contravention of the rules shall be punishable with a fine which may extend to Rs. 50.

S = a figure fixed by the Government for each season for anticipated percentage of extraction of sugar which does not vary by more than 0·25 from the average percentage of extraction of sugar from cane for all sugar factories in the province during the three previous workin seasons;

P = the average fortnightly price in annas per maund as announced by the Director of Industries, United Provinces, Cawnpore, in the local Government Gazette based on the highest wholesale price quotation for white factory sugar made in the United Provinces on a f. o. r. Cawnpore basis minus four annas a maund.

Let us now see the iniquity of the basis of calculation of the price of sugar under the formula adopted by the United Provinces Government, leaving alone the question of the fixation of the average extraction percentage which has been fixed at 8·7 for the year 1933-34. According to these Rules* the price of sugar in annas per maund is

* When these Rules were first published on 25th October 1933, the U. P. Govt. had suggested the adoption, for the value of "P" of the average price of Java white sugar in the *Cawnpore market* (not even the Calcutta market as was recommended by the Tariff Board) as the basis. The Cawnpore price of Java sugar was notably higher than the price of white sugar made in U. P. for various reasons including the keen internal competition as a result of the growth of the factories, the competition of Khandsaris, and the low price of *gur*, the addition of freight and Customs charges in the transport of Java sugar from Calcutta to Cawnpore which amounted to Rs. 1/9 per maund, and the superior quality of Java sugar. The U P. Govt. issued revised rules after strong protests were received against the adoption of such a wrong basis, from the Indian Sugar Mills Association and other bodies.

to be calculated on the basis of the *highest wholesale* price quotation for white factory sugar made in the United Provinces on f. o. r. Cawnpore basis, less 4 annas per maund. In our opinion it is absolutely unfair to determine the value of "P" on such an incorrect basis for various cogent reasons.

(1) Why should the Cawnpore price of sugar be taken, instead of the *ex-factory prices*, for each factory, which is the most equitable and rational basis, particularly when a considerable portion of the sugar is exported to other markets, and does not go to Cawnpore at all?

(2) Why should merely the highest wholesale price for white sugar made in the United Provinces be taken for finding out an average basis of calculation of price realised by all factories? Some factory may get a very high price due to its superior quality and favourable situation. Should the large number of factories which produce sugar which is inferior to that of one or two factories, therefore be penalised by calculating the theoretical rate of purchase of cane on such a wrong and unrepresentative basis? Although these Rules do not fix the price of cane they would certainly create the impression among the growers that the price actually paid by factories is lower than is legitimately due to

them in accordance with this formula, and this creates a bad feeling.

(3) Why should only the highest wholesale price, which means of the best quality of white sugar alone be taken as the basis? what about the second quality of sugar produced in factories. The percentage of the production of No. 1 quality sugar generally varies from 55 to 66 and of No. 2 quality from 45 to 33. Is it then fair to base the calculation of the price of sugar, leaving the lower price of No. 2 quality, which is roughly Rs. 1-8-0 lower per maund than No. 1 quality, out of account?

(4) Is it fair to take the maximum price of sugar for fixing a minimum price of cane?

(5) If at all the Cawnpore price is adopted as the basis instead of ex-factory prices, why should only 4 annas which represents half the average railway freight charges per maund be allowed to be deducted in calculating the value of "P"? If the Cawnpore price of sugar is taken as the basis on the ground that the Cawnpore market furnishes a more reliable basis then a deduction ought to be allowed, equivalent to the maximum freight and handling charges per maund from any factory in the United Provinces for calculating the correct price of sugar.

Several protests were made by the Indian Sugar Mills Association as well as various other factories against the totally wrong, unreliable and fictitious basis of calculating the price of cane according to these Rules.

We therefore suggest that the price of cane should be calculated according to the average ex-factory wholesale price realised by each factory for first and second grade qualities of sugar produced therein. If there are insuperable and administrative difficulties in the calculation of reliable prices from each factory every fortnight, another equitable method would be to adapt the average ex-factory wholesale price of sugar determined from the average prices realised for first and second grade qualities of sugar of 5 or 10 representative factories selected from the different districts in the United Provinces. If either of these courses is not adapted, dissatisfation is bound to prevail amongst the manufacturers and also the cultivators due to the great divergence in the theoretical price of cane as calculated by the Government of the United Provinces, and the actual price as paid by the manufacturers. The theoretical price of cane calculated according to the United Provinces Government Rules which came into effect from 1st December 1933, gives a demonstrably fictitious and unreasonable rate for the purchase of cane, due to the utterly wrong basis of calculating the value of "P" by taking the highest wholesale price quotation for white factory sugar made in the United Provinces as a basis, and by thus ignoring (i) a large number of factories which produce neither the highest quality of sugar nor sugar which fetches the highest price and (ii) the production of second quality of sugar from which the manufacturers realise about Rs. 1-8-0 to Rs. 2-0-0 per maund lower than from first quality. We trust that the United Provinces Government will revise the basis of the calculation of the price of sugar, in the Rules made by them, with effect from the 1934-35 season, in appreciation of these convincing reasons, and adopt the suggestion made herein for calculating a reliable price of sugar in order that the Rules may serve the purpose for which they were framed.*

20. WILL U. P. GOVERNMENT CONSIDER?

We hope that in appreciation of these various practical difficulties which are of no mean order, and the opinions expressed by the Government of the various provinces, the Government of the United Provinces will drop the consideration of any legislation which will doubtless fail to secure the interests of the agriculturists, for whose benefit it is being undertaken, and we trust that the United Provinces Government will allow the natural laws of demand and supply to operate, and allow matters to adjust themselves.

---

*On the 6th March 1934, the U. P. Government issued a notification substituting in explanation of "P" under rule 3, for the words "highest wholesale price quotation..............................four annas per maund (*vide* page 167) the words "average of the wholesale ex-factory price quotations for first grade white factory sugar made in the United Provinces".

Second sugar is not yet taken into account.

21. Tariff Board's Estimate of Cost of Production of Sugar.

The Tariff Board estimated that the total cost of production of sugar during the initial stage of protection would be Rs. 8-3-3 per maund and Rs. 6-10-9 per maund during the final stage of protection. Adding a profit at the rate of 10% on a capital investment of Rs. 13·5 lakhs the Tariff Board calculated that the fair selling price ex-factory during the initial stage of protection would be Rs. 9-5-9 per maund and Rs. 7-12-5 per maund during the final stage of protection. The Tariff Board calculated Rs. 0-10-8 per maund as the price of molasses which would be realised by the factory during the initial stage of protection and Rs. 0-6-9 as the price realised per maund of molasses during the final stage of protection. We are aware that molasses now fetches no price whatsoever. The total cost of production should therefore be computed at Rs. 8-11-11 per maund during the initial stage of protection and Rs. 7-1-6 during the final stage of protection.

22. Decrease of Cost and Benefit to Consumers.

It is a matter of satisfaction, however, to find that the actual cost of production per maund of sugar has been very much lower than what was anticipated by the Tariff Board during the initial stage of protection. The average cost of production of a maund of sugar may be taken at present at between Rs. 7 and Rs. 7-4-0. The price paid for cane during the season 1932-33 may be roughly taken at about 6 annas per maund, delivered at the factory. At the same time it must be observed that the price of sugar in India, has fallen considerably, as a result of keen internal competition and the consumers have been greatly benefited. The average price of sale of sugar for No. 1 as well as No. 2 quality has been only Rs. 8-8-0 or even a little lower during the season 1932-33.

In the season 1933-34 it is not very probable that the factories will realise anything more than Rs. 7-8-0 as the average price of sugar for No. 1 and No. 2 grades. (The production of this is roughly in the ratio of 2 : 1 in most of the factories). This fall in price is due largely to internal competition. The figures submitted by the Sugar Technologist before the Simla Conference early in June 1933 in regard to the profits made by the sugar factories were very much out, inasmuch as among other things, he had assumed a far higher price for the sale of sugar than was realised by most of the sugar factories.

Even if the profits made by the sugar manufacturers during the year 1933 were high, it is easy to see that the profits for the future years will be far less due to the increasing internal competition and the nesessity of the United Provinces and Bihar having to sell sugar to distant markets like Madras, Karachi, Bengal, etc. In spite of any reduction that may be given by the Railways in the matter of freight there is no doubt that the factories will have to spend about Rs. 1-8-0 for the consignment of sugar to Madras, where they cannot realise a higher price owing to competition from abroad, and of factories in Madras Presidency.

23. BENEFIT TO CANE GROWERS.

There is no doubt that the cane growers have been benefited greatly as a result of the development of the sugar industry. They have been getting about 6 annas per maund as the price of cane instead of about $1\frac{1}{2}$ annas to 2 annas per maund which the other sugarcane growers are getting when they sell their cane to Khandsaris or *gur* manufacturers. The fact cannot be denied that the sugarcane grower has been benefited to a considerable extent inasmuch as he realises about 6 annas per maund for his cane. His total realisation per acre has also gone up considerably due to the fact that he has improved the yield per acre. The increase in the acreage under cultivation of cane and the improvements in the quality are both strong evidences to prove that he has benefited considerably during the last two years.

It is not easy to compare the price realised by sugarcane growers for their cane, in relation to their cost of production as the figures of the cost of production are not available. Even then it must be stated that sugarcane growers have been very well off, as compared with cultivators of other crops, as they have realised more than double the prices from factories than they would have done from Khandsaris or *gur* manufacturers, and further that they realised much more than their cost of production. The Director of Agriculture, Bihar Government recently observed at the Sugar Conference held at Patna on the 4th January 1934 that the average cost of production per acre of sugarcane in Government farms in Northern Bihar where 600 maunds of cane were produced per acre, was Rs. 100 and in South Bihar where 800 maunds were produced, Rs.150. The cost of production thus works out to between $2\frac{1}{2}$ annas and 3 annas. It can thus be seen clearly from the prices realised by the cane-growers that the erection of sugar factories has been a great blessing and a boon to them.

24. IS COMPULSORY CONTROL OF CANE-CULTIVATION BY FACTORIES SUITED TO INDIA?

Let us now consider the practicability of this method. The fixation of zones of operation and the licensing of factories have been suggested for the protection of the industrialists. The proposal is designed to protect the factory against competition for cane in the areas in its vicinity from distant factories, and also to prevent the overcrowding of factories where limited areas of cane are available. In this manner it is sought to offer inducements to factories to develop cane cultivation in their vicinity due to the creation of the feeling that any advantage resulting from improvement in supplies or in the quality of cane will be enjoyed by the factory itself. This suggestion is indeed an alternative to what is universally recognised as the best and the most progressive form of cane cultivation, *viz.*, cultivation by the factory of land either in its own possession or under its own control. In Java, the cultivation of the cane and the manufacture of sugar therefrom are carried on by one and the same administration. The benefits derived from such a system are too obvious to need special mention. Indeed the system of cultivation of cane as practised in Java (along with that in some of the Hawaiian Islands) may be considered as the most scientific, the most efficient and the most progressive system of intensive cultivation in the tropics. In Indian conditions, however, save in quite exceptional circumstances, as when waste or reclaimed land is available, such a method of cultivation is impracticable. The Indian Sugar Committee (1920) considered this question thoroughly and came to the conclusion that except in certain special and restricted cases, compulsory acquisition of land would be dangerous in principle and unnecessary in practice. The area of land required to supply a factory with an output of 4,000 tons of sugar a year, might amount to no less than 10,000 acres in Northern India, on a three years rotation. Apart from the legal position referred to by the Indian Sugar Committee (p. 298) the alienation of large areas of land to which our cultivating classes are attached by sentimental and family ties would, in modern conditions, considerably affect the prospects of success of any factory so established. The Indian Sugar Committee also observed that the expedient of providing dispossessed cultivators with suitable land is very difficult to apply in practice partly because suitable land at a reasonable distance from the holdings from which they have been ousted, is seldom easy to find, and partly because of their unwillingness to move to such land even when available. It is difficult to contemplate with equanimity the establishment of a sugar factory in the midst of an aggrieved and sullen peasantry, which would be an inevitable consequence, if land was acquired by Government on any large scale in order to promote the development of the industry. The Tariff Board also did not favour the introduction of compulsion for forcing the cultivators to surrender the control of his land for sugar-cane cultivation to a factory. Any such system of compulsion whether direct, or indirect, such as was suggested in Bombay, *viz.*, provision of water from the canal system being made dependent on the surrender of a portion of the land to a sugar factory, for cane cultivation, will not detract from the resentment which would necessarily follow. It is abundntly clear that in India where the liberty of cultivation is traditional any restriction or encroachment in regard to the same would be sternly resented and therefore we feel that the system, although it is suitable in Java where cane culture is intensive, will be found unsuitable in India. We are in agreement with the Tariff Board and the Sugar Committee however that no objection should be taken and indeed, all encouragement should be given for the acquisition of small areas of land in the vicinity of a factory for set-supply and for demonstration, under the conditions laid down by the Indian Sugar Committee,

But even in this case it would be preferable, if possible, to arrange for the acquisition of such land through private negotiations, instead of Government intervention. If land is acquired by factories, they would be able to distribute to the cultivators in the neighbourhood a supply of sets sufficient to plant a large proportion of the cane it requires, to demonstrate improved methods of cultivation, and also to supplement the work of the Sugar Research Institute and its sub-stations by propagating on a large scale new varieties of cane, as they are evolved, and by distributing them amongst the cultivators. In the interest of a sound development of the sugar industry in India we feel that the factories must interest themselves in suitable cultivation of canes as they are entirely dependent on the same for a profitable working of the factories.

25. FIXATION OF ZONES AND LICENSING OF FACTORIES.

Having discussed the question of the compulsory control of cane cultivation by factories and having stated our arguments against its unsuitability in Indian conditions, we will now turn to the question of fixation of zones and licensing of factories. Licensing of factories and establishment of zones are advocated mainly on the ground that some degree of assurance as regards the supplies of cane is essential before a factory can develop and improve the cultivation of cane in its vicinity. It is also argued that so long as it is possible for a new factory to be located in the neighbourhood of an old established factory, it will not spend money for spreading the cultivation of new varieties of cane, for improving the quality of sets, or for arranging the supply of manure, because the advantages which may accrue from such expenditure, *e.g.*, cheaper or better cane, or larger or more regular supplies, or early or late maturing varieties in order to extend the crushing season, will disappear on the establishment of a rival factory. Further it is also argued that the competition between factories in restricted areas will have a tendency of pushing up the price of cane to uneconomic limits, and apart from this there will be a definite loss resulting from the uneconomic distribution and the consequent increase of the haulage charges. Mr. Noel Deerr in a note submitted to the Tariff Board (printed in appendix No. V of the Tariff Board's Report) showed that it would have been possible to reduce the haulage charges of cane by an agreed system of allocated areas, in the districts of Saran and Gorakhpur in the United Provinces. We are aware that there are advantages which would accrue to the factories by the adoption of a system of licensing coupled with the allocation of definite zones. We are of the confirmed opinion, however, that it is not a subject on which Government could introduce legislation of an all-India application with any definite advantage, particularly because there are many obvious disadvantages which outweigh the advantages, enumerated above. Let us turn to a consideration of these.

26. DISADVANTAGES OF ZONING OUTWEIGH THE ADVANTAGES.

(a) The small holder of cane would no longer be a free agent to sell his produce in the open market, and being bound to one buyer he would be exploited for benefit of the latter.

(b) With the extension of factories and shortage of supplies the grower can force up the price for the cane by playing off one factory against another. Such a system by putting a temporary, fictitious and spurious value on agricultural produce would put a premium on opportunism and cannot be conceived as conferring a permanent and lasting benefit on agriculture, in any way.

(c) The compulsion on the part of the cultivator to sell his cane to a particular factory will open possibility of there being competition between raiyats where there is an excess of supply as to which of them is to be allowed to sell the cane. The disappearance of what little competition there is between factories will place the cultivator at the mercy of the factories and as a result the cultivator may suffer.

(d) From the manufacturers' point of view, zoning has a grave defect, *viz.*, that there is no guarantee that enough cane will be grown within the zone of a particular factory.

(e) Difficulties will arise in demarkating the zones in case of factories already situated within close proximity of each other; *e.g.*, there are already two factories at Pipraich, two at Ramkola, two at Savan, and two at Baheri. With the demarkation of zones it will not be possible for any factory to purchase its cane from outside its area under any circumstances. This may do considerable harm to the factory owner as also the cultivator. After a zone is fixed for a factory, if for some reason the factory does not work during some season either because the managers do not intend to work the factory, or because there might be some defect in the machinery, or due to an unforeseen circumstance, like the recent Earthquake which damaged several factories and threw several out of action, the cultivators interested in that area will suffer as they will be unable to sell their cane to other factories.

(f) It may also happen that if for some reason a factory refuses to buy cane for a cultivator within that area it will not be possible for the cultivator to sell his cane outside his area and thus the cultivator will be in a very disadvantageous position, and it is difficult to understand what would happen if the factory increases the supply of cane in its zone, as in that event the cultivator will be at the mercy of the factory owner.

(*g*) If the factory-owner increases the crushing capacity of the factory and if sufficient cane is not available in his neighbouring area due either to decreased production or to disease in the cane, the interests of the factory owner will suffer as he will not be able to purchase his cane from outside the demarkated area.

(*h*) Zoning will have hardly any meaning without the fixation of minimum price of cane, which as we have shown above, will be impracticable to enforce.

(*i*) Even cane growers, while they are desirous to have a minimum price fixed for cane, strongly object to the system of zoning*.

(*j*) Fixation of zones must be a matter for Government alone and it raises extraordinary difficulties, and is imposing on the Government a very grave liability. The sizes of the zones may in the first instance be sufficient and just sufficient to meet the demand of one factory, but as pointed out above, if a factory

---

*Col. C. G. Lees, representative of cane-growers observed in the Simla Conference that he was in agreement with Mr. H. C. Prior, Revenue Secretary of the Government of Bihar & Orissa, about zoning which was neither necessary nor practicable in Bihar.

increases its supply of cane in the factory, the raiyat will be at the mercy of the mill-owner.

(k) If the raiyat can not sell his cane to the factory, he has no other market, particularly in Bihar, because the *gur* industry does not exist to any great extent in Northern Bihar, as it does in the United Provinces at present.

(l) If owing to economic causes and more profitable cultivation of other crops, the area under cultivation of cane in a particular zone diminishes, Government will be undertaking a serious responsibility in limiting the area from which a factory can draw its cane, thereby making it impossible for the factory to work efficiently, and to pay a fair dividend.

(m) Zoning may perhaps be found desirable in some districts, *e.g.*, Gorakhpur, looking to the crowded nature of the location of sugar factories but it may not be necessary in other parts of the province or in other provinces.

(n) Restriction by zones of a few factories in certain districts or certain provinces will constitute a great hardship to the industry in such places.

(o) Some factories in Behar, purchase their cane from the cultivators in the United Provinces, and *vice versa*. If one province alone introduces legislation, it will be ineffective and create serious complications.

In appreciation of these serious difficulties, we feel, that fixation of zones is a matter which can be settled privately by the factories concerned.

As a matter of fact, several millowners have by private arrangement made such zones, and the Indian Sugar Mills Association, which has been established since June 1932, has assisted several factories in coming to an amicable settlement in regard to this question. The Association has also been instrumental in getting the convention accepted that no factory shall place its weighbridge for purchase of cane at another station where a factory is located, and thus wasteful competition has been eliminated. Even the Railways have co-operated in this matter, and they do not allow any factory to place a weighbridge on Railway land, on outside stations where factories are situated. Thus, natural zones are being established, and there is no difficulty, except perhaps at the fag end of the season, owing to the paucity of supplies, and even this is not very frequent. We suggest therefore, that Government should not interfere and allow the laws of supply and demand to operate freely.

27. LOCATION OF SUGAR FACTORIES.

Peninsular India being in the tropics is climatically more suited for cane cultivation than sub-tropical Northern

India. But the cost of production of cane is higher in the former area than the latter. At the present moment the white sugar belt of Northern India produces the cheapest cane and attracts sugar factory builders. The number of factories in the United Provinces and Bihar represents over 70% of the total factories in India. It would appear, however, that several parts of Northern Bihar and Eastern parts of the United Provinces, particularly the district of Gorakhpur, are congested with factories and competition for cane is becoming more and more keen in these areas. If there is for any reason, a shortage of cane, the factories in these areas will suffer. It is therefore desirable that prospective sugar manufacturers should make the closest enquiry in regard to the selection of site for the location of sugar factories. It would be very advantageous, if any new factories that may be established were located in areas which are not so far exploited and which are capable of producing sufficient quantities and suitable qualities of cane. Among these may be mentioned South Bihar, Rohilkhand and Meerut divisions in the United Provinces, the Deccan, Bengal and Madras where large quantities of cane would be available in selected areas. The location of sugar factories also depends on the cane acreage in each district and the duration of the working season. As we have observed before there has been a continued improvement in the qualities of cane with the result that there is an increase in the expected yield of cane per acre since the Tariff Board reported.

28. Disadvantages of licensing sugar factories.

The advocates of the system of licensing factories urge that unless undue competition is checked by preventing the establishment of more sugar factories in particular areas, the industry runs the risk of collapse. They are therefore definitely of the opinion, that licensing of factories is essential. We are not in favour of any Government intervention for licensing of sugar factories, because we believe that self-interest alone, on the part of the capitalists and spread of knowledge about the conditions of the industry will have the effect of preventing establishment of factories in areas which are geographically in a disadvantageous position and where supplies of cane are insufficient. We are aware of the bad location of a few sugar factories from this point of view, but we still believe that it is unnecessary and undesirable for the Government to intervene in this matter.

Besides, there are several disadvantages in licensing sugar factories :—

1. No system of licensing now introduced could reasonably be applied to existing factories and the position of several factories in the U. P. and parts of Bihar and Orissa where there is overcrowding would not be improved thereby.

2. It is not desirable to seek Government intervention in private enterprise as long as it is possible to avoid the same.

Factories which are or may be located in future in a disadvantageous position will have either to set right their disadvantages soon or will be eliminated because of their poor efficiency as compared with other factories. We would suggest however, that if the advice of the Directors of Agriculture or Directors of Industries in the various provinces were sought by the prospective industrialists in regard to the location of factories, that would be to their great benefit. The Directors of Agriculture as well as the Directors of Industries should be in a position to express an informed opinion on the subject for the guidance and benefit of the industrialists, who in self-interest alone would not like to establish factories at a bad geographical situation. We feel however, that it would be to the great advantage of the industry if the factories were distributed in a manner which would leave sufficient area in their vicinity for their cane supplies. We feel that it would be of great advantage to the industry if no factory would be put up within a distance shorter than 25 miles from another factory. If the daily cane crushing capacity of the factory is larger than the 400-500 tons crushing capacity, the distance should be proportionately greater. The Indian Sugar Committee also expressed the opinion that while admitting that there is much force in the arguments of those who advocate a system of licensing factories, they were not in favour of such a drastic interference with the freedom of the industry as a system of licensing would involve. The Tariff Board also observed that if the Directors of Agriculture had an opportunity of advising the promoters of the sugar factories, the danger resulting from the possibilities of new factories being established in areas where sufficient factories already exist would be much reduced. They further state that the competition between factories is the only definite safeguard which the cultivator possesses for the maintenance of cane rates and it would appear inequitable to deprive him by Statute, of this guarantee, unless effective statutory provision can be made for the rates which should be paid for cane. The Tariff Board also pointed out that such provision would be extremely difficult to enforce. We are in agreement with the Tariff Board that the question of the distribution of the cane, areas of supply, and the fixation of zones, is a matter to be determined by the factories concerned and we believe that the problem is not insoluble if an effective Association of Manufacturers comes into being as a result of the introduction of protection. The Indian sugar Mills Association, a body which now represents about 72 mills, should interest itself in this question.

29. CANE-CULTIVATION INCREASES NEAR FACTORIES.

While discussing the question of location of factories, it is of interest to note that cane cultivation has hitherto tended to increase rapidly in the areas adjoining a factory. This is shown by the increase in the quantity of cart cane received by the several factories in the United Provinces and Bihar during the years 1929-30, 30-31 and 31-32. The increase in the quantity of cart cane clearly denotes an increase in the acreage under cane in the areas adjoining a factory. Prospective manufacturers of sugar need not therefore feel apprehensive on this score if they establish factories even in areas where a sufficient supply is not available.

30. SUITABLE SITE SELECTION ESSENTIAL.

It is of the utmost necessity, however, that they should exercise due caution in selecting suitable sites for the factories in order to prevent over-crowding of factories, which in turn may decrease their efficiency, in other words, their profits, and in consequence be a burden on the country.

31. LICENSING OF CONTRACTORS

Being informed that the price paid by the factory owners for the purchase of cane did not reach the cultivators, the United Provinces Government were considering methods which would ensure that the price paid by the factory owners actually reached the cultivators.

While the best course for a factory is to purchase cane direct from the growers, a fairly large percentage of the factories purchase their cane through contractors in order to ensure regular and constant supplies of cane. Some factories which entered into contracts with individual cultivators for supply of cane found difficulty in regular supplies of cane, because the cultivators did not understand the responsibility in the matter of regular supply. Besides the factories do not consider it proper or worth their while to take action against individual cultivators, who have refaulted in supplies. To avoid all these trouble several factories employ contractors whose main business is to regulate supplies of cane. The United Provinces Government suggested that there ought to be a system of licensing contractors which might provide that the licensee should give the actual grower from whom he gets the cane, at least 90% of the cane he receives from the factory. The license of a contractor who fails to comply with this condition, it is suggested, would not be renewed. It is also suggested that the contractor would be responsible for giving out pass books to all growers in which the amount of cane supplied by them and the money paid to them would be duly entered.

The disadvantages of a system of licensing of contractors are numerous. The system of licensing contractors has been suggested in order to ensure that the cane growers receive the money actually paid by the factories for the cane purchased by them through the contractors. It is anticipated that if they are licensed they will try to be honest and pass off the money to the actual cultivators. In the year 1932-33 most of the cane purchased by the factories was through contractors. Finding, however, that the contractors pocketted a considerable portion of the money paid by them for the cane and that the cultivator received a very small share of their actual payment, a large number of factories started direct contact with the growers and have been purchasing cane from them direct during the season 1933-34.

Purzis are being distributed by the manufacturers amongst cultivators who bring the cane to the factory on the allotted days and they receive payment for the same direct. All the Indian Sugar Factory Owners assembled at a Meeting at Gorakhpur in 1933 passed a resolution recommending to the factories that they should purchase cane as far as possible direct from the cultivators. If at a time when the factory owners are thinking seriously of establishing direct contact with the cultivators, any legislation is passed for licensing contractors it will seriously disturb the relations between the sugar manufacturers and the cane growers. The result of any such legislation would be that the mills would be placed at the mercy of the licensed contractors. It will be a kind of monopoly enjoyed by the contractors and they will try to pay as little as possible to the cane grower and they will have the sugar manufacturer absolutely under their thumb. If contractors are licensed, manufacturers will have to employ only those people who will be licensed by the Government for the purpose of supply of cane and this will constitute a kind of interference on the part of the Government as to the selection of the people through whom purchases have to be made by the factories and whose services must necessarily be utilised for the purpose of working the factories. This system will be neither good for the cultivator nor for the factories. It would be better if the agriculturists have co-operative societies established, as then they will be able to deal better with the factory owners than through these licensed contractors.

Mr. H. C. Prior, Revenue Secretary of the Government of Bihar and Orissa also pointed out at the Simla

Conference of 1933 that he felt that the nature of proceeding for the cancellation of a licence of a contractor when he misbehaves, would be very complicated and stated that it seemed to him that it was likely to be somewhat in the nature of Section 100 proceeding with a large number of witnesses appearing on either side. There is no guarantee about the integrity and probity of the contractors and the system of licensing will only increase the abuses. In fact, it is the most poisonous suggestion and may do considerable harm to factories and to agriculturists. A time may also come when contractors may be able to dictate their terms from the factories and may threaten not to supply cane regularly or create similar other difficulties. It may also be possible that these license certificates of contractors may be sold at a premium and it will be extremely difficult for a factory owner to prove *malafides* of any contractor to the satisfaction of the Government in order to lead to the cancellation of his license. We would therefore suggest that the system of employment of contractors should be done away with by factories as far as possible. In any case the contractors should not be licensed as it will give them an air of authority from the Government, and will postpone the day when direct contact may be established between the factories and the cultivators to their mutual benefit.

The difficulties in making proper selection of contractors and in ensuring that they will give the price to the cultivators which is their due are also numerous and insurmountable. Besides, it would be undue interference with the manufacturers in compelling them to purchase their cane from a few contractors who may happen to get a license from the Government. Their choice of purchase of cane from whomsoever they may like should remain unfettered as at present. From the point of view of the cultivators also, this system will be found unsuitable as a contractor may not purchase his cane from any cultivator and in that event he will have no way left for selling his cane to any mill direct.

32. Establishment of Co-operative Societies of Agriculturists Helpful.

In order to give a feeling of security to the factory-owner that the contract for the supply of cane would be kept faithfully it would be better if small co-operative societies consisting of a group of agriculturists or *Punches* would be formed. That would assist the factory owners in dealing with them and would also remove the danger in their mind about the non-fulfilment of the contract and of absence of regular supply of cane.*

33. No Legislative Interference Necessary.

Having discussed these questions, we have felt that the advantages of protection are being fairly distributed and that it is unnecessary to introduce any legislation at the present moment in order to protect the interests either of the growers, or the sugar manufacturers, or the consumers.

---

*Such organisations, if brought into existence by Government, as proposed in the Sugar-cane Bill, 1934, will not ensure a payment of fair price.

CHAPTER VII.

Research in Sugar Problems.

(AGRICULTURAL, CHEMICAL, ENGINEERING.)

1. RESEARCH AND ITS IMPORTANCE.

The importance of a comprehensive and carefully conceived programme of research and development in connection with the sugar-cane industry cannot be too much emphasised, and may indeed be considered as an essential condition to the success of the scheme of protection. The Tariff Board considered this question in detail and recommended that a grant of not less than ten lakhs of rupees from Central Revenues should be made to meet the purposes which they indicated in chapter 7 of their Report. They also recommended that the Imperial Council of Agricultural Research should act in consultation with the Government and the Legislature in constituting the machinery required for carrying out such measures. It is recognized universally that no real progress is possible for the sugar industry without adequate expenditure on research and development, and a description of the functions of the Research Institutes in Java and Hawaii indicates that much remains to be accomplished in this direction in India. The Tariff Board observed that fourteen lakhs of rupees were spent annually on the great sugar research station at Pasoeroean in Java, where the total area under cultivation (in 1929) was only 4,50,000 (acreage reduced to about 86,000 acres in 1934).

2. SCOPE OF WORK IN JAVA AND HAWAII RESEARCH INSTITUTE.

The scope of the work carried on both in Java and Hawaii is described by Mr. Noel Deerr as follows:—

(*a*) Agricultural;

(*b*) Plant Pathology;

(*c*) Entomology;

(*d*) Manufacture;

(*e*) Statistical.

Under Agriculture is included—

(*a*) Soil surveys;

(*b*) Determination of the appropriate fertilisers;

(*c*) Experimental work with fertilisers and different methods of cultivation;

(*d*) Irrigation problems and the determination of the optimum quantity of water;

(*e*) Cane breeding and the examination of newly obtained sexual varieties.

Under plant pathology is included—

(*a*) The study and means of control of the various fungoid diseases attacking cane.

(*b*) Soil studies connected with such diseases.

(*c*) The quarantining of areas known to be infected with diseases.

(*d*) The distribution of immune varieties.

Under entomology is included—

(*a*) The study of the life histories of insects inimical to the cane.

(*b*) The control of insects mainly by the introduction of their parasites.

(*c*) Quarantine and examination of plants imported from abroad.

Under manufacture is included—

(*a*) Examination of new manufacturing methods, one particular factory being selected for such examination at the expense of all.

(*b*) Advice on the design and installations of new plant.

(*c*) Consulting work with reference to problems as they arise.

(*d*) Periodic visits to factories to inspect results.

(*e*) Distribution of results obtained in each factory for the mutual benefit of all.

3. Agricultural Research.

Generally speaking, the aim of agricultural research, which should be carried on in India, should be to ensure that the right variety of cane is grown on the right soil, to evolve varieties which will combine hardiness with a heavy yield and which will mature early, and late, in the season, and further to secure control or elimination of disease by proper methods of cultivation. In this connection, it will be of great interest to refer to chapter 2 of the Report of the Indian Sugar Committee, dealing with the organization and methods which brought conspicuous success to the sugar industry in Java. It has been pointed out that the Java Sugar Industry was brought to a commanding position due to its admirable organization for mutual assistance in all directions, above all in regard to research, generous expenditure on which is recognized to be a most profitable investment, and by adoption of methods of cultivation and manufacture carried out under highly trained and well-paid supervision on which it would be difficult to improve. The Imperial Council of Agricultural Research has been carrying on research for the last several years and has done much useful work, particularly in testing new seedling canes, and the methods of cultivation and manuring required by them throughout the main Indian Sugarcane belt. For many years the Imperial sugarcane breeding station at Coimbatore has been improving the quality of cane and it was that spadework which enabled the development of the sugar industry to proceed. In connection with the services rendered to the country by the Coimbatore research station by producing improved canes suitable for various provinces, capable of yielding a crop of 600 to 800, and even 1,000 maunds per acre, unlike the *Deshi* variety of 300 tons, we must refer to the very creditable wok of Rao Bahadur T. S. Venkataraman. The Imperial Institute of Agricultural Research at Pusa has also done much creditable work. The investigations at Pusa in regard to mosaic disease of sugarcane promise useful results.

4. TECHNOLOGICAL RESEARCH.

Another thing which the Imperial Council of Agricultural Research work did was to consider methods of developing the Harcourt Butler Technological Institute in Cawnpore into an All India Institute. In order to provide an experimental plan the Imperial Council gave a lump sum grant of Rs. 1,25,000 and a recurring grant of Rs. 20,000 for the running of it, or in other words Rs. 2,50,000 on the whole. The Council also appointed the Sugar Technologist, primarily to give technical advice to the existing sugar factories and to advise prospective factory-owners in buying machinery, etc.

5. RESEARCH GRANT TO PROVINCIAL GOVERNMENTS.

The Imperial Council has also given grants to various Provincial Governments from time to time for carrying on research work in regard to sugarcane. Some of these provincial stations have done creditable work and have evolved efficient canes.

6. CHAIN OF RESEARCH INSTITUTES IN INDIA FOR AGRICULTURAL RESEARCH.

Another welcome step which the Imperial Council took was to establish a chain of research institutions throughout the main sugar belt of India, which extends all along the Central and Northern parts of India. These stations are all meant for agricultural research on sugar cane and include the stations at Karnal, Shahjahanpur, Mushari, Padegaon and Anakapalle. The latest addition is the Testing Station for the North Western Frontier Province at Peshawar, which produces some of the finest canes in Northern India. Thus there is a complete chain of research stations from the North Western Frontier down to the Assam Frontier.

7. Problems of Research in Bombay and Madras.

The problems of sugar cane in Bombay and Madras are rather different. Practically all the improved varieties of sugarcane which are grown in United Provinces and Bihar are from Coimbatore. The indigenous cane of Southern India is different from these. It is a much thicker cane. As we have observed before, the main problem of Western and Southern India is the high cost of producing canes. While it is possible to produce cane at a cost of 2, 3, or 4 annas per maund, in the North, the cost in Madras and Bombay is about 8 to 10 annas per maund. The main problem for research work there is, therefore, to reduce this cost. For this purpose a Research Station has also been established by the Imperial Council on the Bombay-Deccan Canal at a cost of Rs. 4 lakhs. The object of this Research Station is to tackle all the problems of sugar cane research, including plant physiology, water requirements, and suitable varieties and to study the commercial side and to find out where the excess of cost comes in and in what way it can be reduced. In Madras, experiments on similar lines are being carried out at Anakapalle. The problem there is whether a type of cane which requires very much less expenditure could not be produced. The problem of the new hybrid cane is also being tackled. This is supposed to be a cross between sugarcane and sorghum. The results of this experiment are being anxiously awaited.

8. Imperial Sugar Industry Research Institute (Technological).

Another proposal which has been approved by the Sugar Committee of the Imperial Council of Agricultural Research, recently is about the Imperial Sugar Research Institute which is proposed to be started by the Imperial Council of Agricultural Research. It is intended primarily for research work on the technological side. This scheme originated in 1920, when the Sugar Committee made its recommendations. A scheme has now been devised and will be placed shortly before the Governing body of the Imperial Council of Agricultural Research and will be dealt with by the various departments of the Government of India immediately thereafter. The proposed Research Institute will tackle practical problems as also fundamental research. It is not yet certain as to where the proposed Central Sugar Research Institute will be located, but it is likely that it will be located at Cawnpore and that the buildings and equipment of the H. B. Technological Institute at Cawnpore will be utilized as a nucleus for the Institute. If this is done, it will save much time.

The scheme for an Imperial Sugar Industry Research Institute was placed before the Meeting of the Sugar Committee of the Imperial Council, which met at Coimbatore in November 1933 and has been adopted by them. The capital cost of establishing the Research Institute (including the sugar school) and its sub-stations is estimated at about Rs. 35 lakhs.

It has also been suggested that the Imperial Sugarcane Breeding Station, Coimbatore, should be made a part of this Research Institute.

The following tentative programme of work has been suggested for the institute:—

(*i*) Research on Indian Sugar factory problems and in Sugar Technology in general, with specific reference to Indian conditions;

(*ii*) Research on the utilization of by-products of the sugar industry;

(*iii*) The provision of scientific assistance to all factories which need it to supplement the work of their factory chemists and engineers;

(*iv*) The carrying out of extended tests on new varieties of cane, under factory conditions, when such tests are needed by Agricultural Departments;

(*v*) Collection and tabulation of scientific control returns from factories. Critical examination of these returns;

(*vi*) Issue of technical reports to factories on results of the collection of control data;

(*vii*) When desired advice to individual factories;—

(*a*) on faults disclosed by their returns—but without disclosing the results of other individual factories,

(*b*) on difficulties met with or extensions and improvements.

(*viii*) A constant critical study of the working of Indian sugar factories and a comparison of individual results with:—

(*a*) the best established Indian practice,

(*b*) the results obtained in other countries.

(*ix*) Demonstration of new or improved plant or processes;

(*x*) Training of students in all branches of Sugar Technology;

(*xi*) Short refresher courses for men already engaged in the industry.

9. PREVENTION OF DISEASES AND INSECT PESTS IN CANE.

One of the most important questions to be tackled by the Imperial Council is of prevention of insect pests and eradication of diseases in regard to cane. There is no cure for insects as a whole. Insect damage is continuous and varied and when one insect is controlled, others will be still found to be on the increase. Certain insects which depend on the cane for their breeding do not seriously injure the cane, but cause much inconvenience and loss to the industrial concerns. It was recently pointed out that in a large cane area so many of these insects were produced, that they sat on the insulators on high tension electric wires and caused frequent short circuiting which necessitated the Electric Company introducing specially devised insulators to get over that trouble. It has also been estimated that the expenditure of damage done by insects to standing cane is about 40% in a bad year. This insect menace is the greatest obstacle which the development of the Indian Sugar Industry is faced with at the present moment. It has also been pointed out that the chief damage to the cane crop is done by the borers, top, stem and root, leaf sucking insects and beetles.

Termites or white ants represent a type of insects which can be tackled under ordinary conditions. They do a great deal of damage to *newly planted cane.* There are three known methods of dealing with them, (1) deep and frequent cultivation of land, (2) use of crude oil emulsion in the irrigation water, (3) steeping of cane-sets. The first of these has been adopted successfully in Pusa and there is far less white ant attack than formerly and the rotation in which cane follows a thoroughly rotted green manure crop has been helpful in decreasing the incidence of the attack, but it is found that any attempt to grow cane on light land out of the ordinary rotation is certain to produce the attack. These and other similar problems can be dealt with efficiently, if a suitable scheme of research work is initiated. The Imperial Council should give this matter their careful attention.

10. NEED OF RESEARCH ON CANE PESTS.

The necessity of research work on sugarcane pests cannot be too much emphasised. Mr. Wynne Sayer, Offg. Imperial Agriculturist, Pusa is of the opinion that such work can be most efficiently carried out only at a place which is set apart for insect pest research. The Punjab Government also submitted a scheme for research work of pests of sugarcane in the Punjab. Discussing the amount of damage done, they observe that the insect damage to the sugarcane crops begins with the sowing of sets when white ants play a havoc. When the crop has emerged from the soil the stem borers start their action. *Pyrilla* soon follows and is later on helped by mites and white flies. A specific instance of this may be found in what happened at Sonepat in the neighbourhood of the Punjab Sugar Corporation's factory.

In April *Pyrilla* attacked the cane, simultaneously the root and stem borers appeared. In July, the top borer almost completed the work of destruction and the crop had another 6 to 9 months to go.

A sugarcane crop entirely free from insect is, of course, an impossibility, but it is possible to make sugarcane growing profitable by proper control of insect pests. It is not very easy to estimate in money value, the damage done to sugarcane by insects and other animals. In some cases as much as 75% of the crop may be completely lost; 20% is not an uncommon occurrence.

11. Need of cheapening production.

If India is going to retain and improve upon the present position in regard to manufacture of cane it is absolutely essential that her efficiency in sugar production should be increased considerably. It is not in the interest of the consumer that an important foodstuff be produced permanently under protection or by a huge subsidy for all times to come. It is important therefore that all sources of loss should be eliminated, and maximum efficiency introduced. As we have observed before our outturn per acre compares very unfavourably with that of other sugar producing countries and undoubtedly insect pests of sugar cane take a heavy toll.

The absence of irrigational facilities and tube wells, and of sufficient and scientific manure, of adequate ploughing, of rotation of crop on scientific principles, of suitable seeds, etc., are other important factors affecting adversely our quality of cane, and the outturn per acre. The failure of sugarcane in future, will not be a personal loss of a few individual cultivators only, but will affect most seriously a much larger number of cultivators and the factories and through the factories it is bound to have a much wider economic effect. The problem, therefore, of eradicating and controlling sugarcane insects, like borers, which do far greater damage than other pests put together, needs immediate attention. We trust that the Imperial Council will establish a suitable institute for dealing with sugarcane pests.

12. Chemical and Technological Research.

Research work should not merely be confined to the agricultural side; Chemical and Biochemical, Botanical and Physiological and technological researches are also essentially necessary in order to reduce the cost of production of sugar. The Madras Government recently approached the Imperial Council for a grant for a scheme of research on the chemistry of sugar cane. The scheme submitted by the Madras Government emphasises that while development of the sugar industry in India in the direction of breeding and agriculture of sugarcane and manufacture of sugar undoubtedly should receive first consideration, it is necessary to make a systematic study of the chemistry of the sugarcane in the country as soon as the progress in the first two directions has reached a certain stage. Otherwise the development will be lopsided. It will be evident from the history of sugar development in other countries that unless present efforts are supplemented with chemical studies, Indian sugar industry will not attain its rightful position. Technological Research for improving factory-efficiency, quality of sugar, etc., is equally essential. We trust that these aspects will also not escape the attention of the Imperial Council.

Having discussed the necessity of research in various directions, we feel that prompt steps should be taken for effecting improvements in agriculture, and a reduction in the cost of production with a view to enable the industry in India to keep pace with other countries. Then alone will it be possible for the industry to maintain its position. Without scientific research and experiments the industry will not be able to stand on its own legs. We must therefore emulate the excellent examples of Java and Hawaii and try to attain at least as great efficiency as is found in those countries.

13. EMULATION OF JAVA AND HAWAIIAN EFFICIENCY NECESSARY.

The attention of those who are responsible for the development of the industry should, we strongly feel, be drawn towards carrying on vigorous research in the direction of improvement of agriculture and manufacturing methods with a view to decrease the cost of production. The Government are doubtless aware that each acre of land yields 50 tons of cane with 12% sugar in Java instead of about 13 tons cane only with 9% sugar in India. This only means that so far our methods of cultivation are only a *quarter as efficient as that of Java.* If the cultivator can raise the yield from the average 13 tons to even 30 tons it will yield to him more than double the income from the same land. The efficiency of the mills in extraction percentages of sugar cane in Java is 12 while in India it is only 9. We are therefore losing about 3% in extraction and about 37 tons per acre in the yield of the crop. These are the lines in which future developments should take place in order to put the industry on a sound basis. Whereas from every acre of sugarcane in Java they get 6 tons of sugar, we in India get only 1·5 tons, even taking the higher figure of 16 tons of cane per acre (due to improved varieties), instead of the official figure of 13 tons and yield of 9% of sugar extraction. The Government should provide more irrigational facilities for agricultural improvements, by sinking tube-wells and making large quantities of water available to the fields, by supplying better seeds, through research stations, by spreading knowledge about methods of manuring, and by carrying on vigorous and continuous research in the direction of improvement of canes suitable for different climatic conditions in the vaious provinces.

If with proper efforts, it is possible for us to increase our production of cane per acre as in Java the position will be as follows:

If 40 tons of cane be obtained per acre, leaving alone 50 as in Java, where cultivation is very intensive, and even 2½ annas per maund be paid for cane the grower will still receive about Rs. 170 per acre, which will be tant-amount to about 6 annas per maund of its present yield of 16 tons per acre. He will thus be benefited. Similarly if the percentage extraction of sugar can be increased even to 10% (not to speak of 12% as in Java) then with cane at 2 or $2\frac{1}{2}$ annas per maund the factories would be able to sell sugar at a rate of about Rs. 4-8-0 per maund. If this hope materializes, the consumers will be greatly benefited, consumption will be stimulated, and the possibility of exports to foreign countries will also be thrown open.

In this connection we invite the attention of those responsible for the development of the industry in India to the remarkable increase in the yield of sugar in Hawaiian Islands. The most noteworthy and remarkable feature in connection with the sugar industry in the Hawaiian Islands has been the great improvement effected in the yield of cane and sugar per acre through the application of irrigation and fertilization, selection of improved varieties of cane and modern scientific methods of cultivation and the constant study of methods of overcoming insect pests and diseases. Having only a limited area available for cane growing, the Hawaiian sugar producers whose extraordinary task of efficient and systematic thoroughness are remarkable, turned their attention to intensive methods of cultivation and are spending huge amounts of money on research and experiments. As a result of their efforts the average yield of sugar per acre has risen to between *7 & 8 tons* and has reached the remarkable *figure of 16 tons on particular fields.* The yield of sugar per acre in Hawaii far exceeds that of Java even.

The Hawaiian Islands rank highest among the cane countries in respect of extraction results by the milling process. It ought to be our endeavour to follow the illustrious examples of Hawaii and Java and to beat in course of time, the record of these two countries which hold to-day the highest rank in efficiency amongst the cane-sugar producing countries of the world.

14. Research in utilisation of by-products and other uses of sugar.

One of the biggest problems to be tackled immediately will be that of utilisation of by-products, like molasses and bagasse. We have discussed this in another chapter. It would also be useful if research could be carried on for devising other uses of sugar.

15. Cost of production of cane.

In an earlier chapter we have observed that no figures are available of the cost of production of cane, although such information is very necessary and useful. It is gratifying to find that an arrangement has been made by the Imperial Council of Agricultural Research with the Indian Central Cotton Committee under which an economic enquiry into the cost of production of sugarcane has been undertaken. It will extend to ascertaining the cost of production of sugarcane and cotton and their rotation crops. We hope the information will be available by 1936.

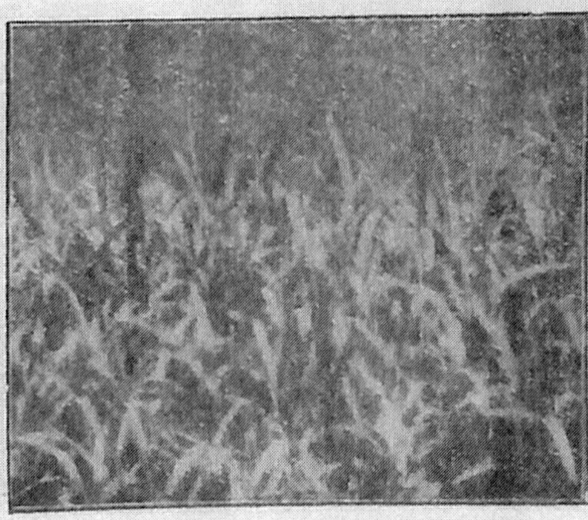

CANE IN THE FIELD.

ON THE WAY TO THE FACTORY.

A MODEL SUGAR FACTORY.

16. Co-operation of Industry and Agriculture for Research Work.

It is essential, for bringing success, to any scheme of research, that active co-operation of manufacturers and cane-growers must be availed of. Unless this is forthcoming, there is a great probability that research will not be directed along most useful lines, and there will be a tendency towards too much fundamental research, divested from practical utility and necessity. While fundamental research work is essential, the endeavour ought to be to carry on continuous research—agricultural, chemical, engineering—bearing in mind its practical aspects. Non-officials should be allowed to have large control over the general policy of any institute for Research. The co-operation of non-officials will be of great advantage. An organisation of an Indian Sugar Board on the Java Model is essential to progress.*

So far, the Government have already spent about Rs. 10 lakhs on sugar-cane Research, and propose to spend about Rs. 10 lakhs more up to 1937-38, through the Imperial Council. This is not enough, and more money should be annually earmarked for further schemes of research and development, as was recommended by the Tariff Board.

In regard to funds, we suggest that a liberal grant of about 25% should be made by the Government, out of the proceeds of the excise duty proposed to be

* *Vide* Indian Sugar Committee Report pages 354 to 374.

imposed on Indian sugar from 1st April 1934. The revenue expected from the excise is about Rs. 147 lakhs in 1934-35. Thus about Rs. 37 lakhs can be easily made available for research work annually.

17. Distribution of Research problems at different Scientific Institutions.

It is also not necessary that all research work should be carried on at one place. Problems for Research can be distributed among scientific institutions, where suitable facilities exist, and grants can be made for this purpose. For instance, some problems can be investigated at the Indian Institute of science, Bangalore, where excellent facilities exist, particularly on the Chemical side. Sir C. V. Raman, the illustrious Director of the Institute, has also expressed his willingness to undertake research work on problems of interest to the industry. A course for training chemists for Sugar industry has also been started there from 1933. Other problems can be distributed to other Universities, like the Benares Hindu University, where a course of Sugar Technology has been started, and where facilities exist for research work in agricultural chemistry.

CHAPTER VIII

Sugar Industry and the Problems of Transport.

1. WELFARE OF INDUSTRIES LINKED WITH TRANSPORT FACILITIES.

It is needless to say that the welfare of the sugar industry like all other large scale manufacturing industries is closely bound up with the question of transport, both of raw materials as well as of finished products. In the sugar industry in particular the importance of cheap and quick transport is very great.

In the first place, sugarcane has got to be supplied from the field to the factory with utmost expedition and at the lowest possible cost in order that the cane may not get deteriorated in quality, maximum sucrose may be had and it may be possible to get supplies of cane from a fairly wide zone at a moderate over-all cost. In the second place the finished products, *viz.*, sugar and molasses, must have such cost of transport as would enable the factories to supply their products to consuming centres situated at various distances at reasonable and competitive prices.

2. NATIONAL ADVANTAGE IN DEVELOPMENT OF SUGAR INDUSTRY.

It is hardly necessary to repeat that the prosperity of the nation is largely dependent on such industrial developments as sugar which provide employment, at outlying rural areas, not only to a large number of landless labourers but also to a very important section of the agricultural population. Thus, in a country like India, the importance of the sugar industry can scarcely be overestimated. And in view of this importance the railways and other carriers of the country have a special duty to perform with reference to this industry, so that the policy of their rates and transportation may be in accordance with the general policy of national economic development.

3. COMPARATIVELY HIGH FREIGHTS.

So far as the importance of railway and other transport charges with reference to sugar is concerned, it will suffice to point out that whereas the present average rates for carrying sugar from manufacturing centres in India to important consuming areas like Karachi, Bombay and Madras (distance about 800 to 1,000 miles) amount to Rs. 1-8-0 per maund, or more than 15% of the cost of production, the ocean freight charged on the transport from Java to Karachi, Bombay and Madras is about 4 to 5 annas per maund only. It should be noted that the Indian sugar industry is a new one and the produce obtained in Indian factories so far is not of the same high quality as that of imported sugar. The market price for Indian sugar, therefore, must be about 6 to 8 annas per maund below those of the imported stuff. It will be clear from this, how with the expansion of sugar industry the necessity for revised rates and methods of transportation has become all the more acute.

4. PRINCIPAL PROBLEMS OF TRANSPORT.

The main problems of transport in the sugar industry may be divided under four heads, *viz.*, (*i*) of sugarcane, (*ii*) of *gur*, (*iii*) of molasses and other by-products, and (*iv*) of sugar. The nature of the problems with reference to each of these is different and the main points to be kept in view are: (*a*) rates of freight, (*b*) expedition in transit, and (*c*) suitable waggon supply. In any study of transport problems with reference to the sugar industry, one has to keep in view all these different aspects.

5. TRANSPORT OF SUGARCANE.

The most important factor with respect to cane is quickness in transport and handling at the terminals. As has been noted elsewhere, sugarcane should preferably reach factories from the field within at most 24 hours of its cutting. Usually our railways do not have such suitable train arrangements as can enable this quick delivery and whenever this question is pressed the Railways argue that, with the short haul at cheap rates, it does not pay them to arrange special trains for this traffic. Unless some solution of this difficulty is found it is obvious that the area for the supply of canes to factories in India will remain rather limited, and it will be difficult for our factories to effect very large-scale production. A possible solution may perhaps be found in the development of road motor services but it is doubtful how far it will be a paying proposition for motor carriers to provide sufficient number of vehicles for seasonal heavy traffic only. In consideration of the importance of the industry, therefore, it is urged that the railways should make every endeavour to carry canes from as large an area as possible, within the shortest time.

In the matter of rates for the carriage of sugarcane also, the exercise of considerable judgment is necessary with a view to see that the cultivation of sugarcane is not cramped into areas just adjacent to factories, and that the minimum charge is levied, making it impossible for road carriers to compete. With lower rates cane can be brought from distances. This will benefit the Railways, and also the raiyats in areas distant from the factories.

6. TRANSPORT OF GUR.

We have observed before that some factories also refine sugar from *gur*, when the cane-crushing season is over. The railways should grant suitable facilities for the carriage of *gur*. Unless it is done cheaply, it is likely that road and water-carriers will compete very effectively in this matter.

7. TRANSPORT OF MOLASSES.

The problem of disposal of molasses has been causing great anxiety to Indian sugar factories. The existing rates of freight as compared with the present prices of molasses are too excessive and are definitely beyond the capacity of the traffic to bear. The railways should carefully watch the situation and whenever opportunity is presented provide such rates and such other facilities, *e.g.*, suitable tank-wagon supply, as would enable movements of this important by-product to the mutual advantage of the factories as well as of the railways.

8. TRANSPORT OF SUGAR.

For sugar traffic, quickness in transit is not so essential as that for cane, whereas the type of waggon stock supply and the rates of freight are of very great importance. The commodity is obviously of such a nature as cannot be left exposed without danger of loss through climatic as well as human agency. The traffic is usually carried in bulk in waggon loads at owner's risk. It is highly desirable, therefore, that suitably protected waggons should be supplied for the transport of sugar in properly locked vehicles.

9. BASIS OF FIXATION OF RATES OF FREIGHT ON SUGAR.

The most important point with regard to transport of sugar, however, is the rate of freight. Hitherto rates for sugar were calculated with a view to provide distribution from the port-towns to various inland consuming centres. The position today, however, is changed and a revision of the rates policy is called for with a view to help a reversal in the movement, *viz.*, from upcountry manufacturing centres to ports and inland consuming areas.

In introducing this revised policy the considerations that have to be kept in view are mainly the following *viz.* :—

(*a*) The price of Indian sugar at the port-towns must remain at 6 to 8 annas below that of imported sugar.

(*b*) As far as practicable no undue preference should be given to any particular area of production over others in India in the matter of access to a particular market.

(*c*) The routing of traffic should be by the most natural course and there should be no attempt by forwarding railways to "block" rates with a view to have a long lead.

(*d*) Rates for internal centres should be governed by the combined rate to the nearest port and differential rule with regard to distance should be applied automatically for places within the sphere of each port.

(*e*) There should be no blocking of rates by the railways with a view to prevent the traffic from going on to inland and coastal steamer services and maximum facility should be provided to the trade to take advantage of any means of transport that provides the best and cheapest conveyance.

(*f*) The longer the distance the lower must be the scale of charges and the advantages of the telescopic rates should be extended over combined through distances on several railways.

(*g*) Possible competitive routes *via* rail-cum-river or rail-cum-river-cum-sea routes should be kept in view, and wherever trade demands it, through booking facilities should be arranged for.

10. CHANGED RAILWAY OUTLOOK NEEDED.

Credit must be given to some of the Indian Railways, particularly the East Indian* for having already realised

---

*The E. I. Ry. has offered some concession in regard to freights and the question of further reduction is under examination. For instance, from January 1934 the following rates of freight are operative from various stations to the following ports.

	Per Maund of sugar
Via Asansol } to Madras & via	0 12 0
„ Gomoh }	
„ Mokameh Ghat to Madras	0 15 0
„ Naini, Cawnpore, Agra, Delhi } to Bombay	0 14 0
„ Delhi to Karachi	0 14 0

An idea of the general reduction on long distance freights on sugar O. R. effected by the E. I. Railway from 1st January 1934 can also be had from the following C/J rate of schedule.

The basis is as follows :—	Pies per Md.	The resulting reduction is as follows :— Miles	2nd class existing rates.	Revised Rates as per C/J scale.	Reduction.
First 150 miles ...	·38				
150 to 250 „ ...	·333				
250 „ 500 „ ...	.20	250	0 8 9	0 7 6	0 1 3
500 „ 700 „ ...	.18	500	1 1 6	0 11 8	0 5 10
over 700 ...	·10	950	2 1 3	0 15 11	1 1 4

the necessity for a change in their policy towards sugar traffic. This change in the outlook appears to have been forced to some extent by the competition of inland steamers and coastal vessels. The railways have urged upon one another the adoption of a "co-operative railway rates policy" under which they propose to carry long distance traffic, particularly to port towns, at specially reduced rates. During the current sugar season (1933-34) the E. I., B. B. & C. I., and the G. I. P. Railways, in conjunction with the E. B., B. N., M. & S. M., N. S., & N. W. Railways have offered certain reductions in the rates for sugar to important long distance centres. The principles generally kept in view in these reductions may be stated as follows :—

(*i*) The opening up of new markets for Indian Sugar at distant places, both with a view to prevent over-production as well as with the idea of promoting railway traffic.

(*ii*) Putting a healthy check to the spread of the sugar industry under the protection of high railway freights, and to prevent the tendency towards over-production by a continuous decentralisation of manufacturing efforts in different parts of India. According to the East Indian Railway this sort of development would be undesirable, because, (*a*) it would encourage the development of the industry on purely local lines leading to the establishment of more factories than what the requirements of the country as a whole warranted; (*b*) it would destroy long lead traffic and leave railways dependent on multifarious short lead traffic movements which are relatively expensive to handle; (*c*) it would expose the railways to increased dangers of road competition.

(*iii*) Co-ordination of the rates policy of different railways with a view to prevent special favour, or discriminatory treatment with regard to a particular manufacturing area, or particular groups of factories. An example in point was the system of reduced rates for sugar from R. & K. Railway to B. B. & C. I. Railway stations *via* Kasganj.

(*iv*) Ensuring as far as possible an equal level of rates on Indian sugar to all ports which are direct importers and distributors of foreign sugar, with a view to enable Indian sugar to compete at the port. Three points were noted by the Railways in this connection, *viz.*:—

(*a*) That all manufacturing areas, as far as possible, were to have an access to ports and adjoining markets on equal terms;

(*b*) the rates to internal centres within the sphere of each port were to be based on a combination of the port rate plus rates from the port; and

(c) railways were for this purpose to be divided into two broad groups—the manufacturing group comprising the B. & N. W., the E. I., the R. & K. and partly the N. W. Railways, and the receiving group consisting of B. B. & C. I., G. I. P., B. N., M. & S. M., E. B., and A. B. Railways and partly the N. W., railway in so far as Karachi and Sind are concerned. It was contemplated that all special rates quoted should be from the junction points of receiving railways, and be applicable to all traffic moving *via* the Junction, it being left to the forwarding railways to preserve the balance between the various producing centres on its line. Equality in rates to be maintained between all junction points and receiving stations where the excess of distance was not more than 25% over the shortest haul.

(v) Rates to internal stations were ordinarily to be governed by mileage, but where a lower combination was obtainable by the port rate plus rates from the port, automatically the rates on the basis of the "key" rates to the ports were to be adopted.

(vi) Suitable all-rail route freights on a co-operative basis were to be introduced with a view to prevent diversion of sugar traffic to water transport.

11. Reduction in B. & N. W. rates essential.*

It must be pointed out, however, that although the railways generally appreciated the position, a proper consideration of all the points was not made in their recent revisions. This was perhaps due to the fact that there was some degree of conflict of views amongst the different railways concerned, particularly between the B. & N. W. Railway and other State-owned and State-managed lines. We hope that the B. & N. W. Railway will in no time realise the necessity of thinking alike with other railways, both in the interest of the factories situated on their lines as well as in their own interest. The B. & N. W. Railway should out of regard for their own interests even, effect further reductions in rate of freight on sugar as well as on sugarcane and should give some encouragement to the factories situated on their line, in disposing of their sugar in distant markets (their production far exceeding the demand of Bihar and United Provinces) by offering requisite facilities. A reduction is particularly necessary in long distance traffic specially to various ports like Madras, Calcutta, Karachi, Bombay, etc.

---

* The following table gives the rate of freight on sugar per maund O. R. from a few factory stations on the B & N. W Railway to Howrah *via* Mokameh Ghat, to Madras *via* Mokameh Ghat, to Allahabad *via* Cawnpore, to Karachi *via* Cawnpore :—

	Howrah *via* Mokameh Ghat.	Madras.	Ahemeda-bad, *via* Cawnpore.	Karachi *via* Cawnpore.	Bombay *via* Allahabad.	Vizaga-patam Town.
Babhnan	-/15/10	1/7/4	1/7/3	1/3/2	...	1/7/4
Narkatiaganj	-/13/7	1/5/1	1/13/11	1/6/8	1/4/11	1/5/1
Marhowrah	-/12/1	1/9/7	1/11/4	1/0/3	1/3/5	1/3/7
Samastipur	-/9/11	1/1/5	1/12/9	1/6/6	1/4/7	1/1/5

12. Reductions to Ports will benefit Railways.

If suitable reductions are offered in regard to rates of freight particularly to the ports by the various railways concerned it will open up the possibilities for extensive traffic to the railways too. For example, a suitable rate of freight to Madras would bring to the railways no less than Rs. 30 lakhs per annum by way of freight alone, as Southern India is a potential market for sugar to the extent of about 150,000 tons per annum.

13. Steamer Company's Freights.

In the transport of sugar from the factories in the United Provinces and Behar, water services are available in addition to the railways. It is true that the railway service is much quicker as compared with water transport but at the same time water service is comparatively cheaper and quickness of transport in sugar is relatively not so essential a factor as it is for sugar-cane. The India General Navigation and Railway Co., Ltd., and the River Steam Navigation Co., Ltd., provide such transport services to Calcutta and to various parts of the Eastern Bengal and Assam, from various steamer stations on the Ganges, at Paleza Ghat opposite Patna, and Semariaghat on the other side of Mokameh, and from Revelganj. It is a matter of regret, however, that the B. & N. W. Railway should adopt a policy which makes it difficult for merchants to utilise the river service, by restriction of sugar booking to steamer ghats. They also place difficulties in the way of through booking arrangements and of interchange of traffic between the B. & N. W. Railway, and the Inland Steamer companies.* Moreover, very often 'block rating' is resorted to by the railways with a view to retain the traffic on their line as much as possible and to divert it from its natural courses to those *via* railway junctions only.

The India General Navigation and Railway Co., Ltd., approached the Government of India for the appointment of a Railway Commission under Section 26,28 and 42(1) and 42(1) and (2) of the Indian Railways' Act of 1890, with the complaint that undue preference or facilities were given by the Railways, particularly by the B. & N. W. Railway.

As far as the sugar trade is concerned, it is evident that it would like to have full facilities for transport of sugar by the water-route if it is convenient and otherwise suitable. It is certainly not reasonable for the railways to subject sugar traffic to any undue disadvantage and difficulty. If a Railway Commission is appointed it may be expected that the question will be properly enquired into and finally settled to the relief of this growing national industry.

---

*The B. & N. W. Rly's contention is that they offer very low freights on raw materials, like cane, lime, etc., and therefore cannot look with equanimity upon the loss of traffic of the finished product *viz.* sugar, from their line to the steamer company. This deserves consideration.

CHAPTER IX.

General review of the world trade and manufacture of sugar.

1. WORLD'S PRODUCTION AND CONSUMPTION.

We now propose to review briefly the general position, manufacture, production and consumption of sugar in the various countries of the world, as that has an intimate bearin on our industry. Before we do it however, it will be useful to see the figures of the world's production and consumption of sugar (cane and beet). The following table (Table No. 32) gives the world's production and consumption of sugar during 1924-25 to 1932-33 and also shows the excess of production over consumption.

TABLE NO. 32.

World Production and Consumption of Sugar.

Year.	Production.	Consumption.	Excess of production over consumption.
	Metric tons.	Metric tons.	Metric tons.
1924-25 ...	24,925,000	23,256,000	1,669,000
1925-26 ...	26,044,000	24,712,000	1,332,000
1926-27 ...	24,718,000	24,880,000	162,000
1927-28 ...	26,579,000	26,492,000	87,000
1928-29 ...	28,898,000	24,479,000	1,419,000
1929-30 ...	28,471,000	27,095,000	1,376,000
1930-31 ...	30,208,000	27,573,000	2,635,000
1931-32 ...	27,771,000	26,920,000	751,000
1932-33 ...	26,331,000	26,302,000	29,000

It will be easy to see therefrom that there was a great excess of production over consumption till 1931-32, and this had a very depressing effect on the sugar markets all over the world. It will be some satisfaction to find, however, that the excess is decreasing slowly due to the restriction of production of sugar.

The world's sugar production, in terms of raw sugar, has been approximately 26,000,000 tons for the last 2 years and is not likely to show any substantial increase, in the near future. The largest production was during 1930-31 when the output totalled 30,000,000 tons. A well-known International Sugar Statistician estimates the world's sugar production during the 1933-34 season at 26,092,000 tons as against a production of 26,331,000 tons in 1932-33 and 27,208,000 tons in 1931-32.* This estimate includes 17,425,000 tons cane sugar and 8,667,000 tons beet sugar. It would be of interest to note that the production of *cane sugar* is roughly *twice* as large as that of *beet sugar.*

2. CANE *vss.* BEET.

Until the eighteenth century cane sugar was without a rival. The sugar beet industry witnessed a rapid expansion particularly on the Continent of Europe, under the stimulus of Government assistance, during the nineteenth century. The following table gives the figures

*There are small differences in figures, which are compiled by various authorities, as it is not easy to compile figures for all countries on any uniform basis, and for the same periods.

of cane and beet sugar for a few years from 1853-54 to 1933-34:—

TABLE NO. 33

Figures of production of cane and beet sugar from 1853-54 to 1933-34.

Year.	Cane.	Beet.	Total.
	Tons.	Tons.	Tons.
1853-54 ...	2,282,000	201,000	2,483,000
1863-64 ...	2,517,000	435,000	2,952,000
1873-74 ...	3,290,000	1,249,000	4,539,000
1883-84 ...	4,860,000	2,436,000	7,296,000
1893-94 ...	6,000,000	3,817,000	9,817,000
1803-04 ...	6,666,000	5,879,000	12,545,000
1913-14 ...	10,744,900	8,871,000	19,615,000
1923-24 ...	15,094,000	5,970,000	21,064,000
1930-31 ...	17,720,000	11,529,000	29,249,000
1931-32 ...	18,256,000	8,952,000	26,963,000
1932-33 ...	18,425,000	7,906,000	25,082,000
1933-34* ...	17,425,000	8,667,000	25,162,000

*Estimated.

A study of these figures will reveal that the sugar beet industry developed fast up to 1913. With the outbreak of the Great War in 1914, the production of beet sugar decreased and this furnished an excellent opportunity for cane sugar countries to increase their production until in 1920 the sugar beet declined to 3,260,000 tons. It was not until 1927 that the beet sugar attained approximately its pre-war production and with the high protective duties particularly in Continental Europe and the United States of America, coupled with the agricultural advantages of the crop, the production increased to over 11,000,000 tons in 1930-31. The subsequent depression in the industry the world over called for drastic measures of restriction of output and under the International sugar agreement (known as the Chadbourne Plan), the production has again gone down.

The following table shows the production of sugar in the various countries of the world during 1930-31, 1931-32 and 1932-33 in thousands of metric tons, raw sugar value.

TABLE NO. 34.

World Production of Sugar during 1930-31 to 1932-33.

(In thousands of Metric Tons, Raw Sugar Value.)

—	Production.		
	1932-33.	1931-32.	1930-31.
Europe.			
Germany	1,075	1,595	2,547
Czechoslovakia	630	814	1,143
Austria	164	163	150
Hungary	105	125	234
France	910	874	1,205
Belgium	245	205	283
Netherlands	240	172	296
Denmark	187	122	168
Sweden	231	144	187
Poland	420	493	782
Italy	322	363	415
Spain	260	423	344
Switzerland	7	6	6
United Kingdom	360	284	479
Soviet Union	1,080	1,493	1,979
Other Countries (*a*)	291	238	437
Total Europe	6,527	7,514	10,655

(*a*) Includes Turkey.

N. B.—Figures in this Table are from Dr. Gustav Mikusch.

TABLE NO. 34—*Contd.*

	Production.		
	1932-33.	1931-32.	1930-31.
Asia.			
British India	4,400	4,264	3,531
China and Hongkong	220	220	180
Japan and Formosa	974	1,181	956
Java (*b*)	2,770	3,004	3,171
Philippine Islands	1,100	1,000	795
Other Countries	57	52	51
Total Asia	9,521	9,721	8,684
Africa.			
Egypt	150	147	122
South African Union	320	296	357
Mauritius	248	167	225
Other Countries	213	170	180
Total Africa	931	780	826

(*b*) Crops of the years 1929-32 inclusive, the crop of 1933 is tentatively estimated at 1,300,000 tons

TABLE NO. 34.—*Contd.*

	Production.		
	1932-33.	1931-32.	1930-31.
North America.			
United States	1,445	1,341	1,411
Hawaii	940	933	905
Puerto Rico	855	904	712
Canada and Newfoundland ...	52	54	48
Cuba	2,050	2,678	3,214
Santo Domingo and Haiti ...	447	459	390
British West Indies	300	292	219
French West Indies	66	67	61
Mexico	235	246	293
Central America	116	127	152
Total North America ...	6,506	7,101	7,405
South America.			
Argentina	344	351	383
Brazil	930	975	937
British Guiana	130	128	130
Peru	380	402	391
Other Countries	96	110	95
Total South America ...	1,880	1,996	1,936
Australia and Oceania.			
Australia	558	616	549
Fiji and Others	140	73	93
World Total	26,063	27,771	30,208

3. Chadbourne Restriction Scheme.

The depression in the sugar industry due to an increase of production as a result of the keen competition which ensued between cane and beet sugar called for immediate attention and the result was that several of the continental capitalists and some of the several large sugar producers met together in order to consider the steps to be taken for arresting the fall in price. According to an International agreement, which was signed on 9th May 1931, by the representatives of Cuba, Java Czechoslovakia, Germany, Poland, Belgium and Hungary, nine of the chief sugar-exporting countries of the world agreed to dispose of their surplus stock gradually over a period of 5 years and in the meanwhile to prevent the accumulation of fresh excess produce during that period. The European signatories have been able to accomplish all that they undertook to do under the agreement but the position is different in the case of Cuba and Java.

Owing to the persistence of economically depressed conditions throughout the world, the demand for sugar failed to reach the proportions estimated and before the end of 1931 it became clear that further reductions in production and exports would be necessary to accomplish the object of the Chadbourne scheme. The political disturbance in China, and a more liberal use of glucose in the United States affected consumption. The result was that while the sugar stocks in Europe declined in 1931-32, those in Java and Cuba became heavier Prices registered a further fall due to the accumulation of sugar in the two chief sugar producing countries. As regards Cuba, their stock increased to some extent, owing to the decreased consumption by the United States and this has counter-balanced the diminution in the segregated stocks under the agreement.

The Agreement was patched up, however, by assigning quotas to Non-American destinations during the remaining years of the plan.

4. The Cuban Industry *Vss.* Philippine Industry.

The sugar industry in Cuba was developed with special reference to the United States market, which was practically assured by the reciprocity treaty, a market there, as against all other foreign sugars, but since 1920 owing to the increase in home production, the United States of America increased the import duties in 1920, 1921 and 1929, the result being that production in the United States, Porto Rico, Hawaii and the Philippine Islands increased rapidly. In 1930 the Philippine sugar was also made duty free and the limit of 300,000 tons per year upon the imports of the Philippine sugar was removed. This gave a great impetus to the sugar industry in the Philippines and the production increased from 229,000 tons in 1913-14 to 1,164,000 tons in 1932-33 with exports to the United States of over 1,000,000 tons. The increase of the Philippine sugar supplies in the United States markets necessarily meant the exclusion of Cuban sugar.* This as well as other minor reasons have been responsible for dragging the Cuban sugar industry to its verge of ruin. It should be noted that Cuba production has fallen to about one-third of its production in 1928-29 and the estimated production for 1933-34 is only 1,700,000 as against 5,517,000 tons during 1928-29. Its annual consumption is 100,000 tons of sugar. The stocks in Java also ran up due to the decrease in demand from India, which has developed its own industry, and Japan which was also dependent on supplies of Java, also reduced its import, by drawing its supplies chiefly from the island of Formosa. Japan is reported to be exporting sugar too. The Indian industry is now practically self-supporting in the matter of sugar supply and she will hardly need any import of sugar with effect from 1934-35. Owing to these factors, *i.e.*, Java's and Cuba's inability to dispose of their stocks, the Chadbourne agreement will necessitate some further re-adjustment. The International Sugar Council is making this adjustment and we hope it will be able to persuade even countries which are at present outside the scheme to join the scheme and ensure an adequate control of production for some years.

5. THE JAVA INDUSTRY.

Let us now examine the sugar industry of Java. The following table shows the production of cane sugar (raw

*It is gratifying to note however that the Philippine Legislature has restricted the production during 1933 to 1935 to 1,480,000 tons. The local consumption there is only 60 000 tons.

values) in British India, Java and Cuba during the past 5 years and the estimated output during 1933-34 as compared with pre-war production.

TABLE No. 35.

Production of Cane Sugar (Raw value) in British India, Java and Cuba from 1913-14 to 1933-34.

Year.	British India. '000 Tons.	Java. '000 Tons.	Cuba. '000 Tons.
1913-14 ...	2,480	1,507	2,596
1928-29 ...	2,990	3,113	5,157
1929-30 ...	3,050	3,066	4,671
1930-31 ...	3,250	3,120	3,570
1931-32 ...	3,520	3,004	2,678
1932-33 ...	4,720	2,759	2,053
1933-34 ...	5,000	1,510	1,700

It will be seen from these figures that the cane sugar industry in Cuba and Java developed enormously and that the production reached in 1928-29 was double the respective pre-war production.

The following table shows the sugar production of Java from 1924/31 according to figures of Dr. Prinsen Geerligs. The number of mills grinding sugar in Java

TABLE No. 36.

Cane acreage and Production of Sugar in Java.

Year.	Cane acreage and production of sugar in Java.		
	No. of factories operating.	Area under cane.	Production of sugar.
		(Acres).	(Tons.)
1924 ...	179	424,945	1,966,273
1925 ...	179	439,695	2,263,479
1926 ...	178	444,038	1,941,649
1927 ...	178	455,806	2,341,538
1928 ...	178	481,863	2,901,751
1929 ...	179	486,799	2,858,054
1930 ...	179	489,984	2,869,943
1931 ...	178	493,721	2,728,776
1932 ...	172	411,888	2,000,000
1933 ...	99	209,000	1,378,000
1934 ...	40	86,000	525,000

has fallen from 170 during 1930-31 to 99 in 1933 and only about 40 in 1934. The Java industry has curtailed its plantings and it has been estimated that in 1934 Java will produce sugar to the extent of only about 500,000 tons as against 1,510,000 tons during 1932-33; 2,759,000 tons in 1931-32 and 2,869,000 tons during 1930-31. It is also estimated that the 1933-34 plantings have been limited to only 86,000 acres calculated to yield about 500,000 tons of sugar under normal conditions, as against 209,000 acres in 1932-33; 411,000 acres in 1931-32 and 496,000 acres in 1930-31. Un-official reports show that in 1935, the production will only be 300,000 tons. This shows that the production of Java during the next year will be just enough to meet her internal requirements. It should be noted, however, that there is a huge stock of unsold sugar which was estimated in March, 1934 at about 2,500,000 tons (roughly equivalent to India's requirements for 2½ years). Estimating that the future crops will not substantially exceed the present estimation, Java will still take over 2 years to clear the stocks, assuming that exports every year reach 1,200,000 tons. On 1st April 1936, Java's stock should be only 28,000 tons. The consumption of Java has been estimated at about 400,000 tons annually.

The export of sugar from Java during 1930-31 and 1931-32 was 235,400 and 154,300 tons respectively.

6. PRODUCTION IN CUBA.

The production in Cuba which had a capacity of 7,000,000 tons of sugar and which had 1200 mills in operation, was only 3,000,000 tons in 1931 produced by 200 mills operating far below their capacity. Its home consumption is about 100,000 tons; but even this huge sacrifice on the part of Cuba has not achieved the expected results. The total export quota for countries other than the United States, had been exported, but exports to the United States failed to reach the 2,577,000 tons allotted. The stocks of sugar in Cuba went on increasing as per report of Chadbourne Plan, resulting in a restriction, by a decree, of production for 1932 to 2,700,000 tons. In Cuba, the total crop of 1933-34 has been officially further restricted to 2,215,000 tons. There was however a stock of 1,456,675 tons in November 1933. Another authority values the figure of stock at 1,870,000 tons. It is likely that Cuba may manufacture only a very small quantity of sugar during 1934 due to the political, economical and particularly the labour situation.

7. Adjustment of Supply and Demand.

It is gratifying to find that efforts are constantly being made to restrict production of sugar and to adjust the supply to the demand. If necessary care and produce are increased, the industry will be able to avoid bad times.

CHAPTER X.

Characteristic Features of Cane-Sugar Countries.

1. FEATURES IN OTHER COUNTRIES.

We desire to state in this Chapter a few characteristic features of countries producing cane-sugar in order to enable a comparison being made of the conditions in other countries with those in India.

2. STANDARD METHODS OF MANUFACTURE.

At the outset we might mention briefly the standard methods of cane sugar manufacture employed in modern factories. These are briefly known as (1) Defecation, (2) Sulphitation, (3) Carbonatation.

Defecation Process.— According to this process sufficient lime is added to neutralize the raw juice, which is subsequently heated under pressure, further "boiled" in open pans (defecators) and then allowed to flow into settling tanks, or subsiders, where the separation of the clean and dirty juice occurs. Of late it has been found beneficial to send the juice through heaters before adding the lime-milk.

Sulphitation Process.—The difference in this process from the above method is that about double amount of lime is added to the juice, whereupon the latter is treated with sulphurous acid gas.

Cabonatation Process.—In this process a considerable amount of lime is added followed by a treatment with carbonic acid gas.

The defecation process is used for making sugar intended for refining. Since carbonatation and sulphitation are the classical processes in the production of white sugar in factories, we will compare their merits.

3. CARBONATATION *vss.* SULPHITATION.

The carbonatation factories generally produce 2·6% more sugar than that of sulphitation factories. This superiority of carbonatation is due to the more intensive and thorough elimination of non-sugar ingredients, so that both the purity and the colour of the clarified juice are strikingly better than in sulphitation. The sugar made in a carbonatation factory realizes a slightly better price than in a sulphitation factory, as the sugar turned out is whiter and more sparkling and retains its qualities much longer. At the same time, the Carbonatation process is somewhat more expensive, costing perhaps about 5 annas more per maund of sugar produced.

The Carbonatation process is not generally as profitable as the Sulphitation process, due to the fact that the difference in price of sugar is not very great.

Out of about 72 factories, which are members of the Indian Sugar Mills Association, 60 are sulphitation factories.

4. FEATURES IN JAVA.

Java has various natural advantages over other cane sugar countries. To start with, the Island is situated most favourably in respect of cane cultivation, lying as it does within the tropical belt. It has been blessed with a climate agreeable to the growth of rich cane of higher sugar content and of heavier yield than is found in India. In point of labour also Java has several advantages.

It has a population of over 35 millions and has an area of 50,000 square miles. Labour is abundant, cheap and readily available.

There is intensive cultivation of cane combined with the application of a well-devised scheme of economic manuring due largely to the fact that only a small portion of the land can be allotted to sugar cane, as a bulk of the land is required for growing food for the population. In regard to cultivation of cane, the universal practice in

Java is to grow exclusively "plant cane"; ratooning as is done in some other countries, is not done in Java. Owing to the necessity of growing rice for the people, Java is forced to adopt a system of rotation of crops, which also implies that the planting of cane is done on irrigated land. *The most important feature, however, is that the cultivation of cane and the manufacture of sugar is done by one and the same administration.* As a matter of fact it can be said that the cultivation of cane as practised in Java may well be regarded as the most scientific and efficient system of cane cultivation in the tropics.

5. MILLING RESULTS IN HAWAII SUPERIOR TO JAVA.

In regard to extraction results by the milling installations, however, Java has not yet reached the high level of Hawaii, which ranks the highest amongst other cane countries.

6. FEATURES IN HAWAIIAN ISLANDS.

These islands lie on the northern fringe of the tropical belt, just within the Tropic of Cancer. The sugar industry is noted for its extra-ordinary degree of efficiency and systematic thoroughness. The relation of applied science to sugar manufactures is most intimate and complete. Over 50% of the total area under cane is irrigated. In respect of extraction results, Hawaii ranks highest amongst cane countries.

7. FEATURES IN CUBA.

The chief reasons for Cuba's pre-eminence as a sugar manufacturing country are the quality and quantity of its soil. The extraordinary fertility of the natural cane lands in Cuba is well-known. Cane, once planted, appears, as it were, to thrive like a weed.

Cuba is similar to Java in some respects. Both are long and narrow islands of roughly the same area (about the size of England). Both of them are within the tropics, north and south of the Equator respectively, and have more or less comparable climatic conditions. It is remarkable, however, that the population of Java is over ten times that of Cuba, although both the islands are of about the same size. On the other hand, the area of cane cultivation in Java is restricted by Government due to the necessity of growing food for the people. Therefore, while land in Cuba is abundant and cheap, and labour comparatively scarce and dear, in Java the land is limited and labour is abundant and cheap. *As a result we find that cultivation of cane in Java is intensive and in Cuba extensive.*

The method of transport of cane by bullock carts in Cuba is not up-to-date.

8. FEATURES IN INDIA.

India is a country of vast dimensions. The differences in climate are therefore great and vary from province to province. The main sugar belt lies in Northern India. It must be observed however that superior qualities of cane are grown in the Deccan and in Madras.

Although the area under cane is large, and of about 3,000,000 acres, cultivation is not concentrated. The figures of the area under cane in various provinces are given in an earlier chapter. India has capricious and often insufficient monsoon. The cultivation also is not scientific. This is responsible for the fact that the production of cane per acre is remarkably low. While Java produces about 50 tons of cane per acre, India produces on an average about 16 tons only.

The provision of irrigation facilities for the fields, of suitable seeds, and of suitable manure, along with instructions in regard to rotation of crops would considerably augment the yield of cane per acre. India has a plentiful and cheap supply of labour, but its inferior quality of cane and inferior treatment of the soil require great improvement. It is also remarkable that a vast bulk of the cane is crushed for the purpose of manufacture of a very impure raw sugar, called *Gur*. We have already referred to the considerable loss of sucrose in this process.

The methods of manufacture show great improvement since 1931 due to the latest plants, and efficient methods of milling introduced within the last 2 years.

9. Crushing or Harvesting Seasons.

The folowing table shows the period of crushing or harvesting seasons for cane:—

TABLE NO. 37.

Period of crushing or harvesting seasons for cane in various countries.

Cuba	...	...	January—June.
Hawaii	...	...	December—September.
Java	...	...	May—November.
Mauritius	...	...	August—December.
Natal	...	...	May—December.
Queensland	...	...	June—November.
Egypt	...	...	December—April.
India	...	...	November—April.

Generally speaking actual crushing period extends from 4 to 6 months, although in districts where exceptional conditions—climatic and otherwise—prevail, *e.g.*, in Hawaii, it extends almost throughout the whole year. The duration of crushing season depends upon a number of factors, the most important of which is maturity of the cane.

10. Age of Crop.

The time taken to grow a crop of cane depends largely upon climatic conditions and the quality of cane grown and varies from country to country. This point has an important bearing on the subject of yield of sugar per acre, when comparisons are drawn between different districts.

Java.—In Java, cane takes 11 to 15 months from planting to harvesting, thus practically constituting one year's crop. "Plant Cane" is exclusively grown; ratooning is not practised. This is due mainly to the system of land tenure in Java, whereby land, although lasting for long periods, is actually kept by the factory during the period of cane cultivation, *i.e.*, from 14 to 18 months.

Cuba.—In Cuba, though ratooning over long periods is practised, crops are usually harvested after an average growth of 12 to 15 months.

Hawaii.—In Hawaii, two seasons are required for producing a crop of cane. Though what is locally termed "Short ratoons" are harvested after 12 months' growth, the bulk of the crop matures in 18 to 24 months. The common practice is to have 3 crops in the ground at the same time; as one crop is being cut, another is being planted or cultivated for ratoons, while a third is growing, to be harvested six months later.

India.—As a rule ratooning is not practised. (See Indian Sugar Committee's Report).

11. SUPPLY OF CANE.

In Queensland and Natal the entire crop of cane is grown by independent European Planters, who supply their cane to the neighbouring mills.

In Mauritius a considerable part of the crop, about 45%, is grown by small Indian Planters.

In Cuba the bulk of the cane is produced by outside planters and sold to mills.

In Java the whole crop is produced by the mills.

In Hawaii about 90% of the crop is produced by the Mills.

In India owing to the smallness of the holdings, large plots of land cannot be put under cane by factories without great difficulty. Small individual cultivators grow cane on their small plots of land and sell their produce to mills as also to the Khandsaries and gur manufacturers. More than 70% of the crop is sold to *gur* manufacturers, whereas only about 10% of the crop is sold to mills for manufacture of sugar direct therefrom. A tendency is, however, noticeable for factories to purchase their land, in close vicinity, for cultivation under their own management.

12. SUCROSE CONTENT.

The crop averages in the different countries indicate practically a uniform percentage of sugar in the cane, *i.e.*, round about 13%. Fibre content is roughly 12 to 13% and the purity of juice is about 87%.

13 YIELD OF CANE AND SUGAR *per* ACRE.

The yields of cane and sugar per acre are necessary in comparing the yield of sugar in one country with that of another. Some confusion is sometimes caused by mixing up Long and Short tons with metric tons*, and other factors also are ignored, *e.g.*, whether the figure is based on a one-year or two-year crop, whether based on white or raw sugar, whether based on plant cane or ratoons, whether on irrigated or non-irrigated land, etc.

In Java.—The average extraction of sugar in Java is about 11·9%. It must be borne in mind, however, in comparing these figures, that in Java the crop consists of plant cane exclusively and is a one-year crop.

In Hawaii.—In Hawaiian Islands, the extraction of sugar percentage of white cane is 12% but it must be borne in mind that ratooning is practised and the cane requires about 18 months to mature. For the sake of a fair comparison, the figure of the tonnage of cane harvested per acre should be based upon the same unit of time as well as area, *i.e.*, tons of cane per acre per annum. The tonnage of cane harvested per acre per annum in Java is about 45 (2,000 lbs.), as compared with about 53 (of 2,000 lbs.) of Hawaii. Both these countries, however, have one factor in common, *viz.*, of intensive cultivation combined with irrigation on an un-paralleled scale. In Java more than 90% of the total cane growing area is under irrigation, while in Hawaiian Island, over 50% of the area is under irrigation.

*Long ton = 2,240 lbs, short ton = 2,000 lbs.
Metric ton = 2,205 lbs.

In Mauritius.—In Mauritius the average yield of cane is about 23 to 24 tons per acre on European estates. In Indian plantations, however, the average is only of about 14 tons per acre. Consequently the average for the whole island is 17·5 tons. This is equivalent to less than 2 tons of sugar per acre. This is due to primitive methods of cultivation of Indian planters who occupy about half of the total area under cane.*

In India.—In India, the average yield of cane is about 16 tons per acre. The yield for improved varieties is more. The production of sugar per acre is about 1·25 tons.

In Cuba.—In Cuba no reliable statistics are available in respect of yields of cane and sugar. But from occasional statements it may be taken that the average yield of cane per acre over the whole island is less than 20 tons and 2 tons of sugar per acre.

In Queensland.—In Queensland the average yield of cane per acre is about 16 tons and 2 tons of sugar per acre.

In Philippines.—No data is available. From an attempt made in 1924 to compile a representative record of the yield of sugar per acre, it was found that 1·28 tons of sugar were yielded by plant cane, 1·38 by ratoons and the total average was 1·1 tons of sugar.

---

*For a detailed study, *vide* Economic Aspects of cane sugar Production.—F. Maxwell.

The following table gives particulars of average yields of cane and of sugar (raw) in terms of short tons per acre for different countries.

TABLE NO. 38.

Broad Average of Yields of Cane and of Sugar (Raw) in Terms of Short Tons per Acre for Different Countries.

Countries.	Cane. Tons per Acre.	Sugar. Tons per Acre.	Approximate period of Growth of Cane.
Java	approx. 45	approx. 5·5	11—15 mths.
Hawaiian Islands ...	" 45	" 5·5	18—24 "
Queensland ...	less than 20	about 2	Practically two years' crop.
Cuba	" " 20	less than 2	12—15 mths.
Mauritius ...	" " 20	" " 2	14—20 "
Philippines ...	" " 20	" " 2	11—14 "
South Africa ...	" " 20	" " 2	2 years' crop.
India	Approx. 16	" " 2	1 year's crop.

This is, however, not up-to-date, and many remarkable improvements have been made therein as observed elsewhere.

14. Methods of Payment for different Countries.

The following table gives the methods of payment for cane is different countries.

TABLE NO. 39.

Modes of Payment for Cane in Different Countries.

Countries.	Payment to the planter for his cane.
Java	50 per cent of the sugar recovered
Mauritius ...	60-70 per cent ,, ,, ,,
Hawaiian Islands ...	\$ 1-\$ 1·20 per ton (2,000 lbs.) of cane for every cent (\$0·01) per lb. of 96° sugar quoted in New York for the month during which the cane is delivered.
Cuba	4·5—7·5 per cent of the weight of cane in the form of raw sugar.
Philippine Islands ...	50-60 per cent of the sugar recovered.
Antigua	4½ lb. of 96° sugar for every 100 lbs. of cane and at end of season a further payment resulting from the division between the cane suppliers of 50 per cent of the profits of the factory.
Queensland ...	Fixed by Government.
South Africa* ..	12s. per ton (2000 lbs. of cane, when the price at Durban of first refined sugar is 18s. per 100 lbs.
Porto Rico ...	6½ to 7 lbs. of sugar per 100 lbs. of cane.
India	No legislation so far. Bill introduced in Assembly on 13th March 1934, enabling Provinces to fix minimum prices of cane, if considered necessary.

*Now on sucrose basis.

It must be remembered, however, that in Java and Mauritius where superior white sugar is made, the percentage to be paid to the planter is on all kinds of sugar turned out. In all other countries (except South Africa) the percentage is based on raw sugar. It is evident that on the same basis a higher percentage can be paid to the planter when the mill is turning out raw sugar than when it is producing 'white'. The Queensland practice is beyond comparison as the price of cane is fixed by the Cane Prices Board and the price of sugar is also controlled by Government and fixed at a very high price.

15. LABOUR SUPPLY.

Mauritius.—Although the island consists of some 700 square miles and has a population of 380,000 people of which 270,000 are Indians, Mauritius is not well situated in respect of labour. The labour shortage affects the welfare of the industry.

Java.—Java is one of the most densely populated countries in the world, and the result is that labour question is greatly simplified.

India.—In India also there is plenty of labour available and at cheap rates too. The factories are estimated to be employing about 90,000 labourers during the crushing season, apart from the khandsaris and *Gur manufacturers.* The total labour force dependent upon cane-cultivation may be estimated at about 15 million, on an average of one acre of cane per family of about 4 to 5 members, in addition to others employed for weeding, harvesting and allied operations.

16. OUTPUT OF SUGAR FACTORIES.

The following table gives average production of sugar in different countries.

TABLE NO. 40.

Average Annual Output per Mill.

Countries.	Average Annual Output per Mill.
Cuba	26,000 tons of sugar.
Hawaii	18,000 ,, ,, ,,
Philippines ...	17,000 ,, ,, ,,
Porto Rico ...	15,000 ,, ,, ,,
Australia	14,000 ,, ,, ,,
Java	12,500 ,, ,, ,,
South Africa ...	9,500 ,, ,, ,,
Mauritius	5,500 ,, ,, ,,
India	7,500 ,, ,, ,,

It must be observed that Cuba stands prominently among the other countries. She stands for large outputs and large milling capacities. In Cuba there are very few factories which produces less than 5,000 tons per annum, and there are a large number of factories which produce over 50,000 tons. There are 3 or 4 factories which produce more than 1 lakh tons. The factories in India are all of a very small size, and the average production of sugar per season may be taken at about 7,500 tons. The Tariff Board recommended the establishment of factories with a crushing capacity of 13 lakhs of maund of cane per annum, *i.e.*, about 4,000 tons of sugar as an "economic unit" in Indian conditions, in view of the scattered and small holdings of cane. It is gratifying to find however that the size of the factories is increasing, and thus cost of production decreasing.

The capacity of a sugar factory is governed by a number of factors which vary from country to country, the main consideration being the amount of cane available, the yield of cane, the duration of the milling season and the quality of cane.

17. CRUSHING CAPACITIES

By crushing or grinding capacity of a factory is meant the amount of cane that goes through the milling plant per unit of time with good extraction and is usually expressed in terms of so many tons of cane per hour or per day. Of course, it would certainly be more rational and desirable to define the capacity as the quantity of cane which can be crushed by the mill with the highest extraction results for after all, the fundamental object of a milling plant is not the mere crushing through of huge quantities of cane, but extraction of the maximum sugar from the cane The cane crushing capacity varies considerably in different countries. In Cuba there are over 50 factories which crush more than 75 tons of cane per hour (of 2,000 lbs.) It appears however that the object of Cuban mills is capacity and not extraction. While the Hawaiian industrialists regard the milling plant as means of extraction of sugar, the Cuban industrialists consider the plant as a means of grinding cane. We find that the highest extraction results are in Hawaiian Islands.

Factories in Java vary widely in milling capacity, the majority ranging from 30 to 55 tons of cane per hour.

In India the average cane-crushing capacity may be said to be about 600 tons of cane per day of 22 hours.

18. Over-all Efficiency.

The over-all efficiency of a factory by which is meant the percentage of sucrose recovered from the total sucrose contained in the cane in the form of commercial sugar varies on account of different conditions. Of primary importance are the richness of the cane, purity of the juice, the fibres in the cane, and method of manufacture. The over-all efficiency combines the extraction of milling efficiency with the recovery or manufacturing efficiency. The following table shows the tons of cane required to make a ton of sugar in different countries.

TABLE NO. 41.

Tons of Cane Required to Make One Ton of Sugar.

Countries.	Tons Cane to One Ton Sugar.	Number of Factories Averaged.	Season.	Observations.
Cuba ...	8·50	80	1924	Raw Sugar.
Hawaii ...	8·20	Practically all.	,,	,,
Java ...	8·80*	,,	,,	Computed on the basis of raw sugar. (Standard muscovado.)
Queensland ...	7·80	,,	,,	Raw Sugar.
Mauritius ...	10·66	20	1919	White Sugar.
South Africa ...	10·90	12	1925	White and partly raw sugar.
India ...	11·5	57	1933	White sugar

*In 1925 this figure was 8·1.

The favourable position of Queensland is mainly attributed to the rich canes there. In other countries, also notable improvements have been made during the last few years.

We expect that India also will be able to increase her efficiency within a short time, with the aid of scientific research, technical experts and latest machinery.

CHAPTER XI.

Single Sugar Selling Organization.

1. PRACTICAL SELF-SUFFICIENCY OF PRODUCTION OF SUGAR.

We have already observed in an earlier chapter that as a result of the development of modern sugar factories, India will be able to produce by 1934-35 practically all the sugar she needs for her consumption. During 1933-34, the Indian production will be slightly smaller than her consumption and it will be necessary to import a small quantity from foreign countries. We except the production of sugar from factories alone, to exceed 800,000 tons during 1934-35.

The quality of Indian sugar is also rapidly improving and can be considered only slightly inferior to that of imported sugar for which there should be a difference of not more than about six to eight annas per maund in price as compared with imported sugar.

2. INDIAN SUGAR SELLS AT UNDULY LOW PRICES.

It is a pity, however, that largely as a result of undue internal competition, Indian Factory-made sugar is not able to sell at such prices and is being sold at a price which is lower by Rs. 1-12-0 per maund, than that of the White Java sugar, prevailing at the ports. For example, Java sugar is being sold in Calcutta at Rs. 10-4-0 a maund and Indian made sugar of almost equal quality after bearing a railway freight of about 12 annas per maund from the Factory to the Calcutta market, is selling at about Rs. 8-8-0 only.

The reason for this abnormally large difference is the competition between Indian Factories themselves in marketing their production. Indian factories, as a rule have insufficient storage accommodation and insufficient capital to carry their produce for more than a few months and there is also the apprehension of the sugar deteriorating, if it is carried through the monsoon. The abnormally low prices obtained now for the Indian sugar represent a loss to the factory industry of not less than 20,000,000 (2 crores) of rupees, estimated on the basis of production of about 600,000 tons. With the increase in production, as a result of the establishment of more factories, conditions are likely to get worse and unless effective measures are taken, in the meanwhile, the aggregate wastage of profits will increase proportionately. It is obvious therefore that a Central Sugar Selling Organization, on the Java model is an urgent necessity for the organised and scientific development of the Industry. If such an organization comes into existence, all factories will benefit considerably by reaping the full advantages of the protective duty granted to the industry by the Government of of India.

3. The Single Selling Organization at Java.

It will be of interest to note in this connection how the present Single Selling Organization of sugar in Java has devolped, as we will be in a position to drive a very useful lesson from the same.

Before the war, factories in Java sold their sugar as the Indian factories do at present. As a rule, forward sales were made through brokers. During the early stages of the War, large purchases of Java sugar were made by the British Royal Commission on Sugar Supply and the old system of sales was thus continued. A change however came in 1917 when Great Britain arranged for most of its supplies, from other sources and when, by a coincidence, other important buyers also withdrew from the Java market. The manufacturers of Java, instead of selling in advance, as hitherto were left with large unsold stocks. Prices went down considerably and a complete demoralization of the market was threatened owing to anxiety of the weak holders to sell. To avert this, the sugar manufacturers of Java established the Java Sugar Association as a Single Seller and almost every holder of a factory joined it. This organization however failed to produce any substantial improvement as the dislocation of shipping owing to the war had brought export business almost to a standstill. By 1918 practically the whole of that year's crop as well as a large part of 1917 was awaiting sales.

At this juncture a new sales organization, called the United Java Sugar Producers' Association (V. I. S. P.) was formed in August 1918 covering about 90% of the industry. As most of the factory owners belonged to Holland and as mail and cable communications were uncertain at that time on account of war, the headquarters of the new Association were transferred from Java to Amsterdam. Although the original object in forming this Association was, to dispose of the old stock without undue internal competition as also the unsold stocks of the 1917 and 1918 crops, the working of this Association proved so very useful that it was continued from year to year till 1932.

Difficulties, however, arose in 1930, when this Sales Organization experienced trouble in marketing the sugar produced by its members due to the fall in prices. Prices were steadily falling till they ceased to be remunerative. Discontent set in amongst the members, and during the end of 1931 eight members left the organization thus weakening its position. On account of the decreased sales, the competition against 17 outside mills had also become increasingly difficult. This organization was therefore on the verge of collapse and in the absence of any organization to take its place and with the accumulation of large unsold stocks, the entire industry in Java was faced with an unprecedented crisis. Notwithstanding a hint thrown out by the Netherlands Indian Government to the effect that it would be highly probable that a dissolution of the V. I. S. P. under prevailing circumstances could not be countenanced without further action on its part in view of the economic interest in the sugar industry on the part of the country and the people, it became known, some time in 1932, that no mutual agreement could be reached by the V. I. S. P. elements and at the end of 1932, its dissolution had become a practical certainty.

These advantages furnished an occasion for the Indian Government to investigate to what extent it would be necessary to take active measures. Even before the producers themselves called the Government to come to their aid so as to prevent, by a general ruling, the unexpected unbridled competition with all its disastrous consequences, Government itself arrived at the conclusion that in the general interest, it would have to step in to save the siutation.

Upon a closer consideration of the problem it was found that the Government's intervention would have to take the shape of a temporary measure only and would have to be limited to the minimum requirements actually necessary to attain the end in view. It was also found that Government would have to assume full responsibility for the working of the organization. Four suggestions were made to the Government in regard to the manner in which they could intervene:—(1) The Covisp Plan, submitted jointly by the Ned. Ind. Handelsbank and the Ned. Ind. Landbouw Mij., which involve a complete change in the existing property relations and the current industrial methods, and under this plan the Government intervention would have to be a protracted one and last many years and would also mean definite financial responsibility for Government.

(2) The Segregation Plan, submitted by the President-Director of the Java Bank proposing the pooling of supplies in a Central Sales Organization combined with a restriction to 50% of the new harvest.

(3) The Minimum Price Regulation Plan, submitted by the Head of the Section of Agriculture, which was closely allied to the previous plan.

(4) The 100% Single Seller Plan, submitted by the Chairman and the Vice-Chairman of the Beniso, proposing that all sugars be disposed of by one Central Sales Organization.

Before making a final decision, the Government held Conferences on 21st September 1932 with a great number of producers and representatives of the sugar trade and it was felt that the Government intervention was essential. The majority of the producers, as also all exporters, declared themselves to be in favour of bringing all sugar into one strong hand. A minority of the producers, seemed to fear that a "Single Seller" would prove to be a continuation of the V. I. S. P. and, on this occasion, exercising coercion.

These expressions of opinion, as also the difficulties which were steadily increasing with the development of political and economic conditions prevailing in British India and in China convinced the Government that a strong organization was essential to tide over the situation. After having studied two different projects devising the technical details for establishing a "Single Seller", the Advisors to Government prepared a memorandum which was submitted on the 16th November to a Working Committee consisting of representatives of producers for their opinion. Representatives of some 40 factories believed that the Government's memorandum contained too much that savoured of the old V. I. S. P. After considerable discussions and after the projected ordinance had been considered by the Council of State and by the Minister for the Colonies, it was presented for discussion in the People's Council, which body adopted the Associated Sugar Ordinance on 23rd December 1932.

Finding that there were several modifications which totally marred the principle that had been the main consideration of the Government, the project could not be accepted. A few alterations were therefore made in the original draft, increasing the Government's influence, etc., after which the Governor-General promulgated the Associated Sugar Ordinance to become effective from 1st January 1933.

Thus on the 31st December 1932 was founded in Batavia the Netherlands Indian Association for the Sale of Sugar (NIVAS) with Head-quarters at Sourabaya. Its constitution was also approved by the Governor-General on the same date. He also appointed this Association to sell the sugar produced in accordance with Article 1 of the Associated Sugar Ordinance.

With this Act the transfer of new sugar, except such as was prepared in the native manner, became subject, from 1st January 1933, to 1st April 1936, to restrictive regulations, the NIVAS for for the period named, obtaining a sales monopoly for sugar.

The NIVAS admits as its members any owners or exploiters of one or more factories in Netherlands India that prepare sugar in a manner different from the native procedure.

Every year the members from among themselves appoint, for the period of one year at least 15 members who, together with the President of the Association (to be appointed by the Governor-General) without his necessarily having to be a member of the Association, and the Java Bank, jointly constitute the Board of Directors. To be designed a member of the Board of Directors, the candidate requires at least 1/25th of the total number of votes that can be cast at any members' meeting, and this is based on each one's share in the total normal production.

The members of the Board of Directors each year appoint six members who together with the President and the Java Bank jointly form the *Diurnal* Board with 2 members of the Board of Directors that may be appointed by the Governor-General.

The executive body of the Association has its headquarters at Sourabaya, which represents the Association both juridically and otherwise, in relation to acts, whether of property or management.

The constitution further contains provisions for establishing a sales office in Holland to be located at Amsterdam, as also a Supervisory and Advisory Council in Holland which is to be composed of members of the Association domiciled in Holland. Through such procedure the necessary contact with the European markets remains constant and the Association does not stand to lose the large experience of owners of sugar factories domiciled in Holland.

The Directorate and the Manager of the Sales Establishment in Holland are responsible for their management to the *Diurnal* Board.

The powers of the Government, in addition to those already mentioned, provide that the Governor-General can annul and prohibit decisions and actions of the organs of the Association. He can also order certain actions to be performed by the various organs of the Association. He appoints a Governmental commission consisting of two members, to which he issues instructions.

One of the members of this Commission will exclusively occupy himself with the sale and commercial aspects of the sugar, whilst the other member will look after the interests of the Industry as such and its relation to the country as a whole and to the population.

As regards the cessation of the Association, the Constitution and the Bye-laws determine that, as long as the Associated Sugar Ordinance remains in force, the Association itself cannot be dissolved. As soon as the ordinance ceases to be effective each member has the right to resign his membership at the end of a certain term which automatically dissolves the Association.

The constitution finally contains an Article providing for the creation of a Sugar Crisis Fund which aims at raising a subvention for such personnel of members of the Association as can reasonably be considered in this connection and have become unemployed since 1st January 1931.

The share of each member in the sugar sold is to be determined by the sugar he must supply, as settled for each member annually, a fraction whose numerator represents the export quantity assigned to him and whose denominator is the total of the export quantities determined for all members conjointly.

In calling for sugar to be delivered to purchasers in the course of any Association year the Directorate, in so far as is possible, will aim at calling upon each member in proportion to his share of delivery. As regards the call it has also been decided that, always observing the proportionate quantities to be delivered the amounts to be called for export and local sales will be divided amongst the members as adequately as possible.

Furthermore the possibility is included of transferring the delivery share or a part thereof. Through this measure a member may be able to obtain a disproportionate share in the call for any Association year, provided he can find another member willing to transfer his delivery share or a part thereof.

As regards the delivery of sugar, it has been ruled that the members shall take care to do so in good time at the usual shipping ports and that each of them will be responsible for the accurate delivery of their own sugars. Costs of transport and delivery, including storage and insurance prior to delivery, are to be borne by the member concerned. Special provisions cover delivery at unusual ports. A ruling is also made to the effect that at a members' meeting it may be decided, in case a reduction has been made on the purchase price in favour of any buyer by reason of delivery at a port inconvenient to him, that such reduction is to be charged to the member concerned. This last provision allows the trade in many cases to remain indifferent as regards the port of delivery of the sugars purchased, thus meeting an old grievance on this score.

To guard against levelling the quality of the sugars down to the average, the Board of Management shall make such proposals to the members in Assembly as will aim at an improvement of the quality produced.

Payment of sugar sold, barring certain exceptions, will be made by purchasers directly to the member having made delivery.

The directorate will keep a "General Sugar Account" on which the members will be debited for the prices received by them from buyers (including possible bonuses for overpolarization), increased by any allowances made and deducting whatever may be due or has been paid out for brokerage, and where necessary, further settlements. The members are to be credited with sugar actually delivered, with a reasonable allowance already or still to be determined, in reference to which provision is made in a combination of regulation.

Settlement is made on the basis of crystal. All sugars therefore, will be reduced to crystal value for which certain forms have been adopted, such as, superior head sugar and superior molasses on a basis of 99·4 per cent. crystal, canal molasses and sugar No. 16 and higher at 97·15% and Muscovado or so called "new assortment" at 95·45%.

The arrangements regarding pre-sales prior to the 8th November 1932, and of which delivery was to be made on or after 1st January 1933, were as follows:—

Such pre-sales, in so far as they relate to sugars ex-harvest 1933, if in the judgment of the Director of Agriculture, Industry and Commerce they were concluded in good faith, and in the manner customary in the sugar trade, are left entirely for the account of sellers under certain conditions:—

1. The quantity of such sugar will be regarded as having been called from the party concerned on the share to which he will prove to be entitled in the total sales

made by the Association from the period covering 1st April, 1933, to 31st March 1934; should it become evident that this share has been exceeded, the additional amount will be regarded as having been called against his share in the total sales effected by the Association in the directly subsequent period.

2. The members so concerned will share proportionately in the disadvantages to which the Association may be subject, as arising from the sale of sugars to markets that can be reached only at the sacrifices of price, that is to say such markets as are situated outside the so-called natural markets of Java.

With the coming into existence of the combination of arrangements, stated above, the Java Sugar Industry has entered upon a period in which all producers whilst setting aside their special group interests, have combined, under the supervision and with the co-operation of the Netherlands Indian Government, by means of a prudent sales policy to avert the crisis now prevailing, with the minimum sacrifices and losses, in the interests of the industry and people as a whole.

4. Sugar Selling Organisation—a benefit to the Industry.

India has an obvious lesson to learn from what Java has accomplished in the domain of sugar sales. If the manufacturers are to get the maximum price which market conditions permit, and to turn to the fullest use the protection granted to the industry, it is essential for them to have a fully representative sales organization with adequate financial backing and ware-housing facilities. The necessity of such an organisation cannot be too much emphasized. It is easy to see however, that the setting up of an effective central sales organization would be difficult, unless all sugar manufacturers could be persuaded to join the organization, unless severe penalties are imposed on members committing a breach of rules and unless a standard quality of Indian made sugar is arrived at as in Java where sales are controlled by "Nivas" and where all factories turn out sugar according to one or two definite classifications. Indian white sugar manufacturers have also to reckon with the competition of an unorganised body of producers of sugar known as the Khansaris who produce about 250,000 tons of sugar and who are too numerous to be included in the organization, owing to the administrative difficulty in dealing with them, as they are small units and spread over various villages. Much of their sugar is sold in the neighbourhood for local consumption, and the selling price of their sugar has an important bearing on the price of white sugar, especially the second quality factory sugar. Due to this competition of khandsari sugar, the sugar factories obtain a very low price for their second grade sugar. The difference in quality and appearance of white sugar factories' first and second sugars is trifling. Their first grade sugar has a sucrose content of 99·7 and their second sugar, of about 99 Considering the slightly inferior quality, the difference in the selling rate should not be more than eight annas a maund, (as was estimated by the Tariff Board) whereas it is about Rs. 1-8-0 to Rs. 2 per maund, at the present time. Due to this, many factories have spent large sums in plants for increasing the production of their first sugar, and to eliminate second sugar as far as possible, by employing various processes like "Norit."

5. Fixation of a Standard of Sugar Essential.

To prevent huge losses in the prices realised by the industry owing to the absence of an organization amongst the manufacturers, and the resultant, unduly keen internal competition in marketing, and waste of protection granted by the state, the necessity of a Central Sugar Sales Organization is paramount. Indian sugar can easily sell at about Rs. 9-12-0 per maund at Calcutta, in competition with Java sugar which sells at Rs. 10-4-0 per maund, but actually it sells at about Rs. 8-8-0 at Calcutta, and thus unnecessarily wastes a considerable amount of protection. But, as stated above, one of the greatest difficulty is the absence of standardization and grading of sugar produced in the various factories in the country. At present, the sugar differs in colour and grain from factory to factory, and, indeed, in some cases in the same factory, from day to day. On account of this, the present quotations in the sugar market are not based on any recognized standard quality. We find that each factory's sugar is quoted separately in its own name, the dealers knowing by their experience and inspection of sugar, the quality of sugar turned out by each. It is clear that a Central Sugar

Selling Organization cannot effect sales on the basis of samples of individual factories. It can only base its transaction on standards of known specifications irrespective of the factory which may produce any particular lot. We trust that the Indian Sugar Mills Association will take up this question in right earnest and make concerted efforts for bringing about a standardization of sugar with the help of experienced chemists. We might suggest that it would be desirable if two or three standards, depending on the different processes in factories *viz.*, one, of Carbonatation factories, another, of sulphitation, etc. were evolved to serve as a basis for transactions. If a few experienced Chemists undertake an enquiry and collect samples from a few factories, the problem of devising an agreed standard would not be difficult.

6. Difficulties to be Surmounted.

We are not unaware of the many and varied difficulties that exist in having an effective organization of all factories in India, owing, *e.g.*

1. To the absence of standardization of sugar;
2. To the fact that the industry is divided into small units, and scattered all over the country;
3. To the possibility of realization of higher prices by a few factories, situated in an advantageous geographical position, by individual sales, than by joint sales;

4. To suspicion and doubts about the successful working of such an organization; and

5. To the possibility of quick sales and immediate realization of money, by sales under personal control, etc.

We also find from experiene that such combination amongst manufacturers is not easily possible unless the industry is faced with difficult times, and unless each manufacturer realizes that if a combination is not forthcoming, it will operate severely to his detriment. For instance, as long as the Jute Industry in India was flourishing, it was not possible to think of a combination. It was only when the Jute Industry fell on bad times, owing to over-production that some agreement was arrived at in regard to restriction of output, with a view to pool up prices, and that, too, with very great difficulty, and after Government intervention. The same happened in the case of the Cement Industry in India. It was only after huge losses were caused to the cement factories, owing to cut-throat internal competition, and foreign cement began to come in, that a Cement Marketing Board could be thought of, with a view to eliminate internal cut-throat competition, and to effect joint sales for all factories. We are glad to note that the Cement Marketing Board is functioning satisfactorily, and has benefited the factories.

We are not very sanguine of any quick response from various factories to such an organization, particularly as long as some factories are able to sell their sugar more profitably than others, and have not tried their skill in selling their own sugar in any market they like for a season or two. We do feel however that in the interest of a scientific and sound development of the industry, such an organization is essential and imperative and would be very helpful. If due to such an organization, the industry is able to utilise fully the protection granted to it, the industry will be able to stand on its legs, within a period far shorter than that envisaged by the Tariff Board. Such an organization alone can effect scientific sales of sugar in suitable centres and can send sugar from factories advantageously situated in respect of various areas, and thus avoid unnecessary freight charges too.

We also trust that the Government of India will, if necessary, lend its helping hand to the industry, in bringing about such an organization. But we must emphasize that the creation of such an organization is largely dependent on voluntary efforts on the part of those engaged in the industry, and on inspiring confidence in the minds of factory owners that their interests will be safeguarded better by a joint and organized selling organization eliminating competition, overlapping, and unprofitable sales in nearest markets, than by individual sales, with the resultant wasteful competition, which will only depress prices to an abnormally low level.

The establishment of a Single Sugar Selling Organization is well worth a trial and sugar factory owners should give this mater their careful consideration.

CHAPTER XII.

Proposed Excise Duty on Indian Sugar, and Regulation of Cane Prices.

I. Proposed Excise Duty on Sugar.

The Hon'ble Finance Member in the Course of his budget proposals *for the Government of India for the year 1934-35 announced that the Government of India propose to impose an excise duty on the production of sugar in India at the rate of Rs. 1-5-0 per cwt. which works out to roughly 0-15-4·5 per maund of sugar. The sugar (Excise Duty) Bill was introduced in the Assembly in March 1934†. The imposition of such a heavy excise duty on the industry within less than two years of the grant of protection to the industry is very unfortunate, and very premature, particularly when it is remembered that relying on the Government's promise of protection to the industry for 7 years in the first instance, the public invested about Rs. 20 crores, and the sugar industry has developed so well and enabled the country to become practically self-sufficient in the matter of sugar within *only two* years of the date of the grant of protection. Besides this, the imposition of the duty considerably reduces the protection to the industry against imported sugar due to the fact

*Relevant Extracts from his speech are given in Appendix II(a).

†The text of the Sugar (Excise Duty) Bill is given in Appendix. II(b).

that since the Tariff Board reported the sugar mills are not able to realise any value from the sale of their molasses. The Tariff Board expected that the factories would be able to reduce their cost of production per maund of sugar by Rs. 0-10-8 due to the realization from molasses during the initial period of protection. As explained in a previous chapter a position has been reached when it necessitates some expenditure on the part of the sugar factories to dispose of their molasses. In addition to that, the high freight charges for selling sugar in distant markets, *e.g.*, from various factories in Bihar and United Provinces to Madras, Karachi, Calcutta, Rangoon, the freight to which exceeds Rs. 1-8-0 per maund, reduces the extent of protection to the industry, due to the fact that prices at the ports cannot be kept at a high level, in view of the competition of imported sugar at the ports.

The Government are also aware that due to the absence of any organization in the industry, and the very keen internal competition, Indian sugar mills have not been able to derive the full benefits of the protective duty, as can be seen from the fact that they sell their sugar at about Rs. 1-8-0 to Rs. 1-12-0 per maund lower than the price of imported sugar at the ports, even when the difference in quality does not warrant a reduction of more than 6 annas per maund. If out of revenue necessities, the Government require money, and if an excise duty has to be imposed, either its extent should be reduced or there ought to be a suitable increase in the import duty in order to make it difficult for foreign sugar to compete with

Indian sugar particularly when India is in a position to supply all the sugar she needs. The Government contend that the present duty of Rs. 9-1-0 per cwt., is Rs. 1-13-0 above the basic duty of Rs. 7-4-0 recommended by the Tariff Board and that even if an excise duty of Rs. 1-5-0 per cwt., is levied it still leaves 8 annas more per cwt. The Government have, however, decided to increase the measure of protection by 8 annas in accordance with the recommendation of the Tariff Board which stated that protection should be increased if Java sugar was being imported at a price less than Rs. 4 per maund at Calcutta In point of fact in March 1934 the landed price of Java sugar was Rs. 3-2-0 per maund without duty and in view of the large stocks that Java holds, and the deterioration in the quality of her sugar produced more than 2 years ago, it is not unlikely that Java may cut her prices further in order to unload her stocks because the sugar is now sold not on the usual standard, but on sample. There is the further possibility of a fall in the prices of Java sugar if she goes off the Gold Standard. It would therefore be advisable if the Government increase the import duty on sugar, which while it may bring no benefit to the sugar industry of the country by effecting an increase in the price of Indian sugar, owing to keen internal competition, will certainly enable it to capture distant markets, *e.g.*, Madras, Trichinopoly, Rangoon, etc.

2. DECLINE IN PROFITS.

It is also not clear to us how the Government have thought fit to impose such a heavy excise duty immediately after guaranteeing protection to the industry for a period of 15 years. It is difficult to acquiesce with the statement made by Sir George Schuster, the Finance Member, that the excise duty is necessary to prevent further expansion. The profits of the industry have already fallen, and there is hardly any danger of "continuing the stimulus," as can be seen from the following table, which will illustrate the position of the Industry in the light of the Tariff Board's recommendations.

TABLE NO. 42.

Position of the industry and its profits.

—	At commencement of Protective Period.	At end of Protective Period. of 15 years.	Actual as in February 1934.
	Rs. As. P.	Rs. As. P.	Rs. As. A.
Fair Price of Sugar ...	9 5 9	7 12 5	7 12 0
Of which, cost of cane ...	5 8 10	4 0 0	4 0 0
	3 12 11	3 12 5	3 12 0
Add back value of Molasses	0 10 8	0 6 9	nil.
Balance to represent manufacturing cost, Overhead Charges and 10% Profit on Capital invested	4 7 7	4 3 2	3 12 0

The figures shown in the last column represent the average market value ex-factory of Indian Factory Sugar in February 1934 and the average cost of cane per maund sugar at Rs. 0-6-0 delivered, with extraction at 9%. Notwithstanding the apparently high protective duty the return to the factory is less by Rs. 0-7-2 than that envisaged by the Tariff Board at the end of the protective period without taking into account the proposed excise duty of Rs. 0-15-4·5 per maund.

The extra protection provided by the surcharge has also become largely ineffective owing to the rapid expansion of the industry in the last two years. In the table below we give balance sheets of a few sugar companies in order to enable the reader to find out the extent of the profit made by the industry, and to appraise the situation in its proper perspective.

TABLE NO. 43.

Balance Sheets of Sugar Companies.

Names.	Paid-up Capital Ordinary.	Gross Block Account.	Dividends per cent. for year.		Return of Percentages on on Block for 1933.
			1932.	1933.	
	Rs.	Rs.			
Basti Sugar ...	11,96,759	27,71,028	30	25	10
Carew (Sugar) ...	16,00,000	14,27,258	12½	15	16
Cawnpore Sugar ...	15,00,000	68,43,810	35	30	6
Punjab Sugar Mills, Co	7,26,000 2,37,000	16,19,015	40	20	11
New Savan Sugar and Gur ...	11,00,000	20,33,082	15	12½	6·6
Purtabpur Sugar ...	9,00,000	28,20,889	10	10	3·2

New Companies Established in 1932.

				1933	
Bharat Sugar ...	5,00,000	8,44,975	...	10	5·9
Ganesh Sugar ...	8,00,000	9,47,372	...	10	8·5
New Swadeshi ...	7,25,000	12,08,991	...	8	4·8
Diamond Sugar ...	10,00,000	10,35,707	...	...	2·6

(Net Profit Rs. 26,000).

First six balance sheets are of companies established before the grant of protection to the industry in 1932. The rest are of Companies established after 1932. An examination of the balance sheets of the newer companies will reveal the fact that their profits are far too smaller. The excise duty will affect adversely particularly the new factories, over 70 factories having commenced operations only this year, and some being even under construction. We are aware that as a result of the policy of protection to the sugar industry the Govenmment's revenue from the import duty on sugar has dried up almost completely and therefore the Government have thought of this source of revenue, but we do feel that the imposition of the excise duty is, to say the least, premature and will surely affect adversely the interests of the manufacturers, particularly the new factories, and also the agricultrists. The Legislative Councils of the U. P., the Punjab, and Madras and the various Chambers of Commerce also have looked with great disfavour upon this imposition of the excise duty by the Government of India at this juncture, as they are apprehensive that it will operate harshly on the industry* as well as on sugarcane producers, and the consumers.

3. BENEFIT TO CONSUMERS.

It is hardly necessary to reiterate that the Indian factories will not be able to pass on the duty, by increas-

---

*The Punjab Legislative Council passed the following resolution unanimously on the 12th March 1934 :—

"In the opinion of this House, the proposed imposition of an excise duty was prejudical to the interests of the sugarcane producers and consumers and manufacturers of sugar in the Punjab"

On the 7th March, 1934, an adjournment motion was carried in the United Provinces Legislative Council against the proposal to levy an Excise Duty on Sugar, and the Government did not challenge a division.

The Madras Legislative Council also passed a similar Resolution denouncing the excise duty, unanimously.

ing the price of sugar, to the consumer, in view of the internal competition. As we have shown in a previous chapter, the burden of the protection granted to the industry, on the consumer has been minimum. The following table will illustrate the price the Indian consumer would have to pay (*a*) for Java sugar, (*b*) for Indian sugar at the average value recommended by the Tariff Board (Rs. 8-13-1) and (*c*) actually paid at present market rates; (in each case Re. 1 per maund has been added to factory or Port price for freight to consuming centres). The consumption is calculated at 6,00,000 tons.

TABLE NO. 44.

Present sugar prices compared with Tariff Board's figures.

Java Sugar. @ Rs. 10/2/- per md. plus freight. 6,00,000 tons.	Tariff Board's recommendation. @ Rs 8/13/1 per md. plus freight 6,00,000 tons.	Actual Price in February 1934. @ Rs. 7/12/- per md. plus freight. 6,00,000 tons.
18,02,25,000	15,90 46,870	14,17,50,000

It is clear that this industry is to-day supplying India with sugar at a saving of Rs. 3,84,75,000 below the present Java price, and of Rs. 1,72,96,870 below the average price recommended by the Tariff Board.

In this connection we would refer the reader to the representation submitted by the sugar manufacturers to the Government of India on the 8th March 1934 relating to the imposition of an excise duty on sugar, and the control of sugar cane-prices to sugar factories in British India.*

* The representation is printed in Appendix II(d).

4. SUGAR CANE-PRICE REGULATING BILL.

The Government of India introduced a Sugar Cane Bill in the Indian Legislative Assembly on the 13th of March 1934, in order to regulate the price of sugar cane for the use of sugar factories*. The actual fixing of prices for canes is left to the Provincial Governments so as to suit local conditions. It is also proposed that Provincial Governments should declare "controlled areas" within which the purchase of cane by factories would be limited to growers of cane or licensed persons and societies at fixed prices.

5. CANE-PRICE FIXING NO ADVANTAGE.

We have dealt with this question exhaustively in Chapter 6† and have come to the conclusion that legislation for fixing of price of cane will be found impracticable, unworkable, and disadvantageous, both to manufacturers and agriculturists. We would also refer the reader to the opinion expressed in the representation of the sugar manufacturers (printed in Appendix II (*d*) wherein the subject has been discussed fully. We earnestly hope that Local Governments will give this matter their most thorough and anxious consideration before introducing legislation for fixing minimum prices of cane for factories.

6. GOVERNMENT DUTY TO HELP GROWTH OF INDUSTRY.

In the end we would urge the Government to consider the possibility of postponing for some time the levy of

---

* The text of the bill introduced in the Assembly on the 13th March is given in Appendix II(c).

† *Vide* pages 155 to 160.

the excise duty on Indian sugar till the next year and also of reducing it to some extent. We would further suggest that the Government should earmark at least 25% of the proceeds of the excise duty for carrying on research work in improving the quality of sugar cane, the utilisation of by-products of the industry, etc., and should spend the amount in such a way as to enable the industry to reduce its cost of production appreciably within a measurable period of time, and to do away with the necessity of protection. We hope that in appreciation of the fact that the Indian sugar industry gives employment to over 80,000 factory-workers, and represents investment on the part of the public of no less than 20 crores of Rupees since the date of the grant of protection,and that the interests of not less than 15 million cultivators are closely bound up with the development and prosperity of the industry, the Government will take a sympathetic interest in its continued progress, and enable it to reach at an early date a stage when it may rank among the most efficient and premier cane-sugar manufacturing industries of the world, able to meet the requirements not only of this country, but also of the British Empire.

APPENDICES

APPENDIX I.

ABOLITION OF SURCHARGE ON SUGAR.*

BY

M. P. GANDHI, M.A.,

Secretary, Indian Sugar Mills Association, Calcutta.

Sugar Industry Accorded Protection in 1932.

With the approach of the Budget Sessions of the Assembly rumours are afloat that the Government of India may remove with effect from 1st April, 1934, the surcharge of 25 per cent. on the import duty on Sugar which was imposed as a revenue measure under the Indian Finance (Supplementary and Extending) Act, 1931. The present duty on imports of sugar is Rs. 9-1-0 per cwt., out of which Rs. 7-4-0 constitutes the prospective duty as recommended by the Tariff Board and Re. 1-13 constitutes the surcharge.

Production of Sugar in Excess of Present Requirements.

Since the grant of protection to the industry, the increase in the number of sugar factories has been very satisfactory in as much as over 100 sugar factories of about 600 tons cane-crushing capacity have been established within a year and a half of the date of the grant of protection. It is true that the quantum of protection recommended by the Tariff Board was Rs. 7-4-0 and that Re. 1-13 is only a surcharge imposed purely for revenue reasons and not with a view to add to the protection accorded to the sugar industry, though the surcharge has had, according to the Government of India, necessarily that effect. While the industry may not ordinarily be able to protest against the suggestion of abolition of this surcharge which is purely a revenue measure, the present position of the industry, as will be shown presently, makes it absolutely imperative that the surcharge should continue, if the industry in which over 15 crores of rupees are invested only during the last two years, is not to come to grief. As the Government are aware the production of sugar in the country has increased from 487,000 tons in 1931-32

* Published in December, 1933.

to about 700,000 tons in 1932-33 and it is expected that during the year 1933-34 the total production will be not less than 11 lakh tons, of which the production from factories alone would come to over 775,000 tons, the balance being production from indigenous methods India can be said to have, practically reached a stage where not only is she self-sufficient in regard to the requirements of sugar for home-consumption, but there is a clear necessity of finding export markets for her production, unless the consumption of sugar in the country goes up as a result of the improvement in the economic condition of the people. The import of sugar has gone down from 516,000 tons in 1931-32 to 401,000 tons in 1932 and only 162,000 tons during the seven months ended October, 1933. India does not need to import any sugar at all except of very special quality to meet the requirements of those having a fastidious taste, and I expect that the import in 1934-35 will be less than 50,000 tons.

Interests of 18 Million Cultivators Threatened.

Protection has been guaranteed to the sugar industry for a period of seven years, in the first instance and further eight years if necessary in order that the industry may be able to develop to an extent which would make her independent of foreign supplies and stand on its own legs. Fortunately for this country such a stage has been reached only within two years of the grant of protection and if instead of appreciating the quick response of the industrialists in implementing the policy of protection inaugurated by the Government, the surcharge is removed, it will create a deplorable plight in the industry and will take away all confidence of the people in the *bona fides* of the action of the Government. What is more, the implications of the grant of protection to the sugar industry must be fully understood. Protection was granted to this industry, not only for the purpose of establishing a sugar manufacturing in the country, but also, and largely, with a view to benefit the agriculturists. In fact the Tariff Board observed that the strongest aspect of the case for protection is that based upon the national importance of promoting the cultivation of sugarcane. The expansion of the sugar industry has been a source of great satisfaction and relief to the ryots particularly at the present time when the prices of almost all crops have fallen to an unremunerative level, inasmuch as it is the only crop which has brought them a fair return, when other crops have failed to do so. The Government are also aware that in a large number of cases it has been possible for the agriculturists to pay their land-revenue also, because of the proceeds realised from the cane crop which is a cash crop. The retention of the surcharge is absolutely necessary if a crisis is to be averted, in the case of the manufacturers as well as the agriculturists. It is estimated that about 18 million people are directly interested in cane cultivation, and their interests will be seriously threatened if circumstances arise in which the area under cane diminishes.

Why Surcharge is Necessary.

It may be argued that the industry enjoys fairly high protection of over 15 per cent. and there is no necessity of the maintenance of this surcharge. It is necessary to point out that there has been one important factor which has necessitated the increase in protection, and that is the calamitous fall in the price of molasses. When the Tariff Board examined the question of protection to the industry, the molasses fetched a price of Re. 1-8 to Rs. 2 per maund. Due to overproduction of molasses a stage has now been reached when it requires some expenditure on the part of the factory owners to dispose of his molasses. Far from bringing a revenue to him, its disposal costs him money and it has become a nuisance. His cost of production has therefore gone up to that extent.

Why Surcharge is not Harmful to any one.

It must also be pointed out that the retention of the surcharge on sugar is in no way harmful to the consumer and it is therefore futile to base any argument on the ground of bringing relief to the consumer, as it is well-known that due to the internal competition there has been a considerable fall in the price of sugar from 1932 onwards and the present position is that the price of *Indian sugar bears no relation whatever to price of imported Java white sugar.* It sells about Rs. 2 per maund lower than imported sugar. If the ruling prices of Indian sugar had any relation with or were as high as the prices of imported sugar one could understand, in the interest of the consumers, the necessity of taking off the surcharge duty, on the ground that it would constitute an unnecessary burden on the consumer, and give an extra protection or profit to the manufacturer. The Government are well aware that the prices of Indian sugar are determined not in relation to the price at which imported sugar from Java is selling, but by internal competition, which is increasing, and constitutes the best safeguard in the interest of the consumer. Since the grant of protection, this cost of production, has considerably gone down, and it is likely that as a result of the growing internal competition, the prices of Indian sugar will witness a further fall. Therefore there is no weight in any argument that may be adduced for the removal of the surcharge. In fact, if the duty on imported sugar were made prohibitive or even if the import of sugar were completely stopped, the interest of the consumers would not suffer at all, and the manufacturer would make no more profit than he can or does at present, owing to the play of keen internal competition. Indeed, it might be observed with truth, that the sugar industry constitutes the best example for proving that the consumers have had to undergo the minimum of sacrifice, due to the rapid growth of the industry and the resultant keen competition.

Unsettlement of Import Trades Inevitable.

The unsettlement caused to the import trade was an inevitable conclusion of the grant of adequate protection to the industry, and could be no argument for removal of the surcharge. The progressive reduction of import of sugar was a foregone conclusion and instead of feeling worried at it, everyone having the interest of his own country at heart should feel jubilant. The proposal of the removal of the surcharge can thus be made only on one ground, viz., of bringing revenue to the coffers of the State. But it is clear that for the sake of earning a small revenue, the State cannot take a measure which would bring calamity and grief to an indigenous industry, fostered deliberately by the Government by the imposition of a protective duty for a long number of years. If after deciding to promote this industry, and taking suitable action on it, the surcharge duty of Re. 1-13 per cwt. which has helped in the speedy development of this industry, and the continuance of which has been rendered necessary in view of the absence of any realisation for molasses, and the retention of which causes no harm to the consumers, is removed at this critical juncture on account of the demand made by a few interested persons engaged in importing sugar, or for purposes of getting revenue for the State, it would be nothing short of a crime against the manufacturers who invested over 15 crores of rupees in establishing factories in the expectation of getting continued help from the State, at least during the period of infancy of the industry, and against the 18 million agriculturists who extended the cultivation of their cane on the expectation of the increase of manufacture of sugar in the country. The area under cultivation has gone up from 29,00,000 acres in 1930-31 to 34,00,000 acres in 1933-34 and the yield of cane is expected to be 50,000,000 tons in 1933-34 as compared with 35,000,000 tons in 1930-31. The Tariff Board also recommended that if any real development in the sugar industry is to be secured, if new factories are to be established, land improvement and irrigation undertaken with a view to cane cultivation, it is essential that both the agriculturist and the industrialist should be assured of protection for at least 15 years.

Retrograde Proposal of Associated Chambers for Removal of Surcharge.

I hope and trust that the Government will pay no heed to the very determintal proposal which is going to be made by the Bengal Chamber of Commerce who have proposed for discussion at the next Annual Meeting of the Associated Chambers of Commerce to be held in January 1934, a resolution inviting the attention of the Government to the critical position of the sugar import trade caused by the crushing burden of taxation imposed upon it, and while *recognising the need for the adequate protection of the indigenous sugar producing industry, urging the removal of the 25 per cent. surcharge* on import of sugar.

Duty of the Imperial Council and Assembly.

I fervently hope that the Imperial Council of Agricultural Research owing to whose strenuous efforts, protection is granted to the industry, will represent strongly to the Government, pointing out how detrimental the suggestion made by the representatives of importer's interest in India for the withdrawal of the surcharge on import of sugar would be, if accepted, to the cause of Indian agriculture and Industry. Any such action, as has been suggested, on the part of the Government can only be interpreted as the index of their desire to let down the manufacturers and agriculturists who extended their activities in the sphere, relying on the Government and their *bona fides*. On the contrary, it is the duty of the Government to watch the prices at which foreign sugar is being imported and if, as a result of Java's going off the Gold standard or of other factors there is any possibility of sugar being imported in the country at a price lower than that manufactured in the country, to increase the production to such an extent that import of sugar would be impossible. As sugar producing countries have high tariffs and regulation of imports, India should also take suitable action in such a manner to aid her industry. For if any imports of sugar are allowed to come into the country, the manufacturers as also the agriculturists would be faced with ruin in all parts of the country.

Growth of Industry will Receive Rude Shock.

Bengal, Bombay, Madras which have not yet made suitable progress in the manufacture of sugar, have now started doing so and it is expected they will establish more factories next year. If however, the Government take any action of the character about to be suggested by the Associated Chambers of Commerce, at the instance of the Bengal Chamber, grave injury would be done to the agricultural and industrial interests in the country. It is surprising that in view of this growing interest in the province of Bengal, which let me incidentally observe, is very well suited for the development of the sugar industry, the Bengal Chamber should have thought it fit to make a proposal which would ruin the cultivators and damp the enthusiasm of the industrialists. I hope that industrial, agricultural, and general public opinion in India will express itself unequivocally in condemnation of this suggestion, and invite the attention of the Government to the great injury likely to be inflicted on the various provinces, as a result of the adoption of the step suggested by the Bengal Chamber. Personally I have no doubt that the Government will summarily dismiss this proposal of the Bengal Chamber of Commerce in the interest of the country. It is, however, their bounden duty to give an immediate and satisfactory assurance to the industry, which they have sought to foster and to continue to take a sympathetic interest in the continued development of the industry with which welfare of the agriculturists and manufacturers is closely bound up.

REMOVAL OF SURCHARGE A CALAMITY.*

Retention necessary for Preservation of Industry.

By

M. P. Gandhi,

Secretary, Indian Sugar Mills Association, Calcutta.

1. The following resolution will be put up by the Bengal Chamber of Commerce for consideration at the next Annual Meeting of the Associated Chambers of Commerce† on the 8th January recommending the abolition of the surcharge on sugar.

> "This Association invites the attention of the Government of India to the critical position of the sugar import trade caused by the crushing burden of taxation imposed upon it ; and while recognising the need for the adequate protection of the indigenous sugar producing industry, the Association urges that consideration be given to the removal of the 25% surcharge imposed as a revenue measure under the Indian Finance (Supplementary and Extending) Act, 1931, thereby reducing the rate of duty from one of Rs. 9-1 per cwt. to one of Rs. 7-4 per cwt. which was the rate of protective duty recommended by the Indian Tariff Board."

2. I understand that the Resolution is being put up at the instance of importers, and will be opposed by several Chambers, including the Punjab Chamber of Commerce and the Upper India Chamber of Commerce, representing the interests of the manufacturers and the general public.

3. I desire to set out briefly a few points why the surcharge on sugar should not be abolished at the present juncture.

(1) The surcharge of Re. 1/13/- per cwt. in addition to the protective duty of Rs. 7/4/- per cwt. has helped considerably the speedy development of the industry and brought it to a stage, within two years of the grant of

* Published 6th January, 1934.

† This resolution was passed by a majority.

protection, when it can render the country independent of foreign countries for its requirements of sugar.

(2) The surcharge has constituted *no additional burden* on the consumer inasmuch as the price of sugar in India has been considerably less than the price of imported sugar, and is determined not in relation to foreign prices, but by internal competition.

(3) The surcharge has been instrumental in preventing imports of sugar from Java which is prepared to sell her sugar at any price in order to reduce its stocks.

(4) The Tariff Board recommended an additional duty in case the landed price of sugar in Calcutta falls below Rs. 4/- per maund. At the present time Java sells white sugar at Rs. 2/15 per maund in the West Coast of India which only shows that Java is willing to sell its sugar below its cost of production and at a loss for the only purpose of reducing her huge accumulated stocks and with a view to deal a blow to the sugar industry of India. It is not generally known that in November 1933 when white sugar was sold to other destinations by Java at Fl. 4·95 and 4·85 per 100 kilograms, it was dumped into British India at Fl. 4·60 on the East Coast and Fl. 4·40 on the West Coast. The present limit for the West Coast is Fl. 4·20. Therefore, even if the surcharge is removed the Government should increase the duty in accordance with the above recommendations of the Tariff Board.

(5) The removal of the surcharge will give a great set-back to the industry and will spell ruin of 18 million of cultivators, for improving whose conditions protection was largely granted. This will also affect the revenue collections of the Government who have been able to realise their rents from the cash money received by the cultivators by the sale of canes. The removal of the surcharge will deal a great blow to manufacturers and investors in this industry. The investment in the sugar industry *after the grant of protection represents* a sum

of not less than Rs. 20 crores and in addition to the investment before 1931, the total investment would be nothing less than Rs. 30 crores in which both Europeans and Indians are interested.

(6) The absence of any realisation for molasses as was calculated by the Tariff Board when framing the recommendations for the grant of protection to this industry has proved a great handicap to the industry, and has increased the cost of production to that extent.

(7) The necessity of having to send sugar over large distances exceeding 800 miles in some cases as for example from the various sugar factories in the U. P. and Bihar and Orissa to distant markets like Karachi and Madras, the freight charges for which per maund amount to Re. 1/8 to Rs. 1/12 renders it necessary to maintain the surcharge as otherwise it will be impossible for the sugar factories in India to compete with foreign sugar at these places, and the industry which is capable of producing from this year all the sugar that India needs, will come to grief.

(8) The removal of the surcharge at this juncture will be a great injustice on the part of the Government and will take away the confidence of the people in the *bona fides* of the desire of the Government to foster industries in India.

(9) The ground urged by the importers for the removal of the surcharge, *viz.*, the unsettlement caused to the import trade was an inevitable conclusion of the grant of adequate protection to the industry, and is therefore entirely unconvincing.

4. I trust that in appreciation of the fact that the imposition of the surcharge constitutes no additional burden on the consumer, that its removal will spell ruin both to agriculturists and manufacturers, who have extended their cultivation and launched in this manufacture relying on the expectation of the Government support and assistance, and will also thwart the development of the sugar industry in provinces like Bengal, Madras, etc., the Government of

India will reject the proposal, take no action which would act like an impediment to the development of sugar industry, with which the well-being of the agriculturists and the manufacturers, is closely bound up, and assure all concerned that they will continue to take all steps for the preservation and development of the industry.

APPENDIX II.

SUGAR INDUSTRY (PROTECTION) ACT, 1932.

ACT NO. XIII of 1932.

The following is the full text of the Sugar Industry (Protection) Act, 1932.

An Act to provide for the Fostering and Development of the Sugar Industry in British India.

Whereas it is expedient, in pursuance of the policy of discriminating protection of industries in British India with due regard to the well-being of the community, to provide for the fostering and development of the sugar industry for a period ending with the 31st day of March, 1946, by determining the extent of the protection to be conferred up to the 31st day of March, 1938, and by making provision for the determination of the extent of the protection to be conferred for the remainder of the period. It is hereby enacted as follows :—

Short Title.

1. This Act may be called the Sugar Industry (Protection) Act, 1932 (Amendment of Schedule II, Act VIII of 1894).

2. (1) In the Second Schedule to the Indian Tariff Act, 1894 (VIII of 1894), there shall be made the amendments specified in the Schedule to this Act.

(2) The amendments made by sub-section (1) shall have effect up to the 31st day of March, 1938.

Statutory Inquiry.

3. The Governor-General in Council shall cause to be made, by such persons as he may appoint in this behalf, an inquiry to ascertain if the protection of the sugar industry during the period from the 31st day of March, 1938, to the 31st day of March, 1946, should be continued to the extent conferred by this Act, or to a greater or lesser extent, and shall, not later than the 31st day of

March, 1938, lay his proposals in this behalf before the Indian Legislature.

Power to Increase Duty Imposed by Section 2.

4. If the Governor-General in Council is satisfied, after such inquiry as he thinks fit, that sugar not manufactured in India is being imported into British India at such a price as is likely to render insufficient the benefits intended to be conferred upon the sugar industries by the duties imposed by Section 2, he may, by notification in the *Gazette of India,* increase such duty to such extent as he thinks fit.

Power to make Rules requiring returns.

5. The Governor-General in Council may, by notification in the *Gazette of India,* make rules requiring the owners of sugar factories in British India to make such returns relating to the production of sugar in their factories as the Governor-General in Council may consider to be desirable, prescribing, the form of such returns, the dates of their submission and the authority to which they shall be submitted.

Power to make Rules requiring Notices of Prices of Sugarcane to be posted up in Sugar Factories.

6. (1) The local Government may, by notification in the local official Gazette, make rules requiring that there shall be affixed, in conspicuous places near the entrances to sugar factories, notices for the information of sellers of sugarcane, and such rules may prescribe the form and languages of such notices ; and the particulars to be included therein relating to prices at which sugarcane is being bought at the factory.

(2) In making such rules the local Government may provide that a contravention thereof shall be punishable with fine which may extend to five hundred rupees.

Explanation.—In this section and in section 5 "factory" has the meaning assigned to it in clause (3) of Section 2 of the Indian Factories Act, 1911 (XII of 1911).

THE SCHEDULE.

(See Section 2).

Amendments to be made in Schedule II to the Indian Tariff Act, 1894.

1. In Part II.

(*a*) For the heading "Sugar" and Item No. 34, the following heading and item shall be substituted, namely:—

Other Food and Drink.

34 Molasses—*Ad valorem* 25 per cent.

(*b*) the heading "Saccharine" above Item No. 34-A shall be omitted; and

(*c*) the heading "Other Food and Drink" above Item No. 35 shall be omitted.

2. In Part VII, after Item No. 156, the following heading and item shall be inserted, namely:—

"SUGAR."

157 Sugar and sugarcandy, excluding confectionary Rs. 7/4/- per cwt.

3. Item No. 156-A shall be re-numbered as Item No. 150.

4. In Part VII under the head "Miscellaneous"

(*a*) in the first column, the figures "157," "158" and "159" shall be omitted;

(*b*) the heading "Matches," Undipped Splints and "Veneers" shall be numbered as Item No. 159; and

(*c*) in the second column, the entries relating to "Matches," "Undipped Splints" and "Veneers" shall be lettered, respectively, as sub-items (*a*), (*b*) and (*c*) of Item No. 159.

Summary of Tariff Board Recommendations.

The following are the sections from the summary of the Tariff Board's Report (1931) in so far as they bear on the protective duties:

Any scheme of bounties is on administrative grounds impracticable. If khandsari manufacturers were included in the scheme, it would be impossible to devise machinery for assessing and checking the bounty. If the khandsari industry were excluded from the scheme, central sugar factories would be given an unfair advantage over this branch of the industry.

We propose therefore that the assistance given should be by way of duty. In order to enable the industry to face initial difficulties and to safeguard the position of the manufacturer of indigenous sugar by the bel method in Rohilkhand we propose that for the first seven years the duty should be fixed at Rs. 7/4/- per cwt., and for the remaining period at Rs. 6/4/- per cwt. The total protection thus granted would be approximately the same as would result from the imposition of a duty of Rs. 6/9/3 for the whole period of protection.

We recommend that the period of protection should be for 15 years.

Since agreement regarding export quotas appears to have been arrived at by the leading sugar producing countries, we have with some hesitation decided to recommend no further immediate increase in duty beyond the protective duty already recommended. We recommend that should the present international negotiations for stabilisation of prices fail or should market prices in Calcutta in the future fall below Rs. 4 without duty, a further duty of annas 8 per cwt., should immediately be imposed.

It is suggested that power to impose this duty should be vested in the Governor-General in Council but that subsequent to the imposition of such duty sanction of the Legislature should be obtained for the continuance of the deferred duty and for the fixation of the period for which it is to be in force.

We propose that the duties should apply to all classes of sugar including sugarcandy.

Expenditure on development and research in connection with sugarcane in India is on a scale which in view of the importance of the sugarcane crop may be considered small, particularly when compared to expenditure in such countries as Java and Hawaii. We propose that increased sums should be allotted to development and research work since without such measures the whole purpose of the protective scheme is likely to be delayed if not defeated. Indeed we regard this as almost a condition precedent to protection.

We would recommend a grant of not less than Rs. 10 lakhs annually to the Imperial Council of Agricultural Research for this purpose. If our scheme of protection is accepted we consider that legislation should be introduced making it compulsory for sugar factories to submit such returns or information as may be called for by the Governor-General in Council or any officer authorised by him in this behalf.

We consider that the scale for cane payment recommended by the Indian sugar committee, namely a sliding scale based on price for cane equal to half the price of sugar manufactured from it subject to a minimum of annas six per maund is generally suitable. But in the first years of protection we consider that this should be increased by one anna per maund.

We would recommend that power should be taken to enable the Governor-General in Council or any authority authorised by him in this behalf to issue rules requiring sugar factories to post in a conspicuous place at the entrance to the factories notices specifying such matters in connection with rates paid for cane as may be thought fit.

Government of India's Communique.

A Communique was issued by the Government of India on the 30th January, 1932, which may be summarised as follows :—

(1) The Government of India accepted the recommendation of the Board that a single rate of duty should apply to all classes of sugar, but considered that an initial protective period of fifteen years was unduly long. They, therefore, decided that protective duty at the rate of Rs. 7/4/- per cwt. be imposed on all classes

of sugar until the 31st March, 1938, and that provision be made in the Statute for a further enquiry, before the end of that period, into the question of continuing protection to the industry.

(2) Government did not accept the Board's recommendation that power should be taken to impose an additional duty in the event of the price of imported sugar falling below a certain level.

(3) Government accepted the recommendations of the Board that the duty on molasses should remain unaltered ; also that power should be taken by Statute to call for such returns from sugar factories as the Governor-General in Council may consider necessary to prescribe.

(4) Government promised careful consideration of the Board's recommendation that an annual grant of not less than Rs. 10 lakhs should be made for sugar research, but owing to financial stringency they could give no undertaking to carry this into effect.

(5) The Government of India were unable to accept the recommendation of the Board that the new sugar companies should be compelled to be registered as public companies. The application of the Board's recommendation that no assistance in the form of loan, grant subsidy or other concession should be given to a new company unless it complies with the conditions laid down in paragraph 292 of the Fiscal Commission's Report was left to the discretion of Local Governments.

Assembly Select Committee's Recommendations.

The Bill was referred for consideration to a Select Committee of the Assembly. Amongst their recommendation, the following may be mentioned :—

(*i*) Government should give a guarantee to the industry that it will be protected for a period of fifteen years as recommended by the Tariff Board, (*ii*) Government should have power to vary the duty to provide against protection being impaired.

(*iii*) In order to safeguard the interests of growers of cane power should be given to Government to require sugar factories to post notices specifying such matters in connection with the prices being paid for cane at the factories as may be considered necessary. A section was added to the draft bill giving local Governments power to make rules to give effect to this recommendation. Small factories, outside the scope of the Indian Factories Act, 1911, were, however, exempted from this provision.

(*iv*) The Customs authorities should watch for any developments whereby sugar may be converted into some product resembling confectionary for the purpose of evasion of import duty, and if any such evasion is reported, Government should take immediate steps to prevent it.

(*v*) Government should provide adequate funds for the Imperial Council of Agricultural Research for schemes of research and development, including the establishment of the proposed Sugar Research Institute, without which the entire purpose of the protective scheme may be delayed, if not defeated.

(*vi*) To guard against the danger of interests outside the British Empire taking advantage of the protective Tariff by establishing sugar factories in India to the detriment of Indian interests, Government should watch developments in this direction, with a view to considering whether any action should be taken to prevent the control of the industry, or of any considerable part of it, from falling into foreign hands.

Several of the above recommendations made by the Select Committee were accepted by Government, and the Sugar Industry (Protection) Act of the Indian Legislature (given above) eventually received the assent of the Governor-General on the 8th April, 1932.

APPENDIX II (*a*).

EXTRACTS FROM THE SPEECH BY THE HON'BLE FINANCE MEMBER IN INTRODUCING THE BUDGET PROPOSALS FOR 1934-35.

* * * * *

17. On the other hand there are certain important items in regard to which special factors will be operative and will produce a loss of customs revenue.

SUGAR.—The most important single item is sugar, in the case of which the very rapid development of local manufacture, to which I have already referred and to which I shall refer again, seems to be leading towards the early extermination of imports on a substantial scale. Indeed it is no exaggeration to say that the success of our protective policy for sugar is the main cause of our budgetary difficulties. In 1930-31 we raised over 10½ crores from sugar. Even in 1932-33 we got nearly 7 crores. In the current year we budgeted for 6,10 lakhs and we actually expect to receive no more that 5,00 lakhs, while for next year we cannot count on more that 2,05 lakhs. Indeed we should normally only have allowed for 1,80 lakhs next year (or an import of about 100,000 tons) but as a result of the earthquake in Bihar the operation of seven factories may be altogether stopped or seriously curtailed and on this account we have increased our estimate of imports. Even so this item accounts for a loss of 2,95 lakhs as compared with the revised estimates for 1933-34 and of 4,05 lakhs as compared with the budget estimate.

* * * * *

MACHINERY.—Then we must be prepared for a substantial drop in the machinery import duty. We expect to get, 1,32 lakhs from this in the current year, or 17 lakhs more than our budget estimate ; but these high receipts are due to the exceptionally large imports of sugar machinery. We cannot count on their continuance and we have reduced next year's estimate to 1 crore which means a drop of 32 lakhs on the revised estimates of the current year.

* * * * *

Proposals for 1934-35.

*   *   *   *   *

26. (*d*) SUGAR.—I came now to a specially difficult case—the case of sugar. I have already had occasion to comment on the tremendous loss of revenue which has occurred under the head of sugar import duties. The import duty which in 1930-31 produced over 10 crores is reduced in our next budget estimates to little more than 2 crores, and as, according to the estimates of production of new factories by the Sugar Technologist, the total production of Indian factories in 1935 is likely to be equal to the present level of India's consumption of white sugar, we must be prepared for losses of revenue still further under this head. The House is well aware that at present there is a surcharge of Re. 1-13 per cwt. on the protective duty of Rs. 7-4-0. The surcharge although its effect combined with the import duty on machinery which gave us a substantial revenue from sugar machinery, may have helped our budget during the period set for the emergency programme, that is to say, up to March, 31, 1933, has led to a very rapid expansion of sugar factories in India. In my budget speech last year I referred to this matter and gave a clear warning to those engaged in the sugar industry that they could not count on a continuance of the existing abnormal level of protection. What has happened since then, has appeared to us to make it necessary to terminate the present situation. On the one hand it does not appear that in all cases the actual grower of sugarcane is getting the full advantage which he was intended to receive from our policy. On the other hand in many cases large profits are being made by sugar manufacturing companies and the attraction of these profits is so great and factories are being set up so rapidly, that there is a real danger of over-production on a scale which may lead to very serious reactions both on the manufacturing industry and on the cane growers who rely on it. There are thus three main points involved.

First, the danger of continuing a stimulus which is in excess of what Government decided to be necessary as a measure of protection ;

Secondly, the need to ensure that the agricultural producer gets his full measure of benefit out of the policy of protection ; and

Thirdly, the replacement of the revenue losses which represents the cost to the general public of India of giving protection to a limited number of manufacturers.

Thirdly, the replacement of the revenue losses which represents the cost to the general public of India of giving protection to a limited number of manufacturers.

After careful consideration of all these points we have decided to propose a dual policy ; on the one hand the imposition of an excise duty on factory produced sugar, and on the other hand the introduction of legislation by the Central Government which will enable the Provincial Governments to apply schemes for enforcing a minimum price for cane to be paid by the factory to the grower. As I have already stated, the present duty of Rs. 9-1-0 per cwt. is Re. 1-13-0 above the basic duty of Rs. 7-4-0 recommended by the Tariff Board. In their report, however, the Tariff Board recommended that there should be power for Government to increase the measure of protection by 8 annas per cwt. when Java sugar was being imported at a price less than Rs. 4 per maund to Calcutta. We propose to assume that the conditions justifying this extra margin of protection are likely to continue in existence for the present, and therefore to leave a protective margin of Rs. 7-12-0 per cwt. and to impose an excise duty of Re. 1-5-0 per cwt. We assume that this will yield Rs. 1,47 lakhs, and out of this we propose to set aside an amount equivalent to 1 anna per cwt., representing about 7 lakhs, as a fund to be distributed among the Provinces where white sugar is produced for the purpose of assisting the organisation and operation of co-operative societies among the cane growers so as to help them in securing fair prices, or for other purposes directed to the same end.

It is only after very carefully weighing all the issues that we have decided to propose an excise duty, for we recognise that it may be criticised as likely to have an adverse effect on the cultivators of sugar cane throughout the country, and that, in the present conditions which are particularly difficult for the agricultural masses, is a result which we could not contemplate with equanimity.* We

* It is important in this connection to appreciate that the sugar refining industry only absorbs a fraction of the sugar cane which is grown in India. Actually in 1932-33 it is estimated that out of a total of about 48½ million tons of cane produced in India only 4½ million tons was taken by factories

of cane produced in India only 4½ million tons was taken by factories

trust however that, as a result of the legislation which we propose to introduce,, the immediate position of the cultivators will be protected, while taking a view of the more distant future we have been compelled to the conclusion that if the present conditions are allowed to continue there is a danger of over production which might in the long run bring disaster to the interests of cultivators and manufacturers alike. We believe that the measure of protection which will remain is sufficient to allow all reasonably well organised factories a fair margin of profit after paying a fair price to the cultivator, and here again we feel that in the long run the industry will enjoy a more healthy life and growth if this change is made now than if the present excessive duty is allowed to continue.. I may mention that we had arrived at our decision in this matter just before the occurrence of the earthquake in Bihar which, as is well known, has affected an important sugar growing area. We consider however, that this does not afford adequate ground for altering our whole plan, though we shall be prepared to consider special measures for the assistance of this particular area. I shall be referring to this again in a later passage of my speech.

Lastly from the point of view of the general tax-paying public of India, who are neither sugar manufacturers nor cane growers, we feel that it is fair that some steps should be taken to preserve revenue from this source. This case of sugar is an illustration of the great cost of protection to the country, and it is essential that the public should realise that if the development of local industries is to be obtained at this cost, then the public services of the country cannot be maintained unless other methods of indirect taxation to replace such loss of customs revenue are adopted.

Before leaving this subject I may inform the House that the proposal for a Sugar Excise duty is not included in the Finance Bill, but in a separate bill, which I shall introduce as soon as possible.

* * * * *

The case is different with the sugar excise, where we have to consider an important long established industry outside power

---

producing refined sugar. Of the balance about 5½ million tons was taken by Khandsari factories leaving 38½ million tons for other purposes.

factories and where the risk of evasion is in any case less because the proposed rate, relatively to value, is much less onerous than that proposed for matches. With sugar again the danger of an unnatural transfer of production to the States is also much less. On both these points, we propose, with the sugar excise, to do what we could not do with matches and to follow the precedent of the cotton excise ; that is to say, the sugar duty will be confined to factory produce, and States which produce sugar in factories will merely be invited to impose an equal duty, for their own benefit, on production in their own territories.

* * * * *

Plan for dealing with Earthquake Damage.

* * * * *

42. I have dealt so far with the problems of permanent reconstruction. The principal necessities for immediate relief have been and are being met, energetically by the Provincial Government out of money which has been made available from the Viceroy's and other relief funds ; but there is one way in which we propose to contribute towards immediate relief from central revenue. Seven of the sugar factories in North Bihar have been destroyed and two more have been very seriously damaged, with the result that cane growers in this area have been deprived of a market for about fifteen million maunds of cane. It is hoped to make arrangements for transferring the bulk of this cane with the necessary expedition to factories in the south of Bihar or the east of the United Provinces, and the Railways concerned are prepared to carry it at very low concessionary rates of freight. But some portion at any rate of the cane cannot be dealt with in this way, and the Provincial Government are therefore providing country mills and other equipment in order to convert it into gur. We have informed them that we are prepared to bear the whole cost of this measure from central revenues ; it will probably not exceed 5 lakhs.

* * * * *

64. At the same time other industries have been growing remarkably. The sugar industry is a case in point. By 1935 it is

estimated that we shall produce in India the whole of the white sugar which used to be imported from Java, and indeed, as I have already said, there is now a danger of this process going too fast and too far. Let me quote yet another interesting example.

* * * * *

* * * * *

Before closing, however, I must revert shortly to the actual Budget proposals. I trust that Honourable Members will give these proposals calm and fair consideration on their merits. I fully recognise that any suggestion of new taxation in present circumstances cannot be very welcome. Nevertheless I trust that further reflection will encourage the view that in all the circumstances these proposals are right and in the interests of the country. They represent a definite plan framed with an eye to the future, and with the idea not only of maintaining equilibrium for the Central Government but of laying, in advance the new constitution, the foundations for a financial position in which the Provincial Governments, in whose hands lies the responsibility for fostering the so called nation building services, may have some possibility of expanding revenue. If this is to be done it is absolutely necessary to broaden the basis of indirect taxation, and this necessity becomes all the greater if industries are to be developed in India thereby reducing her foreign trade and the receipts from customs duties. *The story of sugar is an instructive one as an illustration of the cost of protection to the general taxpayer and consumer. The public may consider the result worth the cost, but the cost has to be met. It is in the light of these considerations that the new excise duty proposal should be viewed.*

* * * * *

APPENDIX I (OF THE BUDGET SPEECH).

* * * * *

The area under sugarcane in India in 1933-34, (*i.e.* for the crop now being crushed) is reported to be 3,305,000 acres, a decrease of ½ per cent. on last year but the yield is estimated to be 5,067,000 tons expressed in terms of gur (jaggery) an increase of 8 per cent. on last year. Full details have not yet been received but from the detailed United Provinces report which covers 1,702,000 acres, it is clear that the increase in production is due to the further spread of improved varieties which in the United Provinces now cover 1,275,000 acres, or 75 per cent. of the total area in that province, with a yield per acre 60 per cent. higher than the old varieties replaced. It is estimated that in season 1933-34 some 586,000 tons of sugar will be produced in modern factories in India as compared to 381,000 tons in 1932-33.

APPENDIX II (*b*).

(Introduced in the Legislative Assembly on the 13th March, 1934.

*A Bill to Provide for the imposition and collection of an excise duty on sugar.**

WHEREAS it is expedient to impose an excise duty on sugar produced in factories and to provide for the collection thereof ; It is hereby enacted as follows :—

Short title and extent.

1. (*1*) This Act may be called the Sugar (Excise Duty) Act, 1934.

(*2*) It extends to the whole of British India, including British Baluchistan and the Sonthal Parganas.

Definitions.

2. In this Act unless there is anything repugnant in the subject or context—

(*a*) "factory" means any premises wherein, or within the precincts of which, twenty or more workers are working or were working on any day of the preceding twelve months, and in any part of which any manufacturing process connected with the production of sugar is being carried on or is ordinarily carried on with the aid of power ;

(*b*) "owner" includes any person expressly or impliedly authorized by the owner of a factory to be his agent in respect of such factory ; and

(*c*) "sugar" means any form of sugar containing more than ninety per cent. of sucrose.

---

* Several amendments to this bill have been suggested by members of the Assembly, the most important being for inclusion of *Khandsaries* in the imposition of duty, for postponement till the September sessions, and for the reduction of the duty.

3. A duty of excise at the rate of one rupee and five annas per cwt. shall be levied on all sugar produced in any factory in British India and either issued out of such factory on or after the 1st day of April, 1934, or used within such factory on or after the said date in the manufacture of any commodity other than sugar, and shall be payable by the owner of the factory.

Imposition of duty on sugar.

4. (1) If any duty payable under section 3 is not paid within the time fixed by rules made in that behalf under this Act, it shall be deemed to be an arrear, and the authority to which such duty is payable may, in lieu thereof, recover any sum not exceeding four times the amount of duty unpaid which such authority may in its discretion think it reasonable to require.

Recovery of duty with penalty.

(2) An arrear of duty, or any sum recoverable in lieu thereof under this section, shall be recoverable as an arrear of land revenue and shall be recoverable in addition to, and not in substitution for, any other penalty incurred under this Act.

5. No person shall issue any sugar out of the premises of a factory, except in accordance with the provisions of rules made in that behalf under this Act, or, until such rules are made, in accordance with the general or special orders of the Local Government.

Issue of sugar from factory.

6. (1) The Governor General in Council may, by notification in the Gazette of India, impose on sugar brought into British India from the territory of any State in India, not being territory which has been declared under section 5 of the Indian Tariff Act, 1894, to be foreign territory for the purposes of that section, a duty of customs equivalent to the excise duty imposed by this Act on sugar produced in British India.

Power of Governor General in Council to impose customs duty on sugar.

VIII of 1894.

(2) The Governor General in Council may, by notification in the Gazette of India, declare that the provisions of the Land Customs Act, 1924, shall apply to the levy of the duty of customs imposed under this section, and on such declaration that Act shall apply as if the expression "foreign

XIX of 1924.

territory" in that Act included territory forming part of a State in India.

Penalty for issue of sugar from factory in contravention of section 5.

7. Whoever contravenes the provisions of section 5 shall be punishable with imprisonment which may extend to six months, or with fine which may extend to one thousand rupees, or with both.

Penalty for evasion of duty or failure to supply information.

8. Whoever evades or attempts to evade the payment of any duty payable by him under this Act, or fails to supply any information which he is required by any rule made under this Act to supply, or knowingly supplies false information, shall be punishable with imprisonment which may extend to six months, or with fine which may extend to one thousand rupees, or with both.

Power of Courts to order forfeiture of sugar.

9. Any Court trying an offence under this Act may order that any sugar, together with the packages or coverings thereof, in respect of which the Court is satisfied that an offence under this Act has been committed, shall be forfeited to His Majesty.

Application of the provisions of Act VIII of 1878 to the duty on sugar.

VIII of 1878.

10. The Governor General in Council may, by notification in the Gazette of India, declare that any of the provisions of the Sea Customs Act, 1878, relating to the levy of and exemption from customs duties, drawback of duty, warehousing, offences and penalties, confiscation, and procedure relating to offences and appeals shall, with such modifications and alterations as he may consider necessary or desirable to adapt them to the circumstances, be applicable in regard to like matters in respect of the duty on sugar imposed by section 3.

Power of Governor General in Council to make rules.

11. (1) The Governor General in Council may, by notification in the Gazette of India, make rules to carry into effect the purposes and objects of this Act.

(2) In particular, and without prejudice to the generality of the foregoing power, such rules may—

(*a*) provide for the assessment and collection of the duty and the authorities by whom functions under this Act are to be discharged, the issue of notices requiring payment, the manner in which the duty shall be payable, and the recovery of arrears ;

(*b*) regulate the issue of sugar out of any factory ;

(*c*) impose on the owners of factories, and on persons engaged in the sale of sugar, the duty of furnishing information, keeping records and making returns, and prescribe the nature of such information and the form of such records and returns the particulars to be contained therein, and the manner in which they shall be verified ;

(*d*) provide for the detention of sugar for the purpose of exacting the duty, the confiscation otherwise than under section 9 of sugar in respect of which breaches of the Act or rules have been committed, and the disposal of sugar so detained or confiscated ;

(*e*) authorize and regulate the search of any place or conveyance used for the manufactures, storage or carriage of sugar ; and

(*f*) authorize and regulate the composition of offences against or liabilities incurred under the Act and rules.

(3) In making any rule under this section the Governor General in Council may provide that a breach of the rule shall, where no other penalty is provided by this Act, be punishable with imprison ment for any term not exceeding six months, or with fine not exceeding one thousand rupees, or with both imprisonment and fine.

(4) The Governor-General in Council may delegate all or any of his powers under this section to a Local Government.

Statement of Objects and Reasons.

This Bill is designed to impose an excise duty on sugar produced in factories in British India. The rate of tax is fixed so as to be equal to the excess of the emergency surcharge over the figure by which, according to the Government's calculations, it would have been incumbent upon them to raise the protective duty in exercise of their power under section 4 of the Sugar Industry (Protection) Act, 1932, had the emergency surcharge not been in force.

2. The Administration of the duty will be entrusted to the Local Governments, working as agents for the Government of India ; but the Bill has been so drafted as to render it possible to revise this arrangement at a later stage.

3. Following the precedent of the Cotton Duties Act, Indian States in which sugar is produced will be invited to impose, for their own benefit, a corresponding excise duty, so as to maintain fair competition. Power is taken to recover duty on sugar imported from States that do not agree to this proposal, but it is hoped that no State in which sugar is produced will adopt that attitude.

New Delhi, GEORGE SCHUSTER.
The 27th February, 1934.

APPENDIX II (*c*).

(Introduced in the Legislative Assembly on the 13th March, 1934).

A Bill to regulate the price of sugar-cane intended for use in sugar factories.

WHEREAS it is expedient, for the purpose of assuring to sugar-cane growers a fair price for their produce, to regulate the price at which sugar-cane intended to be used in the manufacture of sugar may be purchased by or for factories ; It is hereby enacted as follows :—

Short title, extent and commencement.

1. (*1*) This Act may be called the Sugar-cane Act, 1934.

(*2*) It extends to the whole of British India, including British Baluchistan and the Sonthal Parganas.

(*3*) This section shall come into force at once ; the remaining sections of this Act shall come into force in any province on such date as the Local Government may, by notification in the local official Gazette, appoint in that behalf.

Definitions.

2. In this Act, unless there is anything repugnant in the subject or context,—

(*1*) "controlled area" means any area specified in a notification issued under sub-section (*1*) of section 3 ;

(*2*) "factory" means any premises (including the precincts thereof) wherein twenty or more workers are working or were working on any day of the preceding twelve months and in any part of which any manufacturing process connected with the production of sugar is being carried on or is ordinarily carried on with the aid of power ; and

(*3*) "sugar" means any form of sugar containing more than ninety per cent. of sucrose.

Declaration of controlled areas, and fixing of prices.

3. (*1*) The Local Government may, by notification in the local official Gazette, declare any area specified in the notification to be a controlled area for the purposes of this Act.

(*2*) The Local Government may, by notification in the local official Gazette, fix a minimum price or minimum prices for the purchase in any controlled area of sugar-cane intended for use in any factory in that area.

(*3*) The Local Government may, by notification in the local official Gazette, prohibit in any controlled area the purchase of sugar-cane intended for use in any factory in that area otherwise than from the grower of the sugar-cane or from a person licensed by the Local Government to act as a purchasing agent.

Previous publication of notifications under section 3.

4. Not less than fourteen days before the issue of any notification under sub-section (*1*) or sub-section (*2*) of section 3, the Local Government shall publish in the local official Gazette and in such other manner (if any) as it thinks fit a draft of the proposed notification specifying a date on or after which the draft will be taken into consideration, and shall consider any objection or suggestion which may be received from any person with respect to the draft before the date so specified.

Penalty for purchase of sugar-cane in contravention of notification under section 3.

5. Whoever in any controlled area purchases any sugar-cane intended for use in a factory in that area at a price less than the minimum price fixed therefor by notification under sub-section (*2*) of section 3 or in contravention of any prohibition made under sub-section (*3*) of section 3 shall be punished with fine which may extend, in the case of the first conviction for the offence, to one thousand rupees, or, in the case of a second or subsequent conviction for the offence, to three thousand rupees.

Sanction for prosecution under this Act.

6. No Court shall take cognizance of any offence punishable under section 5 except upon complaint made by order of, or under authority from, the District Magistrate.

7. (1) The Local Government may, by notification in the local official Gazette, make rules for the purpose of carrying into effect the objects of this Act.

Power of Local Government to make rules.

(2) In particular and without prejudice to the generality of the foregoing power, such rules may provide for—

(a) the carrying out of inquiries preliminary to the exercise of the powers conferred by section 3 ;

(b) establishing Advisory Committees for any purpose connected with the administration of this Act and defining the powers, functions and procedure of such Committees ;

(c) the issue of licences to purchasing agents, the fees for such licences, and the regulation of the purchase and sale of sugar-cane by and to such agents ;

(d) the organisation of growers of sugar-cane into societies for the sale of sugar-cane to factories ;

(e) the authorities by which any functions under this Act or the rules made thereunder are to be performed ; and

(f) the records, registers and accounts to be maintained for ensuring compliance with the provisions of this Act.

(3) In making any rule under sub-section (1) or under clause (c) or clause (f) of sub-section (2), the Local Government may provide that any breach thereof shall be punishable with fine not exceeding, in the case of a first offence, one thousand rupees, or, in the case of a second or subsequent offence, three thousand rupees.

8. The Governor General in Council may, by notification in the Gazette of India, make rules providing for the exemption of factories or any class of factories from the provisions of this Act.

Power of Governor General in Council to make rules.

STATEMENT OF OBJECTS AND REASONS.

It was announced by the Honourable Finance Member in the course of his speech introducing the budget proposals for 1934-35 that the Government of India would introduce legislation which would enable Provincial Governments to apply schemes for enforcing a minimum price for cane to be paid by the factory to the grower. This decision is consequential upon the imposition of an excise duty on factory sugar. As initiative in the matter of fixing prices for cane must be left to Provincial Governments so as to suit local conditions, it is proposed that the Act should come into force in any province on such date as the Local Government may direct. The scheme of the Bill is that after prior publication of its proposals and due consideration of the objections received, a Local Government should declare controlled areas within which purchase of cane by factories shall be limited to growers of cane or licensed persons and societies at fixed prices. In order to provide for elasticity of procedure in the administration of the scheme, it is also proposed to give wide rule-making powers to Local Governments.

G. S. BAJPAI.
MD. RAFI,
Secy. to the Govt. of India.

NEW DELHI:
The 7th March, 1934.

APPENDIX II (*d*).

Representation submitted by the Indian Sugar Mills Association, and the Indian Sugar Producers' Association on the 8th March 1934 to the Government of India, Finance Department, New Delhi.

Sir,

We have the honour to submit herewith on behalf of our respective Associations a Representation wherein we have endeavoured to illustrate the effect of the proposed Legislation appertaining to (a) the imposition of an Excise Duty on Indian Factory made sugar and (b) the control of sugar cane prices to Sugar Factories in British India.

Representation on behalf of the Indian Sugar Mills Association and the Indian Sugar Producers Association.

1. Introductory : This Representation is put forward on behalf of the combined associations of sugar manufacturers representing 72 white sugar factories in British India.

(1) It is put forward, first, by reason of the announced intention of Government to impose an excise duty on factory produced sugars of Re. 1/5/- per cwt. as from 1st April 1934, Secondly, by reason of Government's implied intention to exclude from this imposition the very large Khandsari industry, Thirdly, by reason of Government's announced intention shortly to introduce a Bill enabling Provincial Governments to fix minimum prices at which factories may purchase sugar cane from growers and, Fourthly, by reason of Press Reports, the accuracy of which it has not yet become possible to verify, of Government's intention to include in the Enabling Bill above referred to, power to Provincial Governments to set up and license, societies or marketing boards, to regulate the price and distribution of sugar cane to factories.

(2) It appears to be the impression of Government and, to some extent, of the Public, that the Indian White Sugar Industry, by

reason of the high Protective Tariff and the imposition of the 25 per cent. surcharge, is enjoying a higher return, or ratio of profits, than was envisaged by the Tariff Board, as a result of whose deliberations and report, the Sugar Industry (Protection) Act of 1932 was passed by the Assembly.

It is the purpose of this Representation to show that, in fact, the return at present enjoyed by the Indian White Sugar Industry falls far below the degree envisaged by the Tariff Board and that in the event of Producers being compelled to bear the full amount of the proposed Excise Duty, the Industry will find itself in a most difficult situation.

2. The Proposed Excise Duty on Factory Sugar :

(1) After full investigation by the Indian Tariff Board, Government accepted their recommendations and in April 1932 the Indian Sugar (Protection) Act 1932 was passed by the Assembly, by which the Industry was granted Protection amounting to Rs. 7/4/- per cwt. in order "to provide for the fostering and development of the Sugar Industry for a period ending 31st March 1946" the intention being to render the country self-supporting in her sugar requirements in due course.

(2) A 25 per cent. revenue surcharge, imposed for a period of eighteen months, subsequently extended and still in force, raised the effective Protection to Rs. 9/1/- per cwt.

(3) This high incidence of Protection has resulted in a development so rapid that the country is now considered to be almost self-supporting and in fact has practically reached the stage visualized by the Tariff Board at the end of the protective period.

(4) This rapid development has led to the investment by the Public of some 15 Crores of rupees and has taken place by reason of the assurance of protection to the Industry for a period of fifteen years. This assurance not only protected the investing public from competition from foreign sources but also implied equality of treatment for all classes of Sugar producers in India.

(5) The following table will illustrate the present position of the Industry in the light of the Tariff Board recommendations:—

Tariff Board Report Page 69.
(Para 64)

	At commencement of Protective Period.			At end of Protective. Period.			Actual as at February 1934.		
	Rs.	A.	P.	Rs.	A.	P.	Rs.	A.	P.
Fair Price for Sugar ...	9	5	9	7	12	5	7	12	0
Of which, cost of cane ...	5	8	10	4	0	0	4	0	0
	3	12	11	3	12	5	3	12	0
Add back value of Molasses ...	0	10	8	0	6	9		Nil.	
Balance to represent manufacturing cost, overhead charges and 10% Profit on Capital invested	4	7	7	4	3	2	3	12	0

The figures shown in the last column represent the average market value ex-factory of Indian Factory Sugar in February 1934 and the average cost of cane per md. sugar @ -/6/- delivered, with extraction @ 9 per cent.

(6) The above table illustrates that notwithstanding the apparently high protective duty, the return to the factory to cover cost of production, overhead charges and profit is less by Rs. 0/7/2 than that visualized by the Tariff Board at the end of the Protective Period, without taking into account the proposed Excise Duty of Re. -/15/4·5 per maund. That is to say that whereas the Tariff Board considered that at the end of the period of protection, factories should, after paying for their cane have Rs. 4/3/2 per maund sugar to cover manufacturing cost (Rs. 2/7/6) Overhead Charges (Rs. -/10/-) and Profit (Rs. 1/1/8), they now only have Rs. 3/12/- and, if they have to bear the whole of the Excise Duty of Rs. -/15/4.5 this may be reduced to Rs. 2/12/7.5 or barely sufficient to cover Manufacturing Costs, with no margin for Overhead Charges or Profit.

(7) Specifically, the Industry's objections to the Excise Duty as at present proposed may be tabulated as follows:—

(a) The Finance Member's statement that the Excise Duty is necessary to prevent further expansion, is not correct.

The above table will clearly show that under existing conditions and without the imposition of any Excise Duty, the industry cannot recover the 10 per cent. profit on its investment indicated by the Tariff Board. There is, therefore, no likelihood of "the danger of continuing a stimulus which is in excess of what Government decided to be necessary as a measure of protection."

(*b*) That the imposition of this duty, which Factories will have to bear in whole or part is manifestly unjust particularly to that large body of investors whose factories have only recently, if yet, actually commenced operations. A large proportion of the Industry is now working its second season and an even larger proportion is working this season for the first time.

(*c*) That the extra protection provided by the surcharge has become largely ineffective owing to the rapid expansion of the Industry in the past two years and that in using this surcharge as a reason for imposing the proposed Excise Duty, Government are basing their arguments on a fallacy.

(*d*) That if, as is implied, the Khandsari Industry is to be excluded from this Duty, a further hardship is imposed on the Sugar Factories. The Khandsari Industry is estimated to represent one-third of the total sugar output. The exclusion of this portion of the industry can only re-act as a further depressing influence on the market price of sugar in India. This discrimination to the disadvantage of one section of the industry is a breach of the equality of treatment implied for all classes of the Industry, when the protection was granted under the stimulus of which the Factory Industry has expanded. It must be pointed out that the Khandsari manufacturer is not an agriculturist, but an industrialist, whose raw material is purchased-juice instead of purchased-cane.

(*e*) That the provision appertaining to Factories in Native States is most unsatisfactory, and may encourage States to utilize the Duty recovered by them in further extensions of State-aided sugar factories to the disadvantage of the Industry in British India. At the least, therefore, provision should be made for the repayment to Central Government of the Duty realized on all Indian States' factory outturn in excess of the Indian States' consumption.

(8) It is fully realized that the loss of Import Duty Revenue on foreign sugar to Government is a matter of great importance and, although this loss was envisaged by Government when the Protection Act was passed, Government may now find themselves unable to find alternative methods of taxation or to revise or reduce the Excise Duty now proposed.

(9) If this is the case, and notwithstanding the injustice to the Industry, this Duty must be imposed, then it is most strongly recommended :—

(*a*) That the Khandsari Industry should be included and the incidence of duty reduced proportionately.

(*b*) That in order to enable Indian Sugars to reach the furthest markets in India and Burma the specific protective duty of Rs. 7/4/- per cwt. should be increased to Rs. 7/12/- per cwt. simultaneously with the imposition of the Excise and during the continuance of the surcharge.

(*c*) That the Duty should not be imposed before 1st November 1934, or if this is impracticable :—

(*d*) That the Duty should apply only to Sugars actually, produced on or after 1st April 1934, and be payable when issued from factories.

(10) With regard to points (*c*) and (*d*) above it should be pointed out that the imposition of this duty within a few weeks of the end of a season will cause and is causing considerable market dislocation, whilst the provision that the duties will be payable on all factory stocks on 1st April will impose an unfair hardship on those factories, which, owing to inadequate railway services, will be unable to clear their stocks by this date.

3. Proposed Bill to enable Local Governments to fix Sugar-cane Prices.

(1) The fixation of minimum prices of a raw material for a large food producing industry, involves a departure from a principle so unprecedented, that it should be the subject of representation from bodies of far greater weight than the Sugar Industry. Upon this important question of constitutional principle it is not, therefore, proposed herein to enlarge beyond the registration of this emphatic protest.

(2) The payment of a fair price for sugar cane to the grower is a principle which the Industry wholeheartedly accepts. Whilst, in a few isolated cases, advantage of excessive cane crops may have been taken by Factories to reduce the price paid to growers, these cases are not only exceptional, but the consequential and inevitable reduction in planting for the following season soon abolishes this tendency.

(3) The Tariff Board laid down, after most thorough investigation, that, "it is clear that no direct measures can be taken to ensure that a definite rate for cane is paid to producers" (P. 99 Para 101). "We fear that no system of scaling prices for cane in accordance with the output of sugar will be understood by the ordinary agriculturist—further that, even if a scale could be devised which would be suitable for the varied conditions of cane cultivation in different parts of India, the methods of evasion are so numerous, that it is impossible that it could be successfully imposed." (P. 100).

They add that "the main requirements for the success of a sugar factory are an adequate and continuous supply of cane of reasonable freshness, a sufficiently long working season and an economic price for cane" (P. 103). This economic price the Tariff Board considered, for Northern India to be -/8/- per maund delivered, at the commencement of the period of Protection (*i.e.* with sugar selling at Rs. 9-5-9) and -/6/- per maund at the end of the period of Protection (*i.e.* with sugar selling at Rs. 7-12-5).

(4) It must be pointed out that, as illustrated above, with conditions considerably less favourable to the Industry than the Tariff Board visualized at the end of the period of protection, the average price being paid for sugar cane is not less than -/6/- per maund delivered at Factory.

F

(5) Any legislation designed to enhance the price now being paid will not only inflict a further hardship upon this Industry, but will certainly increase the price of sugar cane above that "economic price" visualized by the Tariff Board.

(6) It must be pointed out that Provincial Governments' sole interest in the Sugar Industry lies in the prosperity of the agriculturist through the realization of Land Revenue, Irrigation dues &c., &c. This Industry has neither wish nor intention to take advantage of the grower, but the proposed legislation places it in the hands of the Provincial Governments to take advantage of the Sugar Factories, almost up to the point of final extinction. If Provincial Governments had any interest in the proposed Excise Duty, Income and Super Tax, Import Duty on Sugar Machinery or Import Duty on Foreign Sugars, etc., there might be less justification for the apprehension felt at this proposed legislation.

4. Reported intention of Government to create Licensed Societies or Marketing Boards for Sugar-cane :

(1) Until the Bill is published it may be considered premature to comment on this proposal. As reported, however, the proposal is so revolutionary, and is considered by the Industry, so certain to result in complete disaster for the sugar factories, that it is considered essential to review this subject with the least possible delay.

(2) The absolutely vital importance of the constant supply of fresh cut cane to a sugar factory cannot be sufficiently stressed.

(3) The imposition, between the factory organization and the agriculturists from whom the cane is purchased, of any kind of organization, whether controlled by Government or not, with power to fix prices, distribute the cane, receive and distribute payment, cannot possibly do otherwise than duplicate opportunities for corruption and delay. In actual fact the freshness of the sugarcane is of greater importance than the price. Stale cane, even four days after cutting, is not worth purchasing at any price at all. The inestimable losses which would be incurred by delays in supply would in no way benefit the agriculturist, but would make working impossible for the Sugar Factories.

(4) The Industry, holding these views, and with the knowledge of experience that these views are correct, can only oppose any such legislation with all the means at its disposal,

5. The Consumer :

(1) It may be pointed out that this Industry is now responsible for the direct employment of between 80,000 and 90,000 factory workers, from 1,000 to 1,500 graduate executives, a very considerable employment among bullock carters, and revenue to railway and other transport services. It purchases and consumes 60 lakhs of tons of sugar-cane each season, having a value of some 6 crores of rupees, and had stopped an annual drain of some 12 crores of rupees abroad for foreign sugar.

(2) So far as the consumer is concerned, the following table will illustrate the price the Indian consumer would have to pay (*a*) for Java Sugar, (*b*) for Indian Sugar at the average value recommended by the Tariff Board (Rs. 8/13/1) and (*c*) actually paid at present market rate; (In each case Re. 1/- per maund has been added to factory or Port price for freight to consuming centres). The consumption is calculated at 6,00,000 tons.

Java Sugar @ 10/2/- per maund plus freight.	Tariff Board Recommendation @ 8/13/1 plus freight.	Actual price in February 1934 @ Rs. 7/12/- plus freight.
6,00,000 Tons	6,00,000 Tons	6,00,000 Tons
Rs.	Rs.	Rs.
18,02,25,000	15,90,46,870	14,17,50,000

So that it would appear that this industry is today supplying India with sugar at a saving of Rs. 3,84,75,000/- below the present Java price and of Rs. 1,72,96,870/- below the average price recommended by the Tariff Board.

(3) Finally, this representation would suggest that so drastic is the proposed legislation, and so far-reaching will be its effects on the Industry, the agriculturist and the consumer, that if great injustice and great hardship is to be avoided, Government should postpone their legislation at least until the September Session to enable the representation herein put forward to be fully investigated and the results ventilated before proceeding further.

DETAILED LIST OF SUGAR MILLS WORKING INDIA (1933-34)

Mills marked with an asterisk (*) are members of the Indian Sugar Mills Association. Asterisk in the last column indicates the mills that have refineries also.

Name of Factory.	Location.	District.	Nearest Railway Station.	Crushing capacity in tons.
BENGAL.				
1. *Bengal Sugar Mills, Ltd., M/A. Soorajmull Nagarmull, 61, Harrison Road, Calcutta.	Gopalpur.	Rajshahi.	Gopalpur, E.B.R.	500-900
2. *Setabganj Sugar Mills, M/A. Soorajmull Nagarmull, 61, Harrison Road, Calcutta.	Setabganj.	Dinajpur.	Setabganj E.B.R.	450-500
BIHAR & ORISSA.				
3. Sakri Sugar Mills.	Sakri.	Darbhanga	Sakri, B.N.W.R.	400
4. *Lohat Sugar Works of Darbhanga Sugar Co., Ltd., M/A. Octavius Steel Co., Ltd., Old Court House St., Calcutta.	Lohat.	Do.	Do. Do.	800
5. *Ryam Sugar Works Ltd., M/A. Begg, Sutherland & Co., Cawnpore.	Ryam.	Do.	Tarsarai, Do.	600*
6. *Samastipur Sugar Works, Ltd., M/A. Begg. Sutherland & Co., Ltd., P. B. 21, Cawnpore.	Samastipur.	Do.	Samastipur Do.	660*
7. *Semapur Sugar Co., Ltd., M/A. Octavius Steel Co., Ltd., Old Court House Street, Calcutta.	Semapore.	Purnea.	Semapore, Do.	400

8.	Japaha Sugar Factory, M/A. Bicanpur Concern, Muzaffarpur.	Japaha.	Muzaffarpur.	Muzaffarpur,	B.N.W.R.	400
9.	*Motipur Sugar Works, M/A. Motipur Zemindary Co., A. R. Osman & Co., 2, Rajmohan Street, Calcutta.	Motipur.	Do.	Motipur,	Do.	900-1200
10.	*Belsund Sugar Factory, M/A. James Finlay & Co., Ltd., 1, Clive Street, Calcutta.	Belsund.	Do.	Riga,	Do.	500
11.	*Champaran Sugar Co., Begg, Sutherland & Co., P. B. 21, Cawnpore.	Barachakia.	Champaran.	Chakia,	Do.	750*
12.	*Shree Hanuman Sugar Mills, M/A. Daulatram Rawatmull, 178, Harrison Road, Calcutta.	Motihari.	Do.	Motihari,	Do.	400
13.	Sagauli Sugar Co., Ltd., M/A. Md. Henif & Amjadali, 3, Rajmohan Street, Calcutta.	Sagauli.	Do.	Sagauli,	Do.	400
14.	*Motilal Padampat Sugar Mills, Ltd., M/A. Kamlapat Motilal, Chaitai Mahal, Cawnpore.	Majhowlia.	Do.	Majhowlia,	Do.	450-600
15.	*Chanpatia Sugar Factory of Champaran Sugar Co., Ltd., M/A. Begg, Sutherland & Co., P.O. Box 21, Cawnpore.	Chanpatia.	Do.	Chanpatia,	Do.	600
16.	*Pursa Sugar Factory, M/A. Pursa Limited, Pursa.	Pursa.	Do.	Pursa,	Do.	325-365

	Name of Factory.	Location.	District.	Nearest Railway Station.	Crushing capacity in tons.
17.	*New Swadeshi Sugar Mills Ltd., Narkatiaganj, M/A. Birla Bros., Ltd., Jehangir Wadia Building, 2nd floor, Esplanade Road, Fort, Bombay.	Narkatiaganj.	Champaran.	Narkatiaganj, B.N.W.R.	400
18.	*Harinagar Sugar Mills, Ltd., M/A. Narayanlal Bansilal, 207, Kalvadevi Road, Bombay.	Ramnagar.	Do.	Harinagar, Do.	600
19.	*Ramchandram Shah Mustafa Ahmad Sugar Mills, Ltd., M/A. Ramchandram Shah Mustafa Ahmad, Gaya.	Guraru.	Gaya.	Guraru, E.I.R.	350
20.	*The South Bihar Sugar Mills, Ltd., Bihta, M/A. Nirmal Kumar Jain & Co., Arrah.	Bihta.	Patna.	Bihta, Do.	500
21.	Dumraon Raj Sugar Factory, H.O. Dumraon.	Bikramganj.	Sahabad.	Bikramganj, A.S.L.R.	250
22.	*Rohtas Sugars, Ltd., M/A. Inam Jaidayal & Co., (Dinapore), Patna.	Dehri-on-Sone.	Do.	Dehri-on-Sone E.I.R.	1000
23.	Ganga Deshi Sugar Factory, M/A. B. N. Brothers & Sons, Dumraon.	Buxar.	Do.	Buxar, E.I.R.	100*

24.	*Sitalpur Sugar Works, Ltd., M/A. Ghose & Dutt, 93, Dhurrumtolla Street, Calcutta. Indian Press Buildings Allahabad.	Sitalpur.	Saran.	Sitalpur,	B.N.W.R.	450
25.	*Marhowrah Sugar Factory of Cawnpore Sugar Works, Ltd., M/A. Begg, Sutherland & Co., Cawnpore.	Marhowrah.	Do.	Marhowrah,	Do.	880*
26.	Maharajganj Sugar Factory, M/A. Bashir & Co., Cawnpore.	Maharajgangj.	Do.	Maharajganj,	Do.	150*
27.	*Bihar Sugar Works, Pachrukhi, M/A. Bakubhai Ambalal, P. O. Box 28, Ahmedabad.	Pachrukhi.	Do.	Pachrukhi,	Do.	700*
28.	*New Savan Sugar and Gur Refining Co., Ltd., M/A. Andrew Yule & Co., 8, Clive Row, Calcutta.	Savan.	Do.	Savan,	Do.	360-460*
29.	Indian Sugar Works, Ltd., Prop., Moulvi Mohd. Abdul Razzaque.	Savan.	Do.	Do.	Do.	400
30.	*Bharat Sugar Mills, Ltd., M/A. Birla Bros., Ltd., 8, Royal Exchange Place, Calcutta.	Sidhwalia.	Do.	Sidhwalia,	Do.	300
31.	*Sasa Musa Sugar Factory, Prop., S. K. Mohmad Ibrahim Saheb, 3, Damzen Lane, Calcutta.	Sasa Musa.	Do.	Sasa Musa,	Do.	450
32.	*Vishnu Sugar Mills, M/A. Belasrai, Banasilal & Co., Agakhan Building, Dalal Street, Bombay.	Harkhua.	Do.	Harkhua,	Do.	450

	Name of Factory.	Location.	District.	Nearest Railway Station.		Crushing capacity in tons.
33.	*Sri Krishna Gyanoday Sugar Mills.	Hathua.	Saran.	Mirganj,	B.N.W.R.	500
34.	Siwan Deshi Sugar Factory.					
35.	Shree Lakshminarayan Sugar Works, Prop. Gupta Bros., Manoharpatti.	Siwan.	Do.	Savan,	Do.	400
		Manoharpatti.	Bhagalpur.	Nirmali,	Do.	150
	UNITED PROVINCES.					
36.	*Purtabpore Sugar Co., Ltd., Begg, Sutherland & Co., Cawnpore.	Chapra.		Mairwa,	Do.	450-525*
37.	*Noori Sugar Works, Pro., Noori Mian & Co., Sewan.	Bhatni.	Gorakhpur.	Bhatni,	Do.	450*
38.	*Shree Sitaram Sugar Co., Ltd., M/A. Karamchand Thapper & Bros., 5, Royal Exchange Place, Calcutta.	Baitalpur.	Do.	Baitalpur,	Do.	600
39.	*Gauri Sugar Factory of Cawnpur, Sugar Works., Ltd., M/A. Begg, Sutherland & Co., Cawnpore.	Gauribazar.	Do.	Gauribazar,	Do.	275-295* 70
40.	Hanmat Sugar Mill.	Deoria.	Do.	Tahsil Deoria,	Do.	
41.	*Saraya Sugar Factory, Prop., Sardar Bahadur Sir Sundar Singh Majithia, Sardarnagar.	Sardarnagar.	Do.	Sardarnagar	Do.	600-640* 2000

42.	*Diamond Sugar Mills, Ltd., M/A. Murarka & Sons, Ltd., 15, Clive Street, Calcutta.	Pipraich.	Gorakhpur.	Pipraich,	Do.	450
43.	*Pipraich Sugar Mills, Ltd., Prop. Mian Jawad Ali Shah, Mian Bazar, Gorakhpur.	Do.	Do.	Do.	Do.	300-350
44.	*Shankar Sugar Mills, Ltd.,	Captainganj.	Do.	Captainganj,	Do.	600
45.	*Punjab Sugar Mills Co., Ltd., H. O. 5, Montgomery Road, Lahore.	Ghugli.	Do.	Ghugli,	Do.	500*
46.	*Mahabir Sugar Mills Ltd., M. A. Dwarkadas Baijnath, Siswa Bazar.	Siswa Bazar.	Do.	Siswabazar	Do.	400
47.	Vishnuprotap Sugar Works Ltd., M/A. Rai Bahadur Jagdish Narayan Singh Padrauna.	Khadda.	Do.	Khadda	Do.	400
48.	Lakshmi Sugar Mills, Ltd.,	Chhitauni.	Do.	Chhitauni,	Do.	400
49.	*Iswari Khetan Sugar Mills, Lakshmiganj, M./A. Devidutt Surajmull, Padrauna, Gorakhpur.	Lakshmiganj.	Do.	Lakshmipur,	Do.	425-470*
50.	*Ramkola Sugar Factory, H. O. Nawashahr, Via. Abbottabad.	Ramkola.	Do.	Ramkola,	Do.	450
51.	*Maheswari Khetan Sugar Mills, Ltd., M./A. Messrs. Devidutt Chaturbhuj Ramkola,	Ramkola.	Do.	Do.	Do.	400
52.	*Padrauna Rajkrishna Sugar Works, Prop. Raja Shaheb of Padrauna.	Padrauna.	Do.	Padrauna,	Do.	800*

G

Name of Factory.	Location.	District.	Nearest Rly. Station.	Crushing capacity in tons.
53. *Jagadish Sugar Mills, Ltd., Raja Bahadur Brijnarayan Singh & Co., Padrauna.	Kathkuiyan.	Gorakhpur.	Kathkuiyan, B.N.W.R.	400
54.*United Provinces Sugar Co., Ltd., M./A. James Finlay & Co., Ltd., 1, Clive Street, Calcutta.	Bubnowlie.	Do.	Tamkohi Rd. Do.	400-500*
55. *Ganesh Sugar Mills, Ltd., Poddar Jaipuria & Co., Jagannath Ghat Rd., Calcutta.	Pharenda.	Do.	Pharenda Do.	550-600
56. *Ledi Sugar Factory, M./A. Dr. K. K. Bhargava Nichaul,	Nichlaul.	Do.	Siswa Bazar, Do.	60*
57. *Madho Kanhya Mahesh Gauri Sugar Mills, M./A. Badridas Gauridutt.	Jagdishpur.	Basti.	Munderma, Do.	400
58. Basti Sugar Mills Co., Ltd., Hon'ble Dr. G. C. Narang, 5, Montgomery Road, Lahore.	Basti.	Do.	Do. Do.	400*
59. *Basti Sugar Factory, Branch of Basti Sugar Mills.	Walterganj.	Do.	Walterganj, Do.	450
60. Popular Sugar Co., Ltd., M./A. Agarwal & Co., P-115, Cross Road, 6, Strand Bank, Calcutta.	Barhni.	Do.	Barhni, Do.	500
61. *Seksaria Sugar Mills, Ltd., M./A. Govindram Ramnath & Co., 18, Mullick Street, Calcutta.	Seksaria.	Do.	Babhnan, Do.	400

62.	Nawabganj Sugar Factory, Dr. Gocul Chand Narang, 5, Montgomery Rd., Lahore.	Nawabganj.	Gonda.	Nawabganj,	B.N.W.R.	400
63.	*Balrampur Sugar Co., Ltd., M/A Begg, Sutherland & Co., Ltd., Cawnpore.	Balrampur.	Gonda.	Balrampur,	Do.	600
64.	*Kamlapat Motilal Gutaiya Sugar Mills, Messrs. Kamlapat Motilal, Cawnpore.	Nawabganj.	Gonda.	Nawabganj,	Do.	51
65.	*Seth Gulzarimull Jaswatrai Sugar Mills, Ramchand & Lala Jaswantrai & Sons,	Jarwal Road.	Baharich.	Jarwal Rd.,	Do.	400
66.	Burhwal Sugar Mills Ltd., Matadin Bhagwandas, Collectorganj, Cawnpore.	Burhwal.	Barabanki.	Burhwal,	B.N.W.R. and E.I.R.	150
67.	Lucknow Sugar Works, Pro., Dr. K. K. Bhargava, Lucknow.	Aish Bagh.	Lucknow.	Bishbagh,	O. & R.R.	400*
68.	Ratna Sugar Mills Co., Ltd., Kashi Prosad & Co., Benares.	Shahganj	Jaunpur.	Shahganj,	E.I.R.	400
69.	*Shree Krishna Deshi Sugar Works, Kishorilal Mukundlal, Jushi.	Jushi.	Allahabad.	Jushi,	B.N.W.R.	400*
70.	*Tribeni Deshi Sugar Works, Prop., Lala Kanhiya Lal, Naini.	Naini.	Do.	Naini,	G.I.P.	360
71.	U. P. Co-operative Sugar Factory.	Biswan.	Sitapur.	Biswan,	B.N.W.R.	150

	Name of Factory.	Location.	District.	Nearest Rly. Station.	Crushing capacity in tons.
72.	*Oudh Sugar Mills, Birla Bros., Ltd., Jehangir Wadia Building, Esplanade Road, Bombay.	Hargaon.	Sitapur.	Hargaon, R.K.R.	700
73.	The Lakshmi Sugar Mills Co., Prop. Rai Bahadur Seth Ajodhya Prasad, Anarkali, Lahore.	Maholi.	Do.	Maholi, E.I.R.	300
74.	Aira Sugar Factory,	Khamaria.	Kheri.	Lakhimpur, R.K.R.	150
75.	*The Hindusthan Sugar Mills, M./A. Bacchraj & Co., Ltd., Kalbadevi Rd., Bombay.	Golagokarnanath.	Do.	Golagokarnanath, R.K.R.	1100
76.	*Rosa Sugra Works & Distillery, M./A. Lyall Marshall & Co., 5, Council House Street, Calcutta.	Rosa.	Shahjahanpur.	Rosa, E.I.R.	400*
77.	H. R. Sugar Factory, M./A. Lala Ram Sarup, Bareilly.	Nekpur.	Bareilly.	Bareilly, R.K.R.	500-800
78.	Khandke Sugar Mills, Ltd., M./A. D. N. Khandke & Co., Baheri.	Baheri.	Do.	Baheri, Do.	800
79.	*The Kesar Sugar Works, M./A. Kilachand Devchand & Co., Appollo Street, Bombay.	Baheri.	Do.	Do. Do.	500*

80.	L. H. Sugar Factory and Oil Mills, Prop. Raja Lalta Prosad Sahu Harprosad, Pilibhit.	Pilibhit.	Pilibhit.	Pilibhit,	R.K.R.	400
81.	L. H. Bros. Sugar Factory, Prop. Raja Lalta Prosad.	Do.	Do.	Do.	Do.	150*
82.	L. H. Sugar Factories &t Oil Mills, Prop. Raja Lalta Prosad.	Do.	Do.	Do.	Do.	400
83.	*Raza Sugar Factory, M./A. Govan Bros., Ltd., 10, Alipore Rd., Delhi.	Roshanbag.	Rampur.	Rampur,	E.I.R.	600
84.	*Upper Ganges Sugar Mills, M./A. Birla Bros., Ltd., 8, Royal Exchange Place, Calcutta.	Seohara.	Bijnor.	Seohara,	Do.	500-750
85.	Dhampur Sugar Mills Ltd., Prop., H. R. Sugar Factory, Bareilly.	Dhampur.	Do.	Dhampur,	Do.	400
86.	Bhogpur Sugar Works, Raja Hari Kissen Kaul, & Iswardas Lakshmidas, Huges Rd., Bombay.	Bhogpur.	Do.	Naginabad.		50
87.	*Jailakshmi Sugar Works, Prop. Jishnulal, Lahore.	Doiwalla.	Dehradun.	Doiwalla,	E.I.R.	250
88.	Jwalapur Sugar Factory, Prop. Haji Habib Kasam.	Jwalapur.	Saharanpur.	Jwalapur,	Do.	100
89.	The Ganga Sugar Corporation, Ltd., H. O. 17-A, McLeod Street, Lahore.	Deoband.	Do.	Deoband,	Do.	400

	Name of Factory.	Location.	District.	Nearest Rly. Station.		Crushing capacity in tons.
90.	*Upper Jumna Swadeshi Sugar Mills Ltd., M./A. Lala Hariraj Swarup Rajendralal & Bros., Muzaffarnagar.	Mansurpur.	Muzaffarnagar.	Mansurpur,	N.W.R.	400
91.	Upper India Sugar Mills, Ltd.,	Khatauli.	Do.	Khatauli.		400
92.	Amritsar Sugar Mills Co., Ltd., H. O. Amritsar.	Rohnakalan.		Rohnakalan,	N.W.R.	
93.	Upper Doab Sugar Mills, Ltd., M./A. Hariraj Swarup & Rajendralal & Bros., Muzaffarnagar.	Shamli.		Shamli,	A.S.L.R.	600
94.	The Diwan Sugar Mills, Prop. Seth Dhanpatmal Diwanchand, Lyallpur.	Sakhotitanda.	Do.	Sakhotitanda,	N.W.R.	250
95.	*Daurala Sugar Factory, M./A. Delhi Cloth and General Mills Ltd.	Daurala.	Do.	Daurala,	Do.	500
96.	R. B. Narain Singh Sugar Mills, M./D. Sardar Ranjit Singh, 24, Curzon Road, New Delhi.	Baraut.	Do.	Baraut,	A.S.L.R.	600
97.	Indra Sugar Works, M./A. Jucharam & Co., Meerut.	Meerut.	Do.	Meerut.		
98.	Delhi Sugar Mills Ltd. Krishna Sugar Syndicate, Delhi.	Mohiuddinpur,	Do.	Mohiuddinpur.	N.W.R.	

No.	Name	Place	District	Railway Station	Railway	Capacity
99.	*Modi Sugar Mills, Ltd., M./A: Multanimul & Sons, Patiala.	Begamabad.	Meerut.	Begamabad,	N.W.R.	500
100.	Simbhaoli Sugar Factory. Prop. Sardar Raghubir Singh Sandhanmalia, Baksar.	Simbhaoli.		Simbhaoli.		400
101.	Prag Sugar Factory, Pragnarayan Vakil, Rawatpara.	Kiccha.	Nainital.	Kichha.		400
102.	*The Saraswati Sugar Syndicate, M./A. Neoli Syndicate, Alfred Bldg., Lahore.	Manpur Nagaria.	Etah.	Manpur Nagaria (Neoli).		450
103.	Unao Sugar Mills, Ltd., Srikrishnadas Jagannath Prosad.	Unao.	Unao.	Unao,	O. & R.R.	
104.	Baijnath Balmukund Sugar Factory, Bankey Behari and Mandan Behari Lal.	Anwarganj.	Cawnpore.		B.B. & C.I.R.	
105.	Union India Sugar Mills, Ltd., Kamlaput Motilal, Cooperganj, Cawnpore.	Nawabganj.	Cawnpore.	Rawatpur,	E.I.R.	
106.	Cawnpore Factory of Cawnpore Sugar Works, Ltd., M./A. Begg, Sutherland & Co., Cawnpore.	Cawnpore.	Do.	Cawnpore	Do.	
107.	H. B. Experimental Sugar Factory.	Nawabganj.	Do.	Rawatpur,	Do.	24
	PUNJAB.					
108.	*Punjab Sugar Corporation, Ltd., M./A. GaneshFlourMills, Delhi.	Sonepat.	Rohtak	Sonepat,	N.W.R.	300*

	Name of Factory.	Location.	District.	Nearest Rly.	Station.	Crushing capacity in tons.
109.	Jagatjit Sugar Mills Ltd., 5, Montgomery Rd., Lahore.	Phagwara.	Jullundur.	Phagwara,	N.W.R.	600
110.	The Phulerwan Sugar & Oil Mills, Ltd., M./A. Radhakrishna Bros.	Phulerwan.	Sargodha.	Phulerwan,	Do.	
111.	Gujranwalla Sugar Mills, Ltd., M./A. Narang Bros., Lahore.	Rahwali.	Gujaranwalla.	Rahwali,	Do.	300
112.	Bhalwal Sugar Mills, Ltd.	Bhalwal.	Shahpur.	Bhalwal,	Do.	
113.	Harkrishna Sugar Mills., Ltd.	Amritsar.	Amritsar.	Amritsar	Do.	
114.	Amritsar Sugar Mills Co., Ltd., M./D. Sardar Amarat Singh, Amritsar.	Do.	Do.	Do.	Do.	600
115.	Shree Guru Arjundev Sugar Mills, M./A. Seth Sunder Singh.	Butari.	Do.	Butrai,	Do.	500
116.	*Saraswati Sugar Syndicate, H. O. Alfred Buildg., The Mall, Lahore.	Jagadhari.		Jagadhri,	Do.	450
117.	*Pioneer Sindh Sugar Mills Co., Ltd., Mohatta Mukhi & Co., Karachi.	Pritamabad,	Karachi.	Pritamabad.		
118.	Asaka Sugar Works & Distillery, Prop. Messrs. Parmanand Sahu, Lokenath Sahu, Jeewan Sahu and Gopinath Sahu.	Barhampur.	Ganjam.	Barhampur,	B.N.R.	

119.	Shree Ram Krishna Co-operative Industrial Society, Ltd.	Tummapala.	Vizagapatam.	Anakapalle,	M.S.M.	
120.	Etikoppaka Sugar Factory, M./A. The Etikoppaka Industrial and Co-operative & Credit Society.	Etikoppaka.	Do.	Narsapattam Rd.	Do.	
121.	Deccan Sugar and Abkari Co., Ltd., M./A. Parry & Co., Madras.	Samalkota.	Godavari.	Samalkota	M.S.M.	
122.	*The East India Distillers and Sugar Factories, Ltd., M./A. Parry & Co., Madras.	Nellikuppam	S. Arcot.	Nelikuppam,	S.I.R.	
123.	Indian Sugar and Refineries, Ltd., M./A. Ranganatham & Co., Ltd., Armenian Street, Madras.	Hospet.	Bellary.	Hospet,	M.S.M.	400
134.	The Hospet Sugar Mills, Ltd., M./A. Johnson & Co.	Hospet.	Do.	Hospet,	Do.	
125.	Shree Ram Sugar Factory, Prop. A. T. Krishna Swami, Mudaliar.	Podanur.	Coimbatore.	Podanur,	S.I.R.	50-150
126.	Al. Vr. St. Sugar Mills,	Tachanalur.	Tinnevelly,	Tinnevelly,	Do.	
	TRAVANCORE.					
127.	The Travancore Sugar Mills, Ltd., M./A. Vinayaka Kumar & Co.,	Thuckalay.	Trivendrum.	Trivendrum,	Do.	
	MYSORE.					
128.	*Mysore Sugar Co., M./D. Dr. L. C. Coleman.	Mandya.	Mysore.	Mandya,	Mysore Rly.	400-700
	BOMBAY PRESIDENCY.					
129.	Kolhapur Sugar Mills, M./A. Sirgao Kar Bros.	Kolhapur.	Kolhapur.	Kolhapur,	M.S.M.	

	Name of Factory.	Location.	District.	Nearest Rly. Station.		Crushing capacity in tons.
130.	The Saswadmali Sugar Factory, Ltd.	Akluj.	Sholapur.	Pandharpur,	B.L.R.	300
131.	The Phalton Sugar Works, M./A. Kilachand Devchand, Apollo St., Fort Bombay.	Pimpalwadi.	Satara.	Lonand,	M.S.M.	400
132.	*Marsland Price & Co., The Tata Construction Co., Ltd., Phoenix Build. Bellard Estate, Bombay.	Kalamb.	Poona.	Baramati,	B.L.R.	150
133.	*Maharashtra Sugar Mills, Ltd., Prop. M. L. Dahanukar & Co., Ltd., Kalvadevi Rd., Bombay.	Belapur Rd.	Ahmadnagar.	Belapur,	G.I.P.	
134.	*The Belapur Sugar Co., Ltd., M./A. Brady & Co., Bombay.	Harigaon.	Do.	Do.	Do.	700
135.	*The Ravalgaon Sugar Farm, Ltd., Walchand & Co., Phœnix Building, Ballard Estate, Bombay.	Ravalgaon.	Nasik.	Manmad.		150-250 100
	KATHIAWAR.					
136.	*Shree Bhagawat Singhjee Sugar Works, Ltd.	Gondal.	(Kathiawar).	Gondal	GondalState Rly.	

No.	Factory	Place	District	Station	Railway	Capacity
	BURMA.					
137.	The Shahmaw Sugar Factory of the Burmah Sugar Co., Ltd., M./A. Finlay, Fleming & Co., Merchants Street, Rangoon.	Shahmaw.	Mytkyina.	Shahmaw,	Burma Ry.	400
	THE FOLLOWING FACTORIES WILL START CRUSHING DURING THE SEASON 1934-35.					
	BENGAL.					
138.	Radha Krishna Sugar Mills, Ltd., H. O. 138, Harrison Road, Calcutta.	Beldanga.	Murshidabad.	Beldanga,	E.I.R.	400
139.	The Oriental Sugar Works, Ltd., Jayanti Agency, Calcutta.	Majdia.	Do.	Majdia,	E.B.R.	
140.	Desh Bandhu Sugar Mills, Ltd.	Charsindhur.	Dacca.	Narayanganj, E.B.R.		
	BIHAR & ORISSA.					
141.	The New Sugar Mills, Ltd.,	Hasanpur.	Darbhanga	Hasanpur, B.N.W.R.		
	UNITED PROVINCES.					
142.	Bareilly Sugar Works, M./A. Ram Narain Ram, Bharosay, Bareilley.	Bareilley.	Bareilley.	Bareilley,	R.K.R.	
143.	Inchram Sugar Factory.	Meerut.	Meerut.	Meerut.		300
144.	Shiromani Sugar Mills, Ltd., G. W. Daga & Co., Ltd., 8, Canning St., Calcutta.	Khalilabad.	Gorakhpur.	Khalilabad,	B.N.W.R.	
145.	Md. Farooq Sugar Mills.	Campirganj.	Do.	Campirganj, Gorakhpur-Gonda Loop		

A BRIEF BIBLIOGRAPHY

(Arranged Alphabetically)

Accounts of the Sea Borne Trade and Navigation of British India

Bengal Sugar Planter, Calcutta, 1849—S. H. Robinson.

Budget Speech of the Hon'ble the Finance Member, Government of India, 1934-35.

Capital—Industrial Supplements.

Commercial Gazette.

Cultivation of Sugarcane and Manufacture of Sugar—T. Kerr.

Economic Aspects of Cane production—Maxwell.

Facts about Sugar.

Financial News, Bombay.

Imperial Council of Agricultural Research, Annual Reports, 1929-30 1930-31, and 1931-32.

India—1931-32.

India Finance, Industrial Supplements.

Indian Finance, Year Book 1932.

Indian Journal of Agricultural Science, published by Imperial Council of Agricultural Research.

Indian Sugar Industry, the—Khan Bahadur S. M. Hadi.

Indian Sugar Committee Report, 1920.

Indian Sugar Mills Association, Annual Report, 1931-32.

Indian Sugar Mills Association, Memoranda.

Indian Taric Board Report on Sugar Industry, 1931.

Indian Tariff Problem—H. L. Dey.

Indian Trade Journal, 1931 to 1934.

International Sugar Journal, London, various issues.

Lamborn's Sugar Statistical Reports.

Legislative Assembly Debates, 1931-34.

Organisation of Java Industry, Literature on.

Patna Sugar Conference, Summary of representations submitted to.

Phillipine Sugar Association, Annual Report 1932.

Reports of the Departments of Agriculture of various provinces.

Reports of the Departments of Industries of various provinces.

Review of Agricultural Operations in India.

Review of the Trade of India, 1931-32 and 1932-33.

Simla Sugar Conference, Proceedings of 1933.

South African Sugar Journal, various issues.

Sugar Bureau, Pusa, Reports of the Secretary, and various publications.

Sugar in Bengal, Official Bulletin.

Sugar Growing and Refining—G. W. Lock.

Sugar Reference Book and Directory 1932-33—Palmer Publishing Co., N. Y., U. S. A.

Sugar News—Philippines, various issues.

World's Cane Sugar Industry—Prinsen Geerligs.

World Sugar Situation, issued by Economic Committee of League of Nations.

INDEX

(Reference is to pages.)